THE ROOTS OF
COUNTRY

THE ROOTS OF
COUNTRY

ROBERT K. OERMANN

Turner Publishing, Inc.

ATLANTA

Library of Congress Cataloging-in-Publication Data
Oermann, Robert K.
America's music: the roots of country / by Robert Oermann.
p. cm.
ISBN 1-57036-228-9 (alk. paper)
1. Country musicians—United States—Quotations.
2. Country music—History
and criticism.   I. Title.
ML3524.O33 1996
781.642'09—dc20
95-42484
CIP
MN

Published by Turner Publishing, Inc.
A Subsidiary of Turner Broadcasting System, Inc.
1050 Techwood Drive, NW
Atlanta, Georgia 30318

First Edition
10 9 8 7 6 5 4 3 2 1
Printed in the U.S.A.

For my wife, Mary A. Bufwack.
No song ever written can express our love.

And with thanks and affection to Tom Neff,
who helped me make a dream come true with the staffs of
Wild Wolf Productions, TBS, and Turner Publishing.

TABLE OF CONTENTS

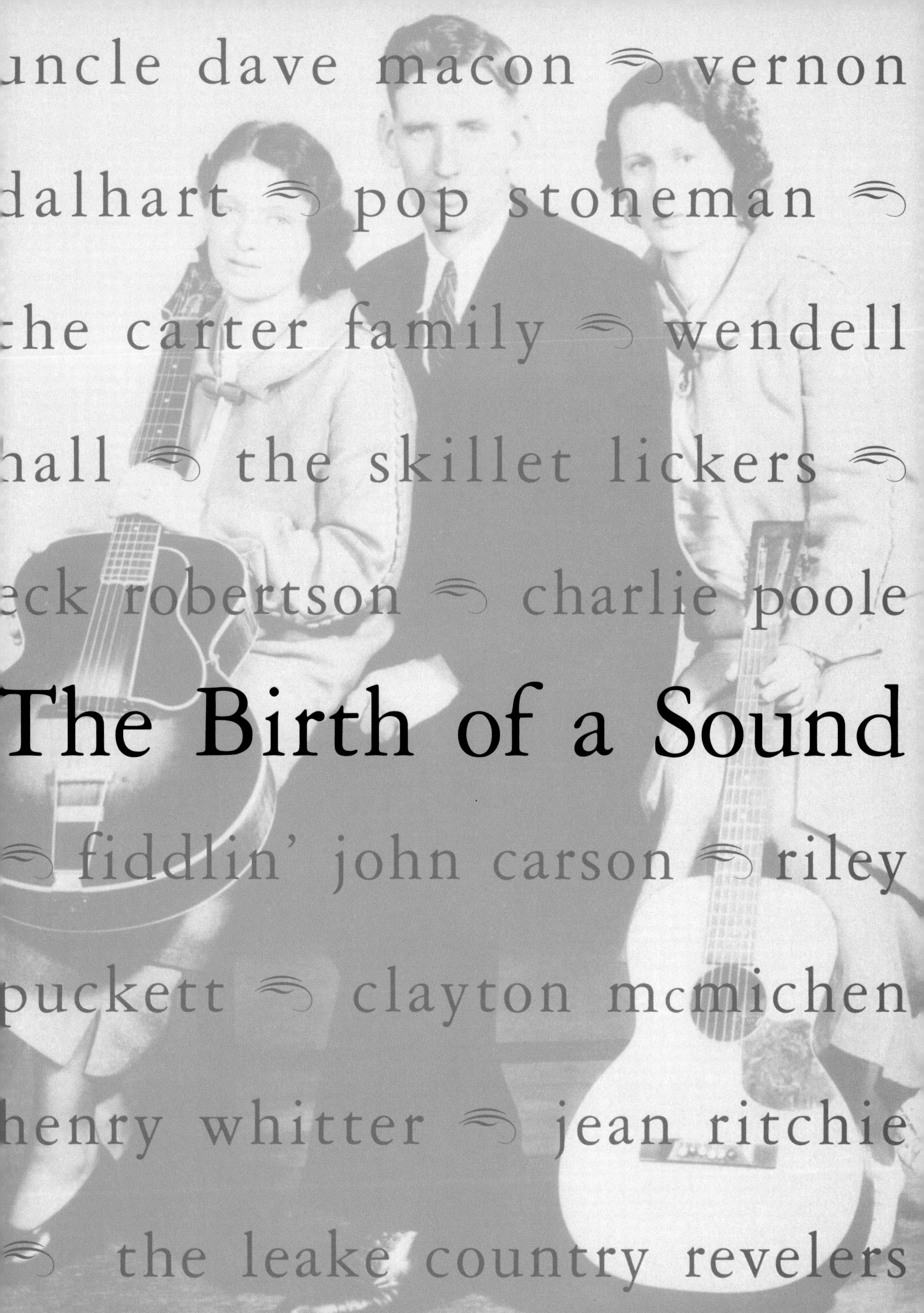

uncle dave macon ≈ vernon
dalhart ≈ pop stoneman ≈
the carter family ≈ wendell
hall ≈ the skillet lickers ≈
eck robertson ≈ charlie poole

The Birth of a Sound

≈ fiddlin' john carson ≈ riley
puckett ≈ clayton mcmichen
henry whitter ≈ jean ritchie
≈ the leake country revelers

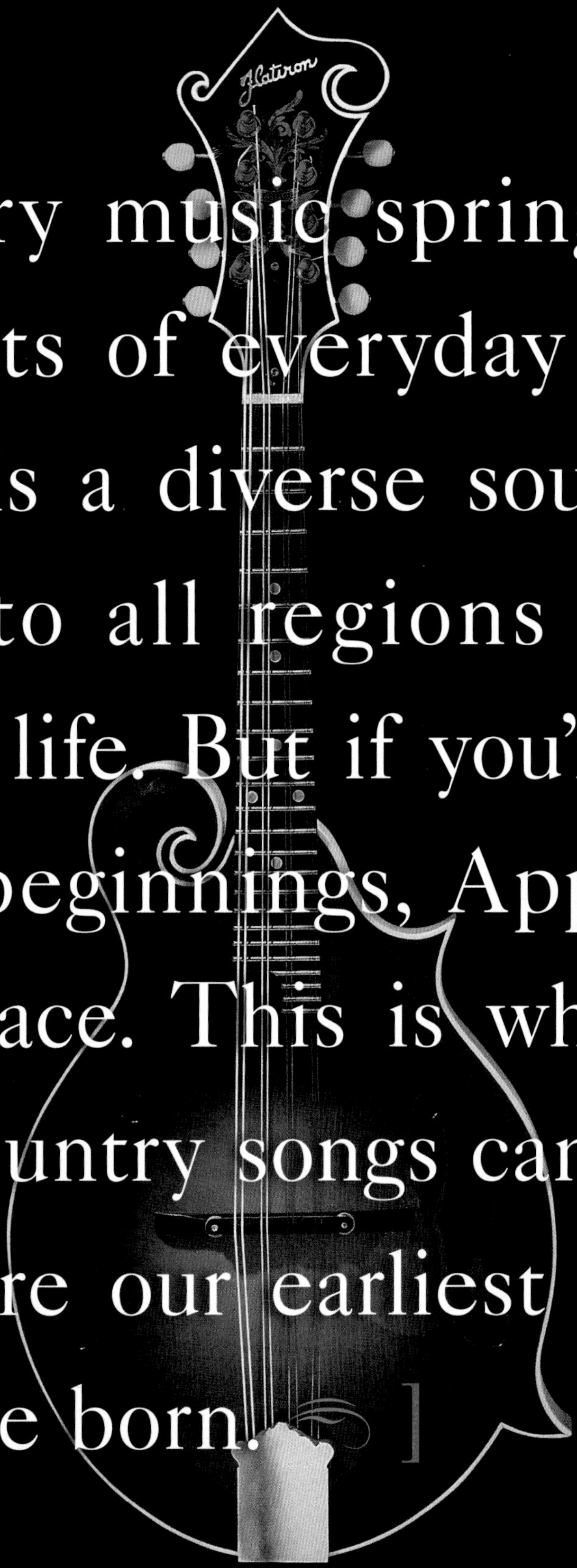

[Country music springs from the hearts of everyday Americans. It is a diverse sound that speaks to all regions and all walks of life. But if you're looking for beginnings, Appalachia is the place. This is where our oldest country songs came from and where our earliest country stars were born.]

[**DOLLY PARTON**] People in the mountains would sing just because they would sing. They sang when they were doin' the laundry, they sang when they were rockin' the babies, at the pie suppers—any social event, and especially at church. My mother was always singin'. It was her way of communicatin' with us, to express problems that she was havin' with my father or just with life in general. And also expressin' her love for us.

[**LORETTA LYNN**] Oh, my mommy sang all the time, and she would always sing when she was sewing on the old Singer sewing machine. I would be rocking the babies while mommy was sewing and making clothes for us to wear. Mommy would sing all these songs about the "Little Orphan Girl" and "Come Up Here, My Little Bessie," and "The Great Titanic," and I would start to cry when she'd sing a sad song. Mommy would always say to me, "Now, Loretta, if you're gonna cry I'll quit singing," and of course I'd try to hide my face, you know, to keep her from seeing me cry.

[**EDDY ARNOLD**] You see, on the farm you have to manufacture your entertainment, 'cause we didn't have a radio, we didn't have a record player. So I learned to play the harmonica.

[**NAOMI JUDD**] In the olden days, I guess as you call it, music was very uncomplicated, just as the folks back then were uncomplicated. So you had the preacher singing, trying to convert the sinners, and the farmers and the factory workers singin' to try to make the work go faster and make the time flow. The lovers sang to each other, trying to win each other's hearts. So many times families gathered together in the evening just to make home-made entertainment.

The songs sung in the mountains in the nineteenth century were handed down from generation to generation. Some ballads and fiddle tunes predate the American Revolution.

Religion also played a central role in people's lives in the 1800s. The sounds of the church created the musical foundation for rural dwellers, and these tunes became the basis of many country music melodies.

[**GOVERNOR JIMMIE DAVIS**] What singin' I did early in life was at the church. Everybody did that.

[**WILMA LEE COOPER**] Gospel goes with our style of country. On my mother's side, all the men were ministers in the Methodist churches. So that's what I wanted to be when I was growing up. I wanted to be a minister, but our church taught that women was to keep quiet in the church. So the gospel singing was very important—I could do that. Might not could preach, but I could do that.

Another common excuse for music making, then as now, is a party. The fall harvest, the spring planting, the raising of a barn, any community activity, could inspire an impromptu

1

"Those mountain people just loved those songs. Those were the songs that really went on back two hundred or three hundred years. Wonderful songs can last forever."

———————

DOLLY PARTON

*dance. The jigs, reels, and old-time dance tunes were most often played on the fiddle, the domi-
nant instrument of early country music.*

*The banjo was introduced to America by African slaves and popularized by touring
minstrel troupes in the mid 1800s. In more prosperous towns and homes, the piano and organ
became prominent, particularly after the Civil War. A mandolin craze occurred around the
turn of the century. The guitar's popularity came later, thanks to mail-order catalogs. Auto-
harps, Hawaiian guitars, harmonicas, and dobros were also introduced this way. But the central melody maker in old-time communities was the fiddle. It was known as "the devil's box"
because of its association with dancing and drinking.*

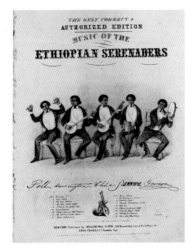

[**LAURIE LEWIS**] I'd say a fiddler was probably
the most important member of any community.
For one thing, the fiddle was an instrument that
is very, very portable. You can't go around carrying
pianos, you know. And a fiddle can be a whole
band, the way the old time fiddlers play—so
rhythmic and so full of life.

[**CLINTON GREGORY**] I learned to play the
fiddle from my father, Willie Gregory, who was
a champion fiddler back in Virginia. His dad was
a fiddler, and *his* dad. It goes back five generations. Playing square dances when I was a kid is

basically how I learned to play. The three main ingredients for a professional square dance is plenty of bootleg whiskey to drink, plenty of food, and good music.

[**ROY ROGERS**] My dad played a mandolin-guitar, and my mother played a guitar, and my three sisters all learned to play the guitar. We lived way back in the sticks, and I started callin' square dances when I was about ten years old.

Almost all early country musicians share memories of hard times. The Great Depression that hit the mainstream United States after the stock market crash of 1929 was already well under way in the rural South. By 1930, one out of every two American farmers worked land they didn't own. Dispossessed farmers poured into northern cities and wound up standing in bread lines and soup kitchens. Thousands migrated west, in search of work in California. This was the socio-economic backdrop for the birth of the commercial country music industry.

[**GOVERNOR JIMMIE DAVIS**] I remember when they had the Depression way back there, why, Bob Miller had a song about "11-cent cotton and 40-cent meat, how in the world can a poor man eat?"

[**EDDY ARNOLD**] I did farm work when the Depression hit. I lost my father in 1929—I was a little boy. And it was tough then. Then it got tougher.

From 1934 to 1937 severe drought hit Oklahoma, Texas, and Kansas, driving more than half the population off the land. The "Dust Bowl" migration of impoverished country people became a metaphor for the Great Depression.

VERNON DALHART
Marion Try Slaughter
(1883–1948)

〰

HOME AREA
Central Texas

SIGNIFICANCE
Country's first million-selling artist. Prior to the rise of rock 'n' roll, "The Prisoner's Song" was the biggest-selling single in pop-music history.

POPULAR SONGS
"The Prisoner's Song" (1924), "The Wreck of the Old '97" (1924), "In the Baggage Coach Ahead" (1925), "The Letter Edged in Black" (1925), "The Death of Floyd Collins" (1926), "Golden Slippers" (1927), "Lindbergh" (1927), "My Blue Ridge Mountain Home" (1928), "Hallelujah I'm a Bum" (1928)

INFLUENCED
Carson Robison, Adelyn Hood, Frank Luther, Welling & McGee

HONORS
Country Music Hall of Fame, 1981

*Texan Eck Robertson
(opposite) is credited as
the first authentic country
artist on record (1922).
Like most country
recording artists, he
came from the home-
made, rural, do-it-
yourself tradition, as
illustrated by the anony-
mous turn-of-the-century
banjo picker below.*

[**MERLE HAGGARD**] I wasn't a hillbilly. I was born out in the edge of Bakersfield, California, out there in the oil fields, and there was cotton fields around there. My mother's very upset about that, about the incorrect concept of people that came in that migration. They were a long way from bein' poor. They didn't have anything to eat, and they didn't have no money, but they weren't poor. They were rich in lots of things, and very proud people.

For many, music became an escape from poverty, a way out.

[**JIMMY MARTIN**] Bill Monroe told me how rough it was to travel in his group. He wanted to try me on the road and see if I could stand the hard work. But I told him that night, I said, "Bill, it ain't no harder than sawing with a crosscut saw wood all day, is it?" I said, "It ain't no harder than getting down in a ditch, and digging a ditch and plowing corn behind a horse all day, is it?" I said, "It ain't no harder than hauling hay to the barn and hauling the stuff away from the barn to put it on a tobacco patch, is it, Bill?" He said, "No." I said, "I think I can take it."

Rural dwellers had limited exposure to professional show business. Touring religious-revival tent shows, minstrel troupes, medicine-show performers, and back-woods vaudevillians would sometimes come to small towns. Showboats occasionally visited the larger river communities. These influences blended with the folk ballads, fiddle tunes, rural blues, and religious traditions to create the early country sound.

The phonograph was invented in 1876, but recordings didn't really begin to penetrate into everyday people's homes until around 1900. The first music recorded was classical, followed by military bands and urban vaudevillians. Around 1915, rube or hick comedians and fiddlers performing folk melodies entered the recording field.

[**JEAN RITCHIE**] In like 1912, '13, or around in there somewhere, my father sent away to a mail-order house for the first record player in our area. It had little long cylinders that you played. He had one called "Whistling Rufus," I remember. He'd play that for people, and they would all go behind and look to see if there was a person hiding behind there playing something. People would come from miles around to look at it. They called it "the talking machine," because there was a lot of talking on the early records, too. They would talk, and then they would sing awhile, and talk in between the verses, and so on.

Gradually, record companies came to understand that there was a distinct market for country sounds. The first black blues act was recorded in 1920, followed in 1922 by the first hillbilly musician, fiddler Eck Robertson. The first hit regional country act was Atlanta's Fiddlin' John Carson, discovered in 1923. But the blockbuster was Texas-bred Vernon Dalhart.

[**DOC WILLIAMS**] The odd part about Vernon Dalhart is that he was an opera singer and sang the modern songs of the day. But when he sang "The Prisoner's Song," Vernon Dalhart became famous and sold up into the millions on old 78-rpm records.

Vernon Dalhart's 1924 recording of "The Prisoner's Song" eventually topped an estimated 20 million in sales. It was an authentic phenomenon, so pervasive that you can even hear the street urchins singing it in the landmark 1937 film of New York City slum life, Dead End.

Ukulele player Wendell Hall also sold millions in 1924, thanks to a simple, two-chord ditty called "It Ain't Gonna Rain No More." The colossal sales of these records opened the door for authentic country music. Record companies scurried to find the next rustic song sensation throughout the mid 1920s. Ernest Thompson's "Little Rosewood Casket" (1924), the Fiddlin' Powers Family version of "Old Joe Clark" (1924), the pioneering singing-cowboy record "When the Work's All Done This Fall" by Carl T. Sprague (1925), Charlie Poole's still-sung "Don't Let Your Deal Go Down" (1925), and performances by Kelly Harrell, the Leake Country Revelers, Bradley Kincaid, Al Hopkins, Carson Robison, the East Texas Serenaders, the Carolina Tar Heels, and other string bands laid the cornerstone for the country industry. Among the most significant was the all-star group the Skillet Lickers. Members Gid Tanner and Riley Puckett traveled to New York to record in 1924. Joined by fiddler Clayton McMichen and banjoist Fate Norris in 1925–26, the group struck pay dirt with "Down Yonder," "Bully of the Town," "Ida Red," "A Corn Licker Still in Georgia," and other top-selling titles.

[**CHET ATKINS**] One of the almost forgotten pioneers from the prewar days of country music was the Skillet Lickers, and their singer was Riley Puckett. I remember Riley. I remember talkin' to him. He was blind, you know. They told him they could do a cornea transplant, and he said, "I'm not gonna do it." He was about sixty then, I guess. He said, "I think I know what my wife looks like. I think I know what a radio looks like. I think I know what my kids look like. And I think the shock would be too great. I don't think I wanna see at this stage of my life."

[**JOE TALBOT**] At times I've been asked, "Why are you so fanatical about country music?" Well, I'd like to tell a little story about how I started loving it. I had a grandfather that I worshiped. He was a railroad man. He cussed, and he drank beer, and I just thought he was wonderful. I was at my grandfather and grandmother's house one day, winding up that Victrola, playing those records, and I ran across this record that had a train whistle on it. I played that record over and over.

▲

Early country songs were spread via songbooks as well as records. Many of Vernon Dalhart's best tunes were composed by his guitarist, Carson Robison.

And from that minute forward I loved country music. I might add the name of the record was "The Wreck of the Old '97."

Originally recorded by Virginian Henry Whitter in 1923, "The Wreck of the Old '97" became a country classic. Its melody has been borrowed many times, notably in the Kingston Trio's 1959 novelty hit "M.T.A." Inspired by Whitter, Ernest V. "Pop" Stoneman created his own early-country monument in 1925, the hit disaster saga "The Titanic."

[**PATSY STONEMAN**] Daddy heard Henry Whitter, who worked in a mill with Daddy. He told Mama, "I think I could do that well," and she said, "Well, Ernest, if you think you can, then go do it. Don't keep talkin' about it."

He saved forty-seven dollars for carfare to New York. He went over to OKeh Records to see Mr. Ralph Peer, and he recorded "The Sinking of the Titanic," a song he had written, and it was a very big seller.

Pop Stoneman was not only a country recording pioneer, he was the patriarch of a dynasty. Of Ernest and Hattie Stoneman's twenty-three children, fifteen survived, thirteen became musicians, and four became stars: Scott, Patsy, Donna, and Hee Haw's Roni Stoneman.

[**PATSY STONEMAN**] When we was growin' up, our favorite song, I reckon, would be an old song called "Somebody's Waiting for Me." Mommy would play "Somebody's Waiting for Me" on the fiddle, and Daddy would play it on the autoharp and the guitar, and all of us young'uns set around and sang it. It became our theme song when we went to Constitution Hall in Washington, D. C., in 1947–48, for television. It was about a fellow's mother waiting at home for him. And we always felt like that way,

Fiddlin' John Carson (below) was the first "star" hillbilly. The Dixie Mountaineers (right) were among the bands assembled by Ernest Stoneman (center) and his fiddling wife, Hattie (second from right).

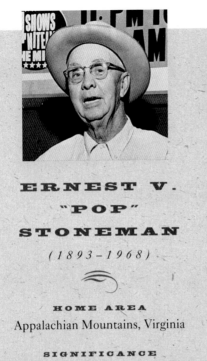

ERNEST V. "POP" STONEMAN

(1893–1968)

HOME AREA
Appalachian Mountains, Virginia

SIGNIFICANCE
Recorded one of the first country hits, "The Titanic." The only country act to have appeared on cylinders, 78s, 45s, LPs, cassettes, and compact discs. Folk-revival star of the 1960s. Own TV series, 1966. Patriarch of "The First Family of Country Music," a dynasty of talented children—Patsy was first woman to lead a bluegrass band; Donna considered a top mandolinist; Scott, a national champion fiddler; Roni, a star on TV's *Hee Haw*.

POPULAR SONGS
"The Sinking of the Titanic" (1925), "Little Old Log Cabin in the Lane" (1926), "The Poor Tramp Has to Live" (1927), "When the Roses Bloom Again" (1927). "Mountaineer's Courtship" (1927), "Sinful to Flirt" (1927), "All Go Hungry Hash House" (1928), "The Five Little Johnson Girls" (The Stonemans, 1966)

INFLUENCED
Patsy Stoneman, Jack Clement

HONORS
Country Music Association Group of the Year, 1967

you know? When Mommy wasn't with us, she was waitin' for us and prayin' for us.

Such sentiments are common in old-time music. They spring from Victorian-era "parlor songs" of the late nineteenth century, which were remembered by early country performers. Prior to the advent of records and radio, most music was circulated via sheet music. Lyrics of motherhood, sympathy for the poor, nostalgia for the antebellum South, and childhood innocence abounded. Many were revived by country's family-harmony groups. They also entered the repertoire of Uncle Dave Macon, the most eclectic showman of his era, a walking museum of nineteenth-century showbiz and early hillbilly culture.

Born in 1870, Dave Macon was fifty-three years old when he began touring on the vaudeville circuit in 1923, but his vigor was ageless. With his gold teeth, whiskers, twirling banjo, gates-ajar collar, and ready stash of country witticisms, Macon was an instant smash. He began recording in 1924, eventually issuing some two hundred titles

The Skillet Lickers were an "all-star" group. Fiddlers Clayton McMichen and Gid Tanner and blind vocalist Riley Puckett (bottom left) were all solo artists as well as band members.

on disc. When WSM inaugurated its Grand Ole Opry radio show in Nashville, Uncle Dave Macon became its first star attraction. "The Dixie Dewdrop" remained an Opry headliner from 1926 until his death in 1952.

[**MAC WISEMAN**] When I first came to the Opry in 1949 with Bill Monroe, Uncle Dave and Kirk McGee were touring with Bill. We were playing a lot of the larger theaters. About the third or fourth night, we're in a big auditorium in Illinois, and Bill said, "You open the show tonight." So I went out with the band and did two or three numbers and introduced Uncle Dave and Kirk to come out, then stood in the wings.

Uncle Dave sat down. He'd get up and twirl his banjo when he finished a tune and doff his hat a bit. So he did this several times, and I thought it was time for him to finish up. I went dashing out, and Uncle Dave stood up and looked at me very sternly and said, "I'm not done yet, boy." It was an awfully long walk back to the wings of that auditorium, I'll tell you.

▲

The rambunctious style of banjo-whacking Uncle Dave Macon and his son Dorris (seated left) is preserved in the 1940 film Grand Ole Opry.

Uncle Dave Macon
was part medicine-
show barker, part
minstrel, part comic,
part evangelist,
and all ham.

▼

The earliest country recording stars all ventured to Manhattan to face the record-company microphones. Most executives didn't even know what to call what they were marketing. One of the most common early descriptions for this music was "Hillbilly." That term was supplanted by "Western" during the singing-cowboy era of the 1940s; "Folk," as the genre's first popular-ity charts were published; and then "Country & Western" in 1950–62. Thirty years ago, the industry finally settled on the simple "Country Music."

Seventy years ago, the market was tiny. That began to change with the development of portable recording equipment in the late 1920s. For the first time, talent scouts could capture country musicians in their natural habitats. Frank Walker, Art Satherley, Ralph Peer, and others began venturing into Appalachia on field trips. Peer's trip to Bristol, Tennessee, in July and August 1927 changed the face of the industry forever.

[**PATSY STONEMAN**] When Ralph Peer left OKeh in 1926 and went to RCA Victor Talking Machine Company, he took with him what he considered his star attraction, Daddy. Pop Stoneman had recorded maybe two hundred records or better by then. Daddy gathered all these people up, and he even took 'em over to the Bluebonnet Hotel over here in Galax and rehearsed them to carry them up to New York. And some of 'em had never been out of these hills.

[**JOE MORRELL, OF WOPI RADIO**] Victor Record Company decided to send a portable studio to the South to get all this folk and hillbilly music. Bristol was the first stop. That's the reason Bristol is called "the birthplace of country music."

[**PATSY STONEMAN**] Daddy set it up to go to Bristol. The engineers set up stuff on State Street at an old hat factory or somethin'. Mr. Peer and his wife came here and spent the night [with the Stonemans] on the way down there. Daddy went down there, and it was in the newspapers about them gonna be there, and how much money Daddy had made the previous year. And they started comin' out of the woodwork. So then Mr. Peer discovered the Carter Family and Jimmie Rodgers.

[**JOE CARTER**] The original trio of The Carter Family consisted of A. P. Carter, Sara Carter, his wife—the lead singer, an alto. And Maybelle Carter, Sara's cousin, played the guitar and the autoharp. She married my father's brother, Ezra Carter. So it was brothers marrying first cousins is how the families got interwoven. That was the beginning of, I guess, the country music.

The Carter Family and Jimmie Rodgers, both discovered by Peer in Bristol in 1927, made the first nationally popular rural records. A. P. Carter col-lected or wrote much of the trio's landmark material. Sara was country's first star female voice. Maybelle sang harmony, and her revolutionary picking style popularized the guitar as a lead instrument. The trio

"With the songs of The Carter Family, there's a poignancy there that's so heartbreaking. I don't know whether we've lost the ability to capture that. I think maybe we have. There is something about the simplicity, the lonely imagery of The Carter Family that I still find very moving."

EMMYLOU HARRIS

From the left are Maybelle, A. P., and Sara Carter, the family wellspring of old-time music.

Maybelle (above left) and Sara Carter spent far more time in domestic pursuits than show business in the early days. But songbooks and 78-rpm records made their songs immortal.

is unmatched as a preserver of Anglo-American ballads, parlor songs, and other melodies of Americana. "Wabash Cannonball," "Are You Lonesome Tonight?" "I Never Will Marry," "Hello, Stranger," "Will the Circle Be Unbroken?" "Lonesome Valley," "Worried Man Blues," and dozens of other Carter Family tunes are now country standards.

[**HANK THOMPSON**] The Carter Family did a song called "I'm Thinking Tonight of My Blue Eyes," and that melody kind of became a traditional thing, because in a few later years, Roy Acuff did "The Great Speckled Bird," and I came along and did "The Wild Side of Life," and Kitty Wells came along with the answer, "It Wasn't God Who Made Honky Tonk Angels." And so that little three-chord melody has been the vehicle for several giant hit songs.

[**JANETTE CARTER**] The records were sold mostly through Sears Roebuck and through Montgomery Ward. They didn't have distributors. They didn't have music stores.

[**RITA FORRESTER**] For each record sold, there was a half-cent royalty. A. P. never renegotiated that contract, and even after his death [in 1960], it was never renegotiated.

[**JANETTE CARTER**] Women was not even involved in music much. They started a whole new trend, Maybelle and mother, by being in music. Way back then, you never seen too many women out making records or doing performances. They played music in the home.

[**JUNE CARTER CASH**] I think my mother and Aunt Sara were probably two of the most liberated women I ever saw. They were liberated inasmuch as they would write the songs they wanted to. But the songs, in the beginning, were all in Uncle A. P. Carter's name. Every one of 'em. That was because he was considered as a head of his house, the head of the Carter family.

[**JANETTE CARTER**] It was all deeply serious singing. They didn't have no comedy like some you've seen. Daddy would get up and announce each song that was going to be, and he would tell a little bit about it: it was a hymn, it was a love song, it was the blues. They were very, very quiet. The people listened.

A. P. became increasingly eccentric, moody, and undependable. Sara and Maybelle were always the dominant musicians, yet he remained in charge. Sara separated from him in 1933. They divorced in 1939. Peer instructed them not to reveal personal matters and to maintain the "family" image. Meanwhile, the trio took its biggest step to national renown by traveling south to broadcast on the mega-watt Mexican-border radio station XERA in 1938–39. Sara and A. P.'s younger children, Janette and Joe, were incorporated into the act, as were Maybelle and Ezra's daughters June, Helen, and Anita.

[**JUNE CARTER CASH**] That would have been an adventure for anybody. It was for me. They offered us a job, if any of the children could sing. So my mother came home and, within about a week's time, I think, taught me to sing. Janette could sing, and Helen and Anita could sing, and I'm the one that they're lookin' at like I'm a snake.

[**JOHNNY CASH**] I think the first time I heard The Carter Family was on the radio at night when I was very small. They were comin' over the air waves from XERA / XERF, Del Rio, Texas. I scanned the radio dial when I was a little kid on the cotton farm in Arkansas, and it was the most wonderful, magical thing in the world to be able to turn that dial and hear different singers in different places. The simplicity of deliverance and the performance in those songs was like my life, you know?

[**JUNE CARTER CASH**] We came back from the Texas

UNCLE DAVE MACON
(1870–1952)

HOME AREA
Middle Tennessee

SIGNIFICANCE
First and best of country music's old-time "songsters." Exponent of the "frailing" banjo style. Humorist, raconteur. The major link between nineteenth-century show biz and the twentieth-century country idiom. The first superstar of the Grand Ole Opry. "King of the Hillbillies," "The Dixie Dewdrop."

POPULAR SONGS
"Keep My Skillet Good and Greasy" (1924), "Chewing Gum" (1924), "Poor Sinners Fare You Well" (1926), "Death of John Henry" (1926), "The Old Man's Drunk Again" (1926), "Rockabout, My Saro Jane" (1927), "Sail Away, Ladies" (1927), "Go 'Long, Mule" (1927), "Buddy, Won't You Roll Down the Line" (1928), "When the Train Comes Along" (1934).

INFLUENCED
Brother Oswald, Grandpa Jones

HONORS
Country Music Hall of Fame, 1966

THE CARTER FAMILY

MEMBERS

Alvin Pleasant "A. P." Carter (1893–1960),
Sara Carter (1899–1979),
Maybelle Carter (1909–78)

HOME AREA

Appalachian Mountains, Virginia

SIGNIFICANCE

Unequaled as preservers of mountain folk
songs, gospel standards, and Victorian
"parlor songs."

POPULAR SONGS

"Bury Me Under the Weeping Willow"
(1927), "Keep on the Sunny Side" (1928),
"I'm Thinking Tonight of My Blue Eyes"
(1929), "Wabash Cannonball" (1929),
"Worried Man Blues" (1930), "Lonesome
Valley" (1930), "Will the Circle Be
Unbroken" (1935), "Are You Lonesome
Tonight" (1936)

INFLUENCED

The Carter Sisters, Carlene Carter,
Joan Baez, Emmylou Harris, Woody
Guthrie, Mac Wiseman, Kitty Wells, etc.

HONORS

Country Music Hall of Fame, 1970;
Nashville Songwriters Hall of Fame, 1970
(A. P. Carter); American Music Award
Favorite Country Group, 1974 (Mother
Maybelle & The Carter Sisters); Music
City News Gospel Group of the Year,
1980 (The Carter Sisters)

border stations, and we went to Charlotte, North Carolina, and that was a big 50,000-watt radio station. We were working there live every morning with Mother Maybelle, Uncle A. P., and Aunt Sara. And Joe Carter was playin' bass for us at that time. And it was kind of a strained situation. My Uncle A. P. and Aunt Sara had been divorced, but they had still been working together. And Aunt Sara had remarried.

By this time, the Carters were legendary. Life *magazine sent a photojournalist to their Virginia homestead in 1941, but the week the story was to run, the Japanese bombing of Pearl Harbor scuttled it. It was too late, in any case. The original trio was no more.*

Sara retired to California. A. P. ran a country store back home. He occasionally tried to relive the past, notably with Sara, Joe, and Janette as recording partners in the 1950s. Maybelle formed a new group with her daughters and kept Carter Family music alive into the modern era in Nashville.

[**JUNE CARTER CASH**] The Carter Sisters and Mother Maybelle, we played show dates all around, for as far as we could drive at night. We played little school houses, we played courthouses, we played anything. We had a public address system that had one microphone.

[**CHET ATKINS**] Maybelle Carter was almost indescribable for me, 'cause she was like another mama. I never saw her lose her temper. She just played her guitar, sang, played the banjo, and sang, and was always happy.

Maybelle played a style that was easy to play, but it was original. I never heard anybody else do it before her. She played melody on the bass strings and rhythm with her fingers. And her "Wildwood Flower" is like the national anthem of country music.

[**JANETTE CARTER**] It took a long, long time for people to realize what they were doing and to put any value on their songs. You've got to keep looking back. The roots is what you have to keep alive and keep a-going. If you let the roots die, there ain't nothing a-going to happen. It's gone.

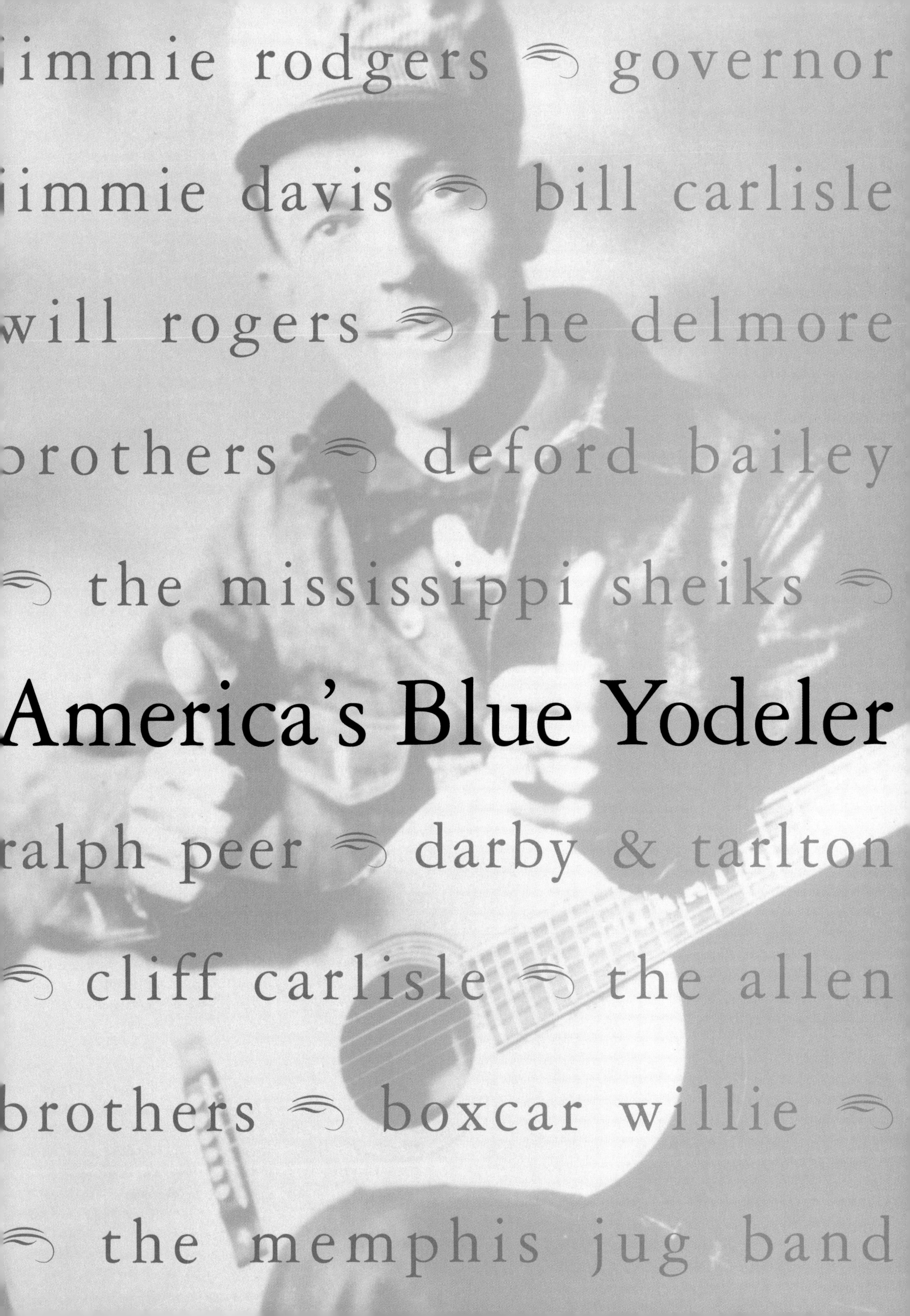

jimmie rodgers ∾ governor

jimmie davis ∾ bill carlisle

will rogers ∾ the delmore

brothers ∾ deford bailey

∾ the mississippi sheiks ∾

America's Blue Yodeler

ralph peer ∾ darby & tarlton

∾ cliff carlisle ∾ the allen

brothers ∾ boxcar willie ∾

∾ the memphis jug band

Black and white musical traditions were intertwined in the turn-of-the-century South. Black fiddlers and banjo pickers were once common in Dixie as square-dance accompanists. Glimmers of this old tradition were picked up on disc during country-music's formative years, notably in the works of such acts as the Memphis Jug Band and Nashville's "harmonica wizard" Deford Bailey

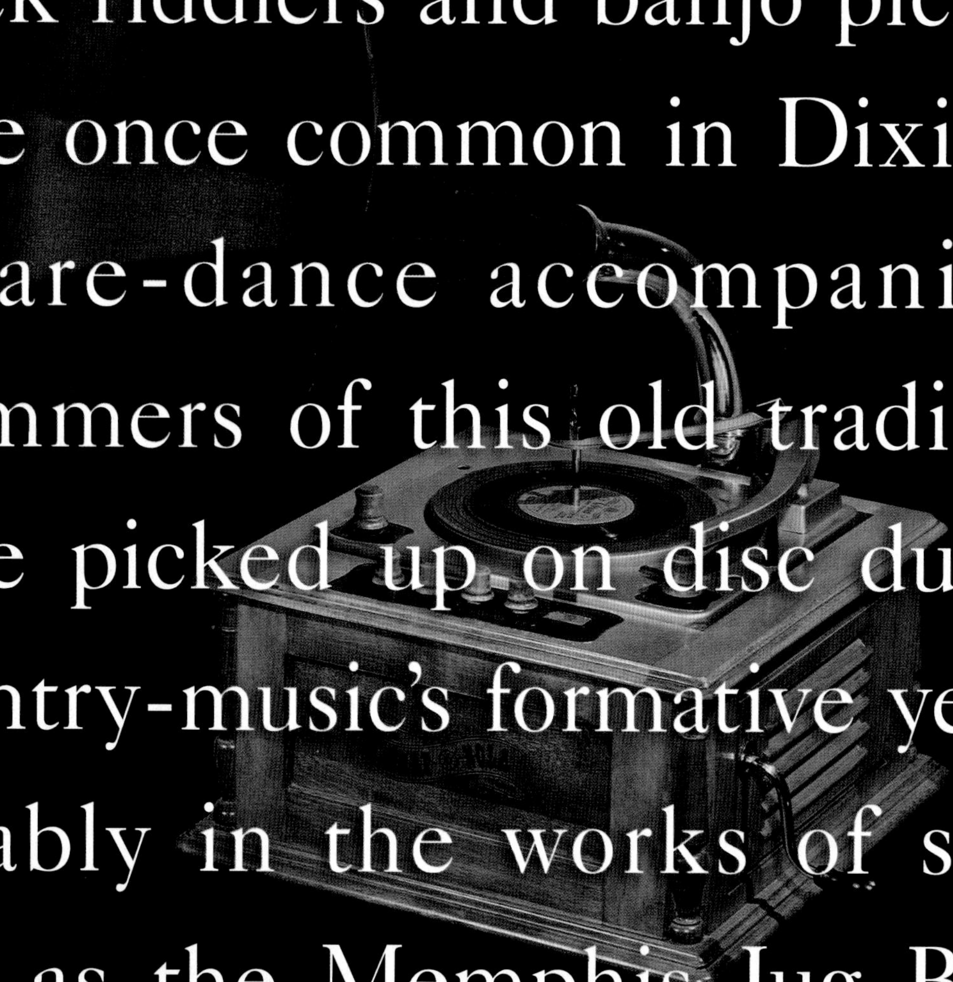

A. P. Carter's song-collecting accompanist was bluesman Leslie Riddles; Bill Monroe learned guitar from black Arnold Shultz and played Kentucky square dances with him; Hank Williams's mentor was Teetot, a black street singer. The Two Poor Boys, the Wright Family, Stovepipe No.1, and Lulu Jackson were all 1920s black performers with country song repertoires. There was even a 1929 act dubbed the Black Hillbillies. Black string bands like the Mississippi Sheiks and the Carver Brothers were marketed in hillbilly record-catalog listings. Conversely, the white Allen Brothers were marketed in Columbia's race-records series. The Delmore Brothers, Darby & Tarlton, and dozens of other country acts specialized in blues tunes. The most popular country star of the era, Jimmie Rodgers, was dubbed "America's Blue Yodeler."

⟐

[**RAY CHARLES**] We can relate to country music because it's so plain. We can relate to the blues because it's so plain. It just talks about what it is—just everyday life and what is goin' on with people.

[**SAM PHILLIPS**] In the South, when you get the black and the white blues goin', I don't know how you could write or hear anything that's better for the soul, better for the spirit, and more educational than this is, fundamentally, in life.

[**JEAN SHEPARD**] Jimmie Rodgers—well, everyone knows he's the Father of Country Music. I learned to yodel off the old Jimmie Rodgers records. The whole valley could hear me singing Jimmie Rodgers and yodeling. I loved him. He was wonderful.

[**DAVID FRIZZELL**] When you listen to Jimmie Rodgers, he was exactly what country music is.

[**BUCK OWENS**] That's where it all came from, you know, from Jimmie Rodgers.

Jimmie's distinctive blend of traditions came from the railroad yards of Meridian, Mississippi. As a worker there, he listened to the black section hands and incorporated their blues into his style. After several seasons kicking around on the small-potatoes Southern vaudeville circuit, Jimmie Rodgers was discovered at Victor Records' famed Bristol Sessions of 1927. Within two years, he was an undisputed hillbilly superstar, "The Singing Brakeman."

[**GOVERNOR JIMMIE DAVIS**] Jimmie Rodgers was the greatest artist I've ever heard, because his diction was so good, and his records usually told a story, you know. Jimmie didn't talk so much about his singin'. He said, "I'm not much of a musician. I can't play my stuff how I wanna play it."

'Course he could.

One time, I was passin' through Kilgore, Texas, and he had a tent out there and

"Jimmie Rodgers drew from the blues that he grew up listenin' to. Everybody likes it because it's so soulful; it's raw, magical."

———

TRACY BYRD

had all the people in it that they could get under there. Some of 'em were on the outside, couldn't get in the tent. Had a show at ten. Stayed out there about an hour. Went up to the hotel, went to bed. About two or three o'clock, he'd come back and have another show. Had a tent full of people again. Just by himself. Nobody singin' but him.

[**SARA CARTER, 1971**] We went out to Louisville, Kentucky, and made these records with Jimmie in 1931. We made "Jimmie Visits the Carter Family" and "The Carter Family Visits Jimmie." We sang these two songs together and yodeled "The Wonderful City"—that was one of Jimmie's songs—and "Why There's a Tear in My Eye"—that was one of the old Carter Family numbers. Oh, we had a good time. Jimmy was real sick then, you know. He was real thin. But he was jolly. He was lively. After we got the records made, Jimmie says, "Well, I'm gonna take you out now for dinner." So he took us out there to a big restaurant. Jimmie ordered up a chicken dinner for us all—had everything to eat with it. And when he got ready to pay the bill, why it was just $5.00 for the whole thing.

During Jimmie Rodgers's short, five-and-a-half year career between 1927 and 1933, he sold more than ten million singles. In the more than sixty years since his death, his records have never gone out of print. Within six months of his 1927 debut, Rodgers's royalties were $200,000 a month. In 1929 he filmed the movie short "The Singing Brakeman" and bought his $50,000 "Blue Yodeler's Paradise" home in Kerrville, Texas. In 1931 he costarred on a concert tour with humorist Will Rogers.

In rapid succession, Jimmie Rodgers turned out "T for Texas," "In the Jailhouse Now," "Muleskinner Blues," "Waiting for a Train," "Frankie and Johnny," and the rest of his timeless tunes. Chronically ill, he knew his career would be brief.

[**BOXCAR WILLIE**] He had tuberculosis, he was a chain smoker, he drank a lot. And back in those days, there was no cure for TB. Matter of fact, he wrote a song called "The TB Blues," and it's still popular today. He could probably have lived a lot longer if he would-a took better care of hisself. He smoked right up to the day he died.

The last recording session, when Jimmie went to New York City in May 1933, he was so weak he would record one song and then he'd have to go lay down on a cot 'til he got his strength back. It was a very tragic ending. Jimmie Rodgers died after he cut his twelfth song there in New York.

When the train left New York City, bringin' his body back to Meridian, the engineer tied the whistle open in a low moan, and people lined the railroad all the way from New York City clear to Meridian, Mississippi. He was such a legend. We think about Elvis and the thousands of people that would mob Elvis. But back in 1933, it was like that with Jimmie Rodgers.

The Mississippi Sheiks (top) were marketed as a hill-billy act. Yet Lulu Jackson's renditions of country tunes can be found in this Vocalion Records blues ad of 1928 (above).

JIMMIE RODGERS

(1897–1933)

HOME AREA
Meridian, Mississippi

SIGNIFICANCE
"The Father of Country Music,"
massively popular as the first national rural
recording star. "America's Blue Yodeler."

POPULAR SONGS
"T for Texas" (1928), "In the Jailhouse
Now" (1928), "Daddy and Home" (1928),
"Waiting for a Train" (1929), "Frankie
and Johnny" (1929), "Muleskinner
Blues" (1930), "Any Old Time" (1930),
"Travellin' Blues" (1931), "Roll
Along Kentucky Moon" (1932),
"Hobo's Meditation" (1932),
"Miss the Mississippi and You" (1932),
"Peach Pickin' Time in Georgia" (1933)

INFLUENCED
Gene Autry, Patsy Montana, Bill Monroe,
Ernest Tubb, Hank Snow, Lefty Frizzell,
Jean Shepard, Hank Thompson, Hank
Williams, Merle Haggard, and virtually
every other country star in history

HONORS
Country Music Hall of Fame, 1961;
Nashville Songwriters Hall of Fame, 1970;
Grammy Hall of Fame, 1985;
Rock 'n' Roll Hall of Fame, 1986

Rodgers's impact was profound. He became the role model for an entire generation of country performers. Gene Autry began his career by emulating the Singing Brakeman and recording "The Death of Jimmie Rodgers." Cliff Carlisle, Bill Cox, Dwight Butcher, Hank Snow, and Ernest Tubb all began their careers imitating Rodgers.

[**JUSTIN TUBB**] My dad thought he was God, I guess. He idolized the man. When he first started, he patterned his style after Jimmie, yodeled, and every song he sang, he sang just like Jimmie. He wrote songs about Jimmie.

So he called Mrs. Rodgers up on the phone. She lived right there in San Antonio, where we lived. And my dad had a little radio show in the morning on KONO in San Antonio, for fifteen minutes, just him and his guitar. And he worked in a drug store, deliverin' prescriptions on a bicycle. He called her up and said, "Mrs. Rodgers, I'm Ernest Tubb, and I'm a big fan of your husband's, and I have a radio show in the morning, and if you would listen some morning, I'd like for you to hear me sing." She liked what she heard, and she kind of took him under her wing. She gave him Jimmie's guitar to use. And when he first started, she would go out on the road with him. She would go out and introduce him on the show, saying, "I'm Mrs. Jimmie Rodgers, and this young man I have found I picked to carry on my husband's singing and his musical career."

And that was their show. She got him on Bluebird records, which was the subsidiary of RCA, and she was instrumental after that in getting him on Decca Records in 1940. He asked her once, "What can I ever do to pay you back for all you've done for me?" And she told him, "Just pass it on." And that's, I think, what he did the rest of his life. He passed it on.

[**BILL MONROE**] Jimmie knew how to sing and keep the timing of his music right. All of his music had some blues in it, and I've always loved the blues. "Muleskinner Blues" was the first one I ever sung on the Grand Ole Opry, and, I'm not bragging, but I got three encores the first time I ever sung it there. So, I always liked Jimmie's singing. He had a good voice.

Monroe's 1940 revival of "Muleskinner Blues" is one of dozens of recordings that have kept Rodgers's legacy alive. Webb Pierce

topped the charts with "In the Jailhouse Now" in 1955. Hank Snow saluted his idol with a 1960 album. Jimmie Skinner, Elton Britt, Yodeling Slim Clark, and Grandpa Jones also issued collections of Rodgers songs. Lefty Frizzell hit the charts with "Travellin' Blues" in 1951, and his Rodgers tributes, too, were assembled for an LP. One of the landmark tribute records was Merle Haggard's double album Same Train, Different Time. *This 1969 release alerted a whole new generation to Jimmie Rodgers's genius.*

[**MERLE HAGGARD**] His music was like newsworthy. It was about the Depression. It was about the blues of the people that lived during that Dust Bowl. And I thought it was for me. Jimmie Rodgers was one of the best newscasters of all. He did it all in key.

▲

Mr. and Mrs. Ralph Peer (center) visit Jimmy and Carrie Rodgers and their daughter Anita at "Blue Yodeler's Paradise" in 1930.

"I sang 'T For Texas.' I heard it by Jimmie Rodgers. I learned it from Jimmie. I imitated him. Dad thought that all the songs I should do were like Jimmie Rodgers's old songs that his generation would love to hear redone."

CLINT BLACK

Two national icons pose together during their Texas tour of 1931. Jimmie Rodgers (left) and Will Rogers.

Superstar Dolly Parton scored her first top-ten hit in 1970. It was the Jimmie Rodgers classic "Muleskinner Blues."

[**DOLLY PARTON**] Jimmie wrote wonderful songs. Buck Trent is a man that played in Porter Wagoner's group for many years and was famous for mastering and creatin' that electric banjo, and I remember once he said, "Why don't you do 'Muleskinner Blues' as a girl song?" Porter did produce it and had wonderful ideas. So they got a big ole whip, and we had that in the studio. We had a lot of laughs, crackin' the whip and doin' the song. And it was a big hit for me.

[**CRYSTAL GAYLE**] When I recorded the album *Miss the Mississippi*, we had a lot of fun working on it. But the title song, Jimmie Rodgers's song "Miss the Mississippi and You"—it was special. We took it and did it in, I guess you could say, the Crystal Gayle way. 'Cause I can't yodel. But I tried. It was just the feel of it, the lonesome feel, you know. You're out there, working the road, but you still miss that home.

"In the Jailhouse Now" was revived by Johnny Cash (1962), Sonny James (1977), and Willie Nelson (1982). "T for Texas" entered the repertoires of Grandpa Jones (1963), Tompall Glaser (1976), and Lynyrd Skynyrd (1976). Maria Muldaur sang "Any Old Time" in 1974. As recently as 1989, Tanya Tucker was on the popularity charts with "Daddy and Home." The last song recorded by the Grateful Dead's Jerry Garcia before his death in 1995 was "Blue Yodel No. 9."

One of the earliest to pick up Jimmie Rodgers's bluesy, rambling-boy, "rounder" image was Bill Carlisle. His older brother, Cliff, accompanied Rodgers on disc.

[**BILL CARLISLE**] I guess some of you folks wanna know when I did start thinkin' about gettin' into this business. We had a show in Louisville, Kentucky, there called *The Carlisle Barn Dance*, and I wrote a tune about that time called "Rattlesnake Daddy." (I wrote songs back when I first started out recording, but I did 'em for free, you might say. Made fifty dollars on "Rattle-snake Daddy.") And we'd have to do it three or four times every Saturday night. I don't do it anymore. It's kind of a risqué tune.

▲

Trains and hobos are staples of country songs, thanks to old-time artists like Jimmie Rodgers and modern stylists like Boxcar Willie.

"Rattlesnake Daddy" kicked off Bill's recording career in 1933. He followed it with items like the bluesy, ribald "String Bean Mama," "Copper-Head Mama," and "Sally, Let Your Bangs Hang Down," and was promoted as a successor to Jimmie Rodgers. Still exhibiting the good-natured "rounder" personality he'd developed in the '30s, Bill Carlisle entered the '50s with his biggest hits of all, the novelties "Too Old to Cut the Mustard" and "No Help Wanted." In 1954, he reinterpreted the r&b hit "Honey Love" as a country tune. In turn, Bill's "Leave That Liar Alone" of 1953 became the Ray Charles r&b favorite "Leave My

Governor Jimmie Davis became country's longest-tenured star, thanks to hits like 1935's "Nobody's Darlin,'" publicity like this 1944 magazine cover story, and radio broadcasts like the one pictured above.

Woman Alone" four years later. *Another Jimmie Rodgers disciple who went on to have an extraordinarily long career was Louisiana's Jimmie Davis. After beginning his recording career in 1928, Davis became one of the biggest country stars of all time.*

[**GOVERNOR JIMMIE DAVIS**] In the early days, I was singin' blues then a whole lot. I had a couple of blacks in my band. One of the greatest bluesmen was Ed Schaffer. Took another one, Oscar Woods. He played dobro; he played it with a small bottle as a slide.

Schaffer and Woods can be heard on Davis's naughty 1932 single "Red Nightgown Blues." Like Bill Carlisle, Jimmie Davis specialized in off-color hillbilly blues tunes during his early recording career, 1928–35. "Jellyroll Blues," "Bear Cat Mama From Horner's Corners," "Tom Cat and Pussy Blues," and "Organ Grinder Blues" were typical. When Davis went into politics in the 1940s, these numbers came back to haunt him. But not for long.

[**GOVERNOR JIMMIE DAVIS**] They were not dirty songs. There was no cussin', no four-letter words, just a lot of silly songs. I had a song called the "Bed Bug Blues"—things like that. Political opponents put down the words and passed 'em out as anti-Davis campaign literature. One of the fellows running put it in the paper: "I wanna tell you about a man's runnin' for governor up here. I want you to know somethin' about him, because ain't no tellin' what mess we gonna be in if he gets in there. I'll be out there at a certain park at 2:00." Well, I got to where it was gonna be, and the people, they was scattered all over the place out there. Just a big crowd.

He said in the paper, "I don't want the children to come. I don't want 'em to hear these songs. I want the ministers to come, all the preachers." He had a Victrola nearly high as I am, and a stack of my records. He put one on there—a song I had—"Comin' Through Town in a Red Nightgown." And when he started that, they started pairin' off, everybody dancin' except one man didn't have a partner, so he was soloing it. Some of 'em was dancin' all into the woods.

He said, "If that's the way you feel about it, why you can just have it! I'm goin'! He stomped the records, broke 'em all up on the ground.

In 1934, Jimmie Davis ascended to country superstardom with "Nobody's Darling But Mine," one of the biggest hits of the Depression.

[**CLINTON GREGORY**] I've always loved the song. It's a beautiful song about somebody dying. My dad used to play it, and when he'd get to drinking a little, he'd sing it. And that's where I learned it. In 1994, I thought, "I'm gonna give this a shot." It's a good showoff thing for some harmonies and some fiddle playing, and maybe a little bit of soul you could add into it. And it's one of my favorites.

[**PATSY MONTANA**] The first break I ever got at all, was Jimmie Davis. I came home one year for my first vacation, and my folks had never heard me on the air. We didn't live too far from Shreveport, Louisiana, and KWKH. So I go down there one day, walk in and say, "I wanna go on the air for two weeks"—something I would never dare do today.

Jimmie was the City Clerk of Shreveport. He heard a

JIMMIE DAVIS
(1902–)

HOME AREA
Shreveport, Louisiana

SIGNIFICANCE
Early white blues stylist, apparently the first country star to tour and record regularly with African-American sidemen. Originated several standards during the Depression. Rose from music star to the governorship of Louisiana (1944–48 and 1960–64). The first country artist to have his life made into a motion picture, 1947's *Louisiana*. Attained gospel stardom later in life. Longest recording career of anyone, from 1928 into the mid 1990s.

POPULAR SONGS
"Bear Cat Mama From Horner's Corners" (1930), "Nobody's Darling But Mine" (1934), "I Wish I Had Never Seen Sunshine" (1936), "It Makes No Difference Now" (1938), "You Are My Sunshine" (1940), "There's a New Moon Over My Shoulder" (1945), "Supper Time" (1953), "Where the Old Red River Flows" (1962)

INFLUENCED
Patsy Montana, Red Foley, Hank Williams, Clinton Gregory

HONORS
Country Music Hall of Fame, 1972; Nashville Songwriters Hall of Fame, 1971

BILL CARLISLE
(1908–   )

HOME AREA
Central Kentucky

SIGNIFICANCE
Brother/partner Cliff Carlisle (1904–83) was an early popularizer of the steel/dobro guitar sound and one of the most prolific record makers and songwriters of the 1930s. Both became solo hillbilly blues stylists. Noted for outrageous showmanship. Gave Chet Atkins his first music job and introduced him to Nashville as a session musician.

POPULAR SONGS
"Rattlesnake Daddy" (1933), "Rainbow at Midnight" (with Cliff, 1946), "Tramp on the Street" (1948), "Too Old to Cut the Mustard" (1951), "No Help Wanted" (1953), "Knot Hole" (1953), "Is Zat You Myrtle" (1953), "Leave That Liar Alone" (1953), "T'Ain't Nice to Talk Like That" (1954), "Honey Love" (1954), "I'm Rough Stuff" (1957), "What Kinda Deal Is This?" (1965)

INFLUENCED
Chet Atkins, Martha Carson, George Riddle

HONORS
Grand Ole Opry cast, 1953

The irrepressible Bill Carlisle (center) has been knockin' 'em dead for more than sixty years.

broadcast and called up one day. Wanted to know if I'd like to go to New York. I wasn't gonna bite on somethin' like that, thinking, "He's just some guy tryin' to get smart." I hadn't ever heard of Jimmie Davis. I was tellin' my brother about it. Oh, he just liked to had a fit: "Hey, that's *the* Jimmie Davis." With Jimmie Davis—that's the first break I got in the business.

[GOVERNOR JIMMIE DAVIS] If I had to pick a favorite of all the country music singers, I would pick Jimmie Rodgers. Like so many people, I tried to yodel like he did, but nobody can really replace him, his yodelin' and singin'. I think he was most complete artist of his kind.

[TRACY BYRD] Jimmie Rodgers's music was the beginning of everything.

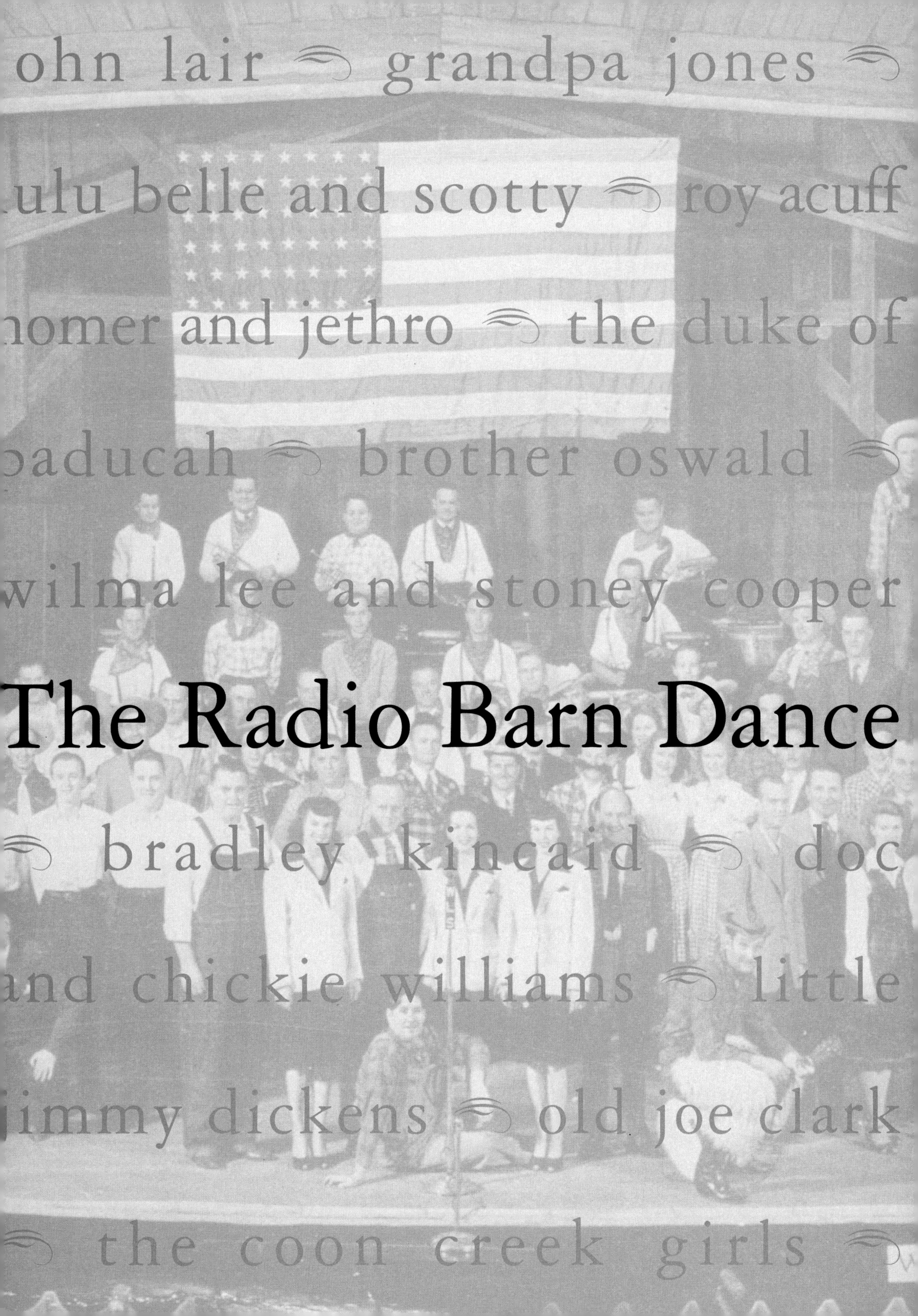

ohn lair ∾ grandpa jones ∾

ulu belle and scotty ∾ roy acuff

homer and jethro ∾ the duke of

paducah ∾ brother oswald ∾

wilma lee and stoney cooper

The Radio Barn Dance

∾ bradley kincaid ∾ doc

and chickie williams ∾ little

jimmy dickens ∾ old joe clark

∾ the coon creek girls

[The emerging country-music industry grew side by side with the development of radio in the United States. KDKA, the nation's first commercial radio station, crackled to life in Pittsburgh in 1920. In 1922, the year of the first country recording, there were 30 U.S. stations; by 1923 there were 556. ⌒]

Country was on the air from the start. KDKA, Ft. Worth's WBAP, and Atlanta's WSB were among the stations with country shows during 1922–24. The magical experience of hearing music over the airwaves had a profound impact on country people.

—◦—

[**SAM PHILLIPS**] There was somethin' that came outta that speaker that I don't believe can be re-created to the mind today. I don't believe there's one thing that I can think of that stirred the imagination like: "Hey, I know a little somethin' about the world! I'm hearin' somethin' from Nashville, Tennessee."

[**BILL ANDERSON**] My mother and dad told me that I could find country music on the radio a long time before I could tie my shoelaces. The songs painted pictures with words.

[**EDDY ARNOLD**] You know what I did? Now this is gonna sound like a made-up story, what I'm about to tell you. I came from as far back as anybody. I grew up on a dirt-road farm, and I'd sit on my porch in the spring and the summer with my guitar, and I'd strum for anybody that came along. There was a man that drove up in front of our place. He was selling subscriptions to a newspaper in Jackson, Tennessee, and he heard me. I played him a little tune. He said, "Son, I probably can get you a little audition on the radio station." And he did, on a station called WTJS. So I went down there, and they let me on that station.

[**DOC WILLIAMS**] I started in Cleveland, Ohio, WJY, on a program called *The Barn Busters*. Morey Amsterdam was the announcer. I made a dollar a night.

[**PHIL EVERLY, OF THE EVERLY BROTHERS**] My brother started in radio before I did. He had a little show in a town called Shenandoah, Iowa, on a station called KMA—*The Little Donny Show*. He was in the third grade. On Saturday we'd go down there, and he would sing for fifteen minutes. And all the third-grade little girls just thought he was swell. And I was smart enough to notice that. So it wasn't that much longer that I joined him. I guess it's like going to the "University of Music."

[**CLIFFIE STONE**] In the twenties and thirties, almost each local station had a cowboy band. Usually we were on from five to seven in the morning, and we sold vitamins and tonic.

[**WILMA LEE COOPER**] The radio station at WSVA, Harrisonburg, Virginia, offered my dad and mother—as we came through that town—a daily radio program. Dad said, "Oh, we couldn't do that. The girls are all in school. Now, we might could come over and sing for you on Saturdays." Like we was doing them a big favor. And so that's how they hired us, and we started in radio.

Country entertainers were gypsies. You'd build up your popularity over the radio airwaves and promote your shows throughout the listening area. When you'd "played out" a region, you

"The radio was my only way of finding out what was out there beyond the cotton fields of home."

———

CHARLEY PRIDE

WLS National Barn Dance Cast, Octobe

The WLS National Barn Dance from Chicago ruled the radio airwaves of the 1930s and 1940s, generating hundreds of souvenir items like this square-dance instruction booklet, "Family Album," and cast photo.

moved on to the next station. The live country radio shows were called "barn dances." They flourished from 1925 to 1955 as a show-biz institution. At one time, virtually every sizable station had one.

[**JIM GASKIN**] A classic radio barn dance involved a pretty large group of very closely associated entertainers. They had worked together and knew each other so well they were almost like a family. There were certain classic barn dance acts: a brother duet, a sisters' group, a western group, the baggy-pants comedian who was usually a banjo picker, a quartet, the ballad singer, the love-song crooner. There was also the boy/girl courtship situation. Always had that in the show. And all that was knitted together by the master of ceremonies, a folksy, down-to-earth kind of person.

In the 1930s and 1940s there were dozens of such touring troupes. The prototype was Chicago's National Barn Dance on WLS, which began in 1924. In 1933, the show became radio's first network barn dance (NBC) and the first to send its cast out on road shows. Bill Monroe, now famed as the father of bluegrass music, was a square dancer in the WLS troupe.

The National Barn Dance launched Gene Autry, Patsy Montana, Rex Allen, George Gobel,

Red Foley, Bradley Kincaid, and many other country greats. During the show's heyday, its king and queen were Lulu Belle and Scotty.

[**REX ALLEN**] Originally, Lulu Belle's partner was Red Foley, and they called them Lulu Belle and Burr Head. But she married Scotty, and they were the toast of that whole part of the country for many, many years.

I was workin' with a group out of Philadelphia called The Sleepy Hollow Gang. I was their fiddle player and worked their radio shows and the park every Sunday up at Allentown, Pennsylvania. Lu and Scotty used to work there in the summer, and they asked me one day, "Did you ever think about maybe goin' on National Barn Dance?" I said, "Wheeew, I've thought about that a lot, but never seriously." They said, "Well, why don't you come over and take an audition?" And I just beat them home to Chicago, got the job, and everything went from there.

Another legendary family act that traces its heritage back to WLS is the Everly Brothers.

[**PHIL EVERLY**] At the National Barn Dance out of Chicago, my father worked with a man named Red Green. They did a duet and had an early morning WLS radio show where the two of them sang together. Our father was an extraordinary man. He was a thumb picker. He is responsible, along with a man named Mose Rager, for teaching Merle Travis how to play. He carried that to WLS and worked with Gene Autry. And from WLS, that thumb-pick style went to Chet Atkins, and then just spread across the country.

The National Barn Dance's format was copied by hundreds of similar radio shows. It survived into the TV era, broadcasting as The ABC Barn Dance *during the 1949 season, but its popularity diminished during the onslaught of rock 'n' roll. WLS switched to teen music in 1960, and the* Barn Dance *folded in 1969 on WGN. Today, there are only three survivors from the old days: The Wheeling Jamboree in Wheeling, West Virginia, the Renfro Valley Barn Dance*

Lulu Belle and Scotty were "The Sweethearts of Country Music" on radio and in eight Hollywood films, including 1944's The National Barn Dance.
▼

LULU BELLE & SCOTTY

near Versailles, Kentucky, and Nashville's Grand Ole Opry.

[**DOC WILLIAMS**] The Wheeling Jamboree started in 1933, kind of by a fluke. The movie didn't arrive at the Capitol Theatre in downtown Wheeling. They called the radio station upstairs in the building above them and wanted to know if they could get a stage show together. So they did. They put their country radio show, which had started in 1927, on the Capitol Theatre stage. And thirty-five hundred people got in, and maybe two or three thousand more never even got inside the door.

The Wheeling Jamboree became an important force in popularizing country music in the Northeast. Among the cast's notable graduates are such celebrities as Grandpa Jones, Hawkshaw Hawkins, Red Sovine, Reno and Smiley, Elton Britt, Jimmy Martin, Kenny Roberts, and Jimmy Dickens.

[**KATHY MATTEA**] My great-uncle was a buck dancer, a buck-and-wing dancer on the Jamboree. When I was a kid, they would talk about him dancing on the radio. And I couldn't figure out how he would dance on the radio. How did they know? It wasn't 'til later that I really appreciated what he did.

[**WILMA LEE COOPER**] We went in July of '47 into WWVA, Wheeling, West Virginia, where we stayed for ten years. You come out and you do the song, and those people really give you a hand, right in the song. We rocked that place.

In 1977, WWVA inaugurated a summer festival called Jamboree in the Hills. Today, it is the largest annual country music event in the

The Duke of Paducah (Benjamin "Whitey" Ford) and the comedy team of Homer & Jethro (Henry Haynes, left, and Kenneth Burns) were among the many alumni of Kentucky's Renfro Valley Barn Dance.

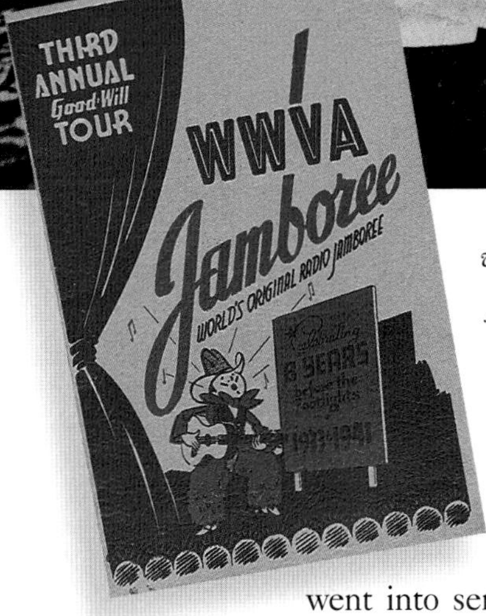

THIRD ANNUAL *Good-Will* TOUR — WWVA *Jamboree* — WORLD'S ORIGINAL RADIO JAMBOREE

world. At the other end of the barn-dance spectrum is Renfro Valley, founded in 1937 by WLS/National Barn Dance executive John Lair. Although Renfro also hosts modern outdoor summer festivals, its Sunday Mornin' Gathering *is the surviving broadcast that is closest in spirit to the barn-dance days of old.*

[**ANN LAIR HENDERSON**] John Lair was a farm boy. My father said he never left the Renfro Valley until he went into service for World War I. When he came home after the war was over, for the first time he began to appreciate what he had grown up with and looked around him and thought, "This is all going to disappear. All these log homes I see, all this way of life is changing after the war."

There was a two-story log house here in Renfro Valley that was the home of a great-uncle of his. It had been standing in 1800. That became the Renfro Valley "home" in his mind. My father decided about 1937 it was time to make the break. He brought, from WLS to Cincinnati, some people he had under contract: Red Foley, Lily May Leadford, the Girls of the Golden West, Slim Miller. They were

▲

Fan mail poured into West Virginia's WWVA as a result of its radio jamboree, which was a significant force in popularizing country music in the Northeast.

"The very first time I ever played the old Ryman, I was seventeen years old. Boy, what a great time. That was 1973, before the Opry moved out to the suburbs. I'm so proud that I was a part of that era of country music, when it was still the Opry at the Ryman Auditorium."

STEVE WARINER

WSM's Grand Ole Opry broadcast live from the Ryman Auditorium between 1943 and 1974. Crowds lined up for blocks to see it at "The Mother Church of Country Music."

about two years building the barn and restaurant and the cabins in Renfro Valley. November 4, 1939, was the first broadcast.

The Renfro Valley Barn Dance spawned such stars as Little Eller and Shorty Long, The Coon Creek Girls, Homer and Jethro, Aunt Idy, Granny Harper, and the Duke of Paducah.

[**PETE STAMPER**] Red Foley was really my idol in country music. When he sung a gospel song, he felt it. When he sang a love song, he felt that. There was no put-on about Red Foley.

[**OLD JOE CLARK**] Aunt Idy was vaudeville. She was big-time vaudeville. The Duke of Paducah? Well, he was another vaudeville act. See, that's what Mr. Lair done here. He brought people in that knew show business. The Coon Creeks was natural-born country people. Good people, hard workin' people. And so when they went out on the road, they were not puttin' on. It was real. Granny Harper was an old lady from over here in Nicholasville. We called her right off the street. That's where she used to play. Played the fiddle on the street durin' tobacco-season time, in Lexington. Granny was a real trophy. I mean, she was good. She played the fiddle and the French harp and danced. She loved Old Joe Clark. Bless her heart. I worked with her about eighteen years, and she never got no older. No tellin' how old she was when she died. You never get old in this business. You just die up against a stump somewheres.

Renfro Valley hosts more than three hundred thousand visitors a year nowadays. Its Saturday night shindig is a contemporary-country show in a state-of-the-art hall, but Sunday's show is still in the old barn, just the way John Lair left it when he died, at age ninety-one, in 1985.

[**DOLLY PARTON**] Music played such a wonderful part on the radio. I think all mountain children pretend that they're stars. And tin cans make great microphones. I'd drive a tobacco stick down in the porch and then put the tin can on top of it and poke little holes in it to make that like a real microphone. That was where I really used to do a lot of my performin'.

For Dolly and thousands of other country musicians, the ultimate fantasy was playing on the stage of the Grand Ole Opry. Broadcast weekly on WSM since 1925, it is the world's longest-running radio show. WLS/National Barn Dance alumnus George D. Hay ("The Solemn Old Judge") began broadcasting a rural fiddler named Uncle Jimmy Thompson on WSM in Nashville, on November 28, 1925. Other local

Phil (left) and Don Everly began their careers as country radio entertainers with parents Ike and Margaret Everly in the 1940s.

▼

entertainers—notably *Uncle Dave Macon, The Crook Brothers, Dr. Humphrey Bate's band, and black "harmonica wizard" Deford Bailey—were gradually added. In 1927 Hay named his Saturday night show* The Grand Ole Opry. *Its popularity grew after WSM's power was increased to 50,000 watts in 1932.*

The Opry groomed several stars in the 1920s and 1930s. In addition to Uncle Dave Macon, the McGees, and Deford Bailey, the cast included The Delmore Brothers, Sarie and Sally, Texas Ruby, Curly Fox, and The Vagabonds. The Opry outgrew the WSM broadcasting studio in 1934 and moved to the eight-hundred-seat Hillsboro Theater. Between 1936 and 1939, it was in the barnlike Dixie Tabernacle in East Nashville. This is where its first modern superstar debuted in 1938.

[**ROY ACUFF, 1988**] I had wanted for a long, long time

George D. Hay, the "Solemn Ol' Judge," was the founding father of the Grand Ole Opry. He also appeared in the 1940 movie spun off from the radio show.

to come to Nashville and try to get on the Opry. And when I was given the opportunity, we were at the Dixie Tabernacle. It was just a gospel tabernacle, where they would walk down the sawdust trail and sit down on just a board.

I realized I had to do something to get the attention of the people. I didn't have any idea when I sang "The Great Speckled Bird" that I'd get the response that I did. But I sang differently from anybody back then. There were crooners back then that'd get up close to the microphone, but I rared back like I was going after the cows, the same way when I used to drive cows out to pasture on the farm. In them hills up there in Union County, I sang loud. I've knocked a lot of small stations off of the air. I took four or five encores that first night, and my mail came in in bushel baskets. Then WSM called and asked me if I'd take a regular job.

Acuff's full-throttle mountain sound electrified audiences. Within two years he was the Opry's biggest headliner, and he remained its living symbol for more than fifty years.

[**KITTY WELLS**] Roy was responsible, really, for the artists gettin' out of the little schoolhouses and going to the bigger auditoriums. He had a great influence on country music.

[**STONEWALL JACKSON**] I would like to pattern myself after Roy Acuff. He could be with the president of the United States or, say, the richest man, Ross Perot, or we'll say anybody—Ted Turner for example, anybody like that. One of the boys come in that worked with me out on the farm, maybe doesn't have but a third-grade education. Roy Acuff would take up as much time and as much attention to this person. He was just as comfortable with that guy as he was with the guy that was president of the United States. That was Roy Acuff.

His showmanship, his singing, and the force of his personality were not Roy Acuff's only contributions. Along with Wilma Lee and Stoney Cooper's Clinch Mountain Clan, Acuff's Smoky Mountain Boys band was notable for popularizing the slurred-note sound of the dobro, paving the way for the steel guitar.

[**CHARLIE COLLINS**] The dobro was really the sound of Roy Acuff and the Smoky Mountain Boys. Roy was one of the first bands to use the dobro, and I always credit Bashful Brother Oswald—whose real name is Pete Kirby—for the sound.

[**BROTHER OSWALD**] A dobro is a Hawaiian guitar with a

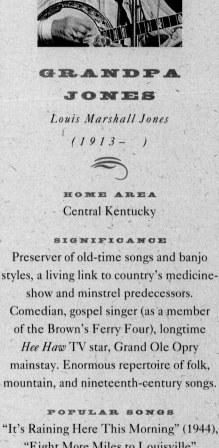

GRANDPA JONES

Louis Marshall Jones
(1 9 1 3 –)

HOME AREA
Central Kentucky

SIGNIFICANCE
Preserver of old-time songs and banjo styles, a living link to country's medicine-show and minstrel predecessors. Comedian, gospel singer (as a member of the Brown's Ferry Four), longtime *Hee Haw* TV star, Grand Ole Opry mainstay. Enormous repertoire of folk, mountain, and nineteenth-century songs.

POPULAR SONGS
"It's Raining Here This Morning" (1944), "Eight More Miles to Louisville" (1946), "Mountain Dew" (1947), "Old Rattler" (1947), "Are You From Dixie?" (1948), "T for Texas" (1963), "The Christmas Guest" (1969)

INFLUENCED
Merle Travis, Joe Maphis, Ramona Jones, Stringbean

HONORS
Country Music Hall of Fame, 1978

▲

East Nashville's Dixie Tabernacle had a sawdust floor and wooden benches, but that is where the Grand Ole Opry rose to fame in 1936–39. As suggested by the 1938 Rural Radio *magazine cover shown at lower right, down-home Opry stars such as Sarie & Sally were like neighbors visiting your living room.*

resonator with an amplifier cone in it. You don't use no electricity to it at all, but it sounds like an electric guitar when you put the mike down on it real close.

[**BILL ANDERSON**] I idolized Roy Acuff. We became very, very close because of a song "I Wonder If God Likes Country Music," which is the story about an old man coming into a venue one night prior to a concert and picking up the younger artist's guitar, knowing that his life is about over and wondering if when he gets up to heaven if God is going to like country music. Roy and I sang this song together many, many times on the Grand Ole Opry stage.

I never will forget the last time that we did it. It was in October of 1992, and Roy was eighty-nine years old at the time, and he had been hospitalized for a few days with the problems that ultimately led to his death. He was so determined to be on the Opry this particular night that, against the doctor's wishes, he got up out of the hospital bed and came to the Grand Ole Opry. I saw them leading him out to the stage, and he was so feeble, I thought, "There's no way this man can possibly perform." And yet the minute that curtain went up, something came over him. I turned to him, and I said, "Mr. Roy, we didn't have a chance to rehearse or anything, but would you sing the song with me tonight?"

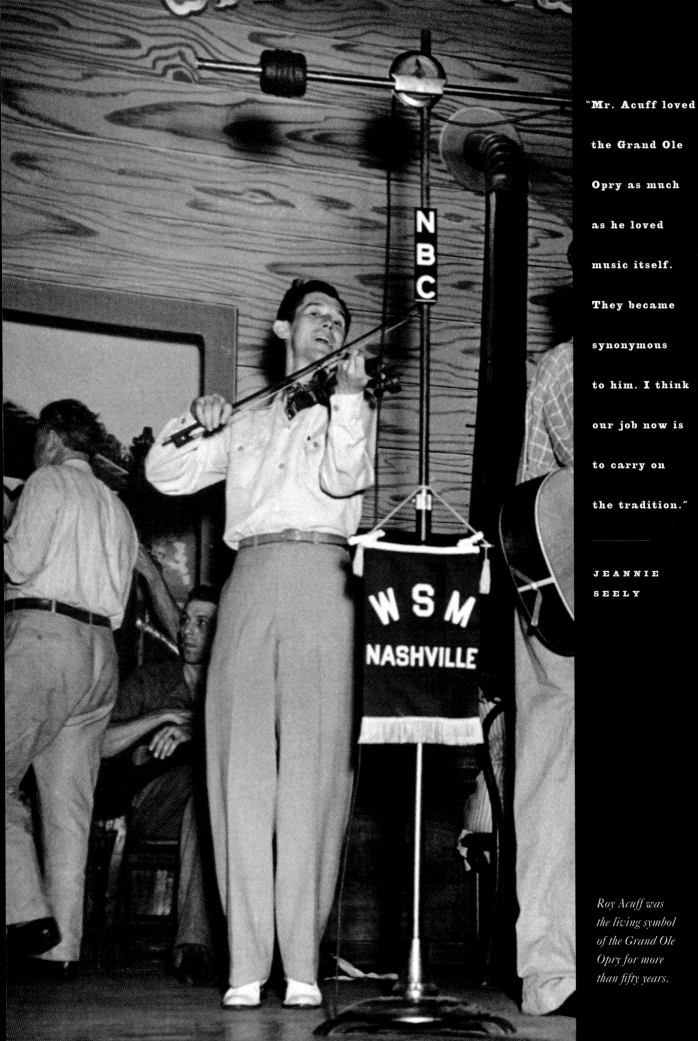

"Mr. Acuff loved the Grand Ole Opry as much as he loved music itself. They became synonymous to him. I think our job now is to carry on the tradition."

JEANNIE SEELY

Roy Acuff was the living symbol of the Grand Ole Opry for more than fifty years.

ROY ACUFF
(1903–1992)

HOME AREA
Maynardville, Tennessee

SIGNIFICANCE
"The King of Country Music." Major mountain-music stylist. His Smoky Mountain Boys band included Brother Oswald (Pete Kirby), seminal dobro stylist. Father figure on Grand Ole Opry for more than fifty years. His Acuff-Rose Publishing the founding firm of the Nashville music business. Considered to be the Opry's first superstar singer.

POPULAR SONGS
"The Great Speckled Bird" (1938), "Wabash Cannonball" (1938), "The Precious Jewel" (1940), "Wreck on the Highway" (1942), "Fire Ball Mail" (1942), "Night Train to Memphis" (1942), "Wait for the Light to Shine" (1944), "The Prodigal Son" (1944), "I'll Forgive You But I Can't Forget" (1944), "Blue Eyes Crying in the Rain" (1945), "Jole Blon" (1947), "Waltz of the Wind" (1948), "Once More" (1958), "I Saw the Light" (1971)

INFLUENCED
Hank Williams, George Jones, Boxcar Willie, Willie Nelson

HONORS
Country Music Hall of Fame, 1962; Lifetime Achievement Grammy Award, 1987; Hollywood Walk of Fame

My guitar player kicked off the song, and Roy jumped in when it came his time.

But it was different that last time because he leaned against the microphone stand and never opened his eyes. He kept his eyes closed the entire time he was singing, "I wonder if God likes country music? / Will there be a place up there to sing my song? / Will they make my fingers nimble like they used to be? / Will I play my guitar and sing along?"

Acuff's arrival coincided with the Opry's ascendance to the front ranks of the radio barn dances. In rapid succession, the show recruited Bill Monroe (1939), Minnie Pearl (1940), Ernest Tubb (1942), Eddy Arnold (1943), Red Foley (1946), Hank Williams (1949), and Hank Snow (1950), giving it an unparalleled cast of stars. The show went coast-to-coast on NBC in 1943; three years later the network dropped WLS's National Barn Dance, solidifying the Opry's new eminence.

[**JUNE CARTER CASH**] When we first came, we were quite young, Helen and Anita and I. And it was amazing to me that I was finally gonna get to work where Uncle Dave Macon and Sam and Kirk McGee, Bill Monroe, Roy Acuff, Ernest Tubb, and some of those people were.

[**MARTY STUART**] I knew if I ever came to Nashville that I was gonna make somethin' out of it. I was so excited, I stood up in the front of the Greyhound bus from Philadelphia, Mississippi, to Jackson, Tennessee, which is about five hours, and talked to the driver the whole way. I finally fell asleep at three in the morning, thereabouts. The old Greyhound bus station was right across the street from the Ryman Auditorium in Nashville. I got off of that bus, and I stood real still. It froze me. I thought, "I know where I came from, and I'll never forget, but that's where the future is for me." The next weekend, I was on stage playin' with Lester Flatt. My peers became Ernest Tubb, Grandpa Jones, Stringbean, Bill Monroe, Little Jimmy Dickens—the guys that invented country music.

After a 1939–43 stint at Nashville's War Memorial Auditorium, the Opry found its true home, the three-thousand-seat Ryman Auditorium. Known as "the Carnegie Hall of the South," the Ryman housed the show from 1943 to 1974. No one who saw the Opry there ever forgot it.

[**BILLY WALKER**] The Ryman Auditorium was a marvelous, marvelous place to sing in. It really didn't have to have a sound system to hear yourself sing. I get a chill every time

JAM UP & HONEY

UNCLE DAVE MACON

GEORGE D. HAY

DAVID COBB

GRAND OLE OPRY

THE DANIEL QUARTET

BILL MONROE

PURINA'S GRAND OLE OPRY
SAT. 6:30 & 8:00 P.M. (CWT)

THE BLUE GRASS BOYS

I hear some of those old shows that we used to do in there.

[MARTY STUART] You know, the Ryman Auditorium to me represents what it's all about. It's the Mother Church of Country Music.

[LORETTA LYNN] When I first stepped on the stage at the Grand Ole Opry, they had to push me out on the stage because I was so bashful and backward. I remember patting my foot to my song. And I remember, after the song was over, running out the back and meeting my husband. He was listening to it in the car, and we were hugging. I said, "Honey, I've just sung on the Grand Ole Opry!"

[FARON YOUNG] The first time I went on the Grand Ole Opry, I was so nervous, I could have threaded a sewing machine with it running. When I got through with the song, I ran off the stage, and Ernest Tubb grabbed me. He said, "Get back out there. You're getting an encore." I went back out and sang the same song over again. Then, when I came off, Hank Williams Sr. came over and said, he said, "Hey, boy, you know, you just might make it in this business. You're pretty good, boy." That was like Jesus saying, "Boy," you know, when Hank told me that.

Radio barn dances were sponsored by rural products like Purina livestock food, as illustrated by this Opry souvenir photo (above), or Stuart's Dyspepsia Tablets, sponsors of the WJJD souvenir fan (below left).

ATLANTA
The WSB Barn Dance (WSB)
CHARLOTTE
The Crazy Barn Dance (WBT)
CHICAGO
The National Barn Dance (WLS)
CINCINATTI
The Boone County Jamboree,
The Midwestern Hayride (WLW)
DALLAS
The Big D Jamboree
DESMOINES
The Iowa Barn Dance Frolic (WHO)
FT. WAYNE
The Hoosier Hop (WOWO)
KANSAS CITY
Brush Creek Follies (KMBC)
KNOXVILLE
The Tennessee Barn Dance (KNOX)
LOS ANGELES
Hometown Jamboree, Hollywood Barn
Dance (KNX), Covered Wagon Jubilee
(KFUD), Lucky Stars (KFWB)
LOUISVILLE
Renfro Valley (WHAS)
MINNEAPOLIS
Sunset Valley Barn Dance (KSTP)
NASHVILLE
The Grand Ole Opry (WSM)
NEW YORK
Village Barn Dance
OKLAHOMA CITY
Bluff Creek Round-Up (KOMA)
PASADENA
The Dinner Bell Roundup (KXLA)
PHILADELPHIA
Sleepy Hollow Ranch (WFIL)
RICHMOND
Old Dominion Barn Dance (WRVA)
ST. LOUIS
The Old-Fashioned Barn Dance (KMOX)
SHREVEPORT
Louisiana Hayride (KWKH)
SPRINGFIELD
The Ozark Jubilee (KWTO)
TULSA
Saddle Mountain Round-Up (KVOO)
WHEELING
The Wheeling Jamboree (WWVA)

Grandpa Jones has been a "grandpa" since he first put on the old-timer outfit at age twenty-two in 1935. He's rousing a Virginia radio audience in this 1949 photo.

[**HAL KETCHUM**] There's a section of wooden stage that was moved from the Ryman Auditorium out to the Opryland site, the present Opryland site, that holds a lot of the soul and a lot of notes that were played at the Ryman. And the first time I hit the Opry stage, I stood on that spot and felt the soul of all the people that had stood there before.

[**PATTY LOVELESS**] To me, when I stand on that piece, I'm like, "Patsy Cline stood here, Loretta Lynn has stood here so many times, Hank Williams stood here." And I tell myself that.

[**MARTY STUART**] This is the place where Hank Williams encored "Lovesick Blues" seven times. This is the place where Patsy Cline was. This is the place where country music as we know it was pulled together.

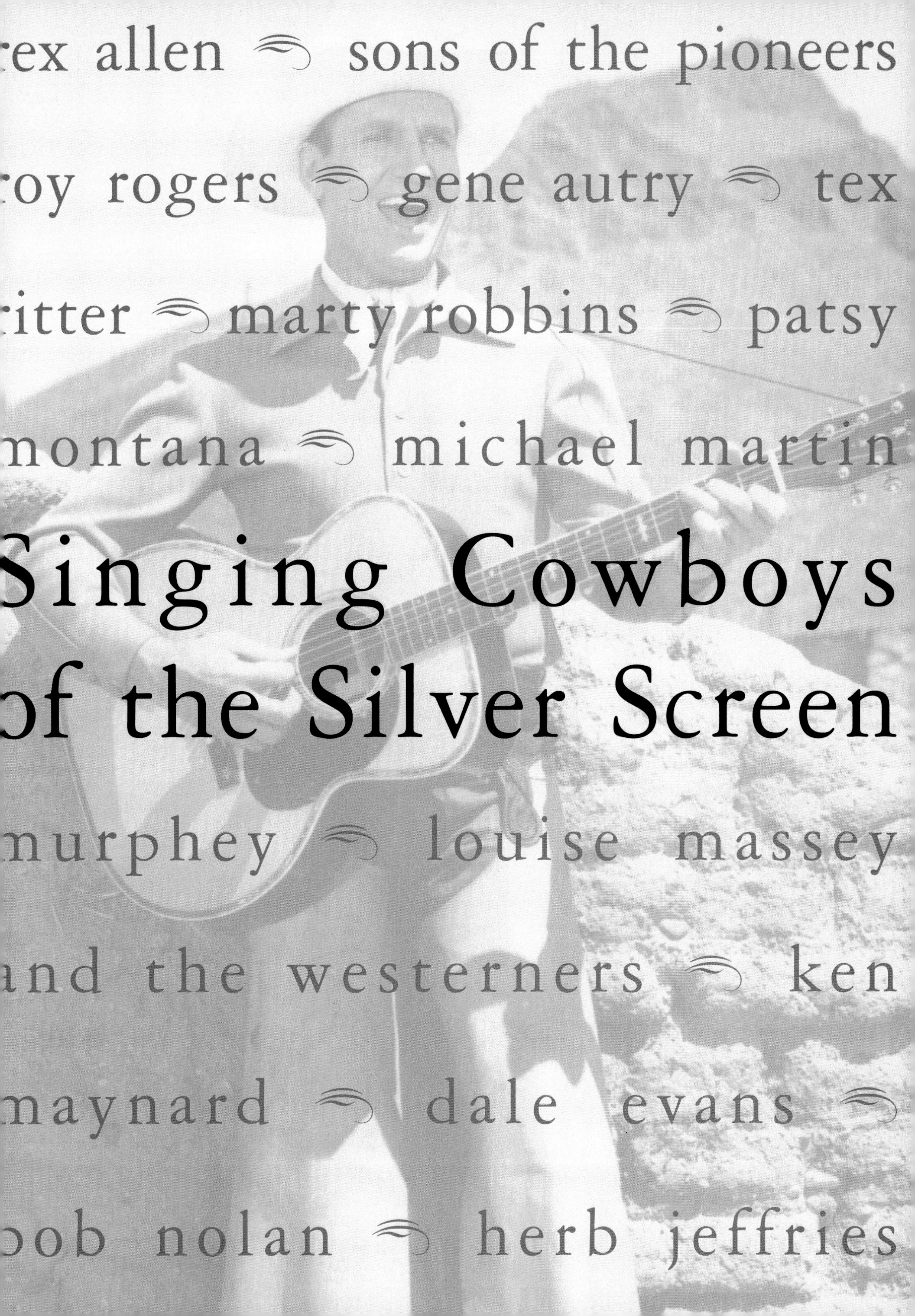

tex allen ～ sons of the pioneers
roy rogers ～ gene autry ～ tex
ritter ～ marty robbins ～ patsy
montana ～ michael martin

Singing Cowboys
of the Silver Screen

murphey ～ louise massey
and the westerners ～ ken
maynard ～ dale evans
bob nolan ～ herb jeffries

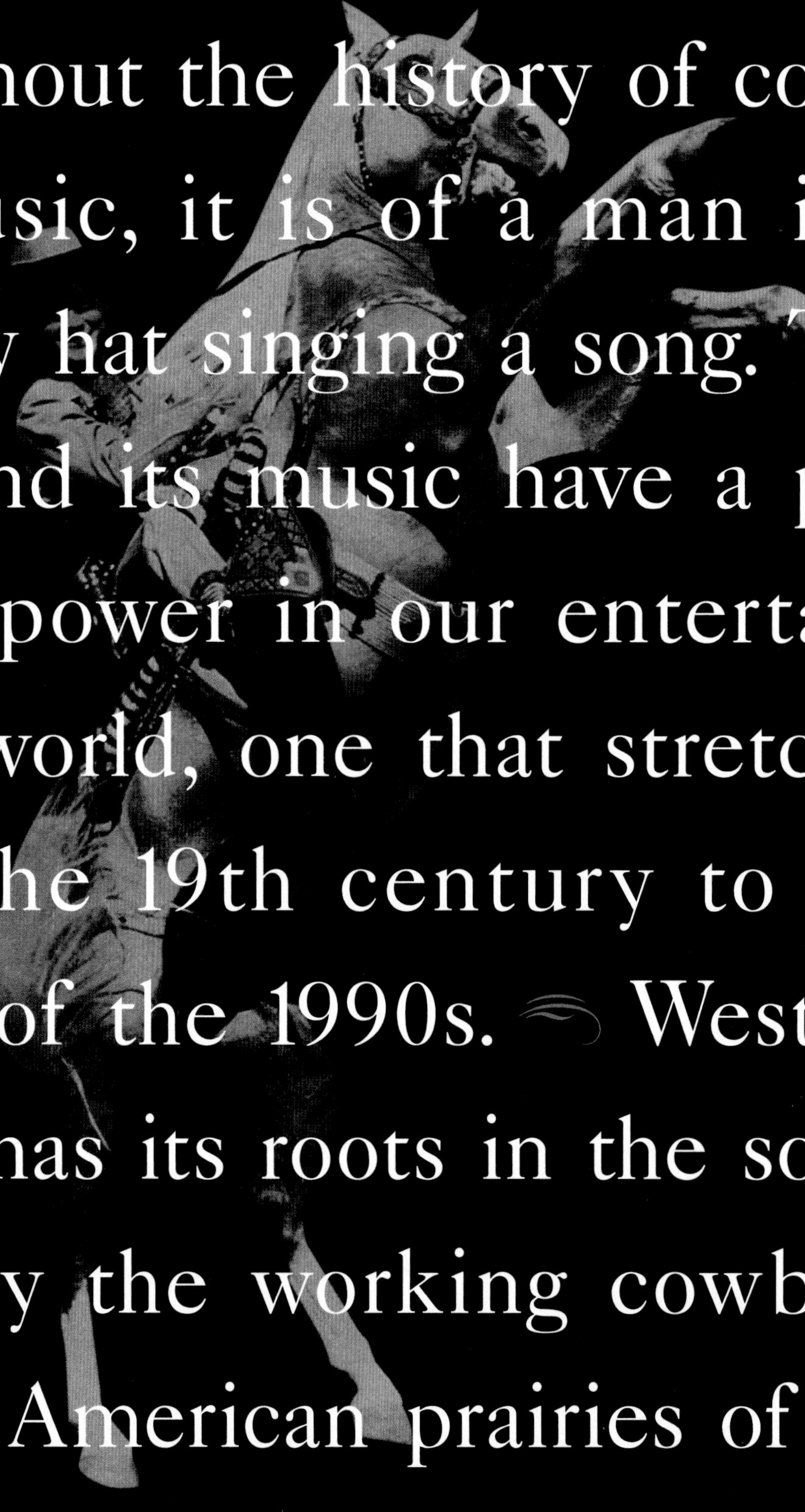

[If there is one enduring image throughout the history of country music, it is of a man in a cowboy hat singing a song. The west and its music have a profound power in our entertainment world, one that stretches from the 19th century to the music of the 1990s. ꩜ Western music has its roots in the songs sung by the working cowboys on the American prairies of the mid 1800s. ꩜]

[**MICHAEL MARTIN MURPHEY**] The cowboy is, in fact, the most powerful image associated with America. When our Olympic team marches in a parade in an international setting, they wear cowboy hats. Our skiers and our runners wear cowboy hats. That's our national uniform.

[**RED STEAGALL**] A lot of what we call country music evolved from the cowboy songs. The cowboy songs originated primarily with the people of Celtic stock who came to the western part of our country from the East Coast or the mountains. You mix that with the German settlers who brought us all the dances, the gospel sounds of the black South, the Appalachian with the banjo and the fiddle, the Hispanic sounds of the guitar from Mexico. You boil all that down into one big pot—our cowboy music evolved from that.

[**BAXTER BLACK**] Why does the cowboy sing? Probably because he's in the company of animals that are not very discriminating.

[**MICHAEL MARTIN MURPHEY**] Now the Hispanic people really invented everything that we have today that we associate with cowboys—from the sombrero hat that we wear, to the slant-heel boots, to the spurs, to the chaps. When Texas became a Republic in 1836, right after the Alamo, the cowboy was written about all over the American press, and then everybody suddenly said, "Wow, there's this amazing new thing out there called a cowboy." And then it became a romantic figure.

[**PETER ROWAN**] I think the influence from Mexico was very strong. In fact, the term "Gringo" is supposed to be from the old song "Green Grow the Lilacs," which was a song they sang in the covered wagons coming across. It's probably an old Irish or Scottish air. That melodic influence went into Mexico and mixed with the old Spanish waltzes, you know.

Historians estimate that one out of every four cowboys in the late 1800s was nonwhite.

[**HERB JEFFRIES**] How the black cowboy came about was during slavery. The escaped slaves would find refuge in the Indian territories. Many of the Indian tribes took the slaves in. They had quite a compassion for the slaves in those days. They were sort of country cousins in a way. And they learned how to ride. Just fantastic riders—without saddles, you know. When they did move out of the Indian tribes into the civilized territories who accepted blacks, such as up in Montana and Canada, they moved as liaisons, who'd bring the trappings from the Indians, sell them at the trading post, and then take food and stuff for the winter back into the Indian tribes. Then some of them became drovers. The cattlemen realized that these men could move their cattle through—the black drovers—and the Indians wouldn't attack them, as they would the paleface.

The appeal of western music is sort of in our blood. It's what this country is all about."

EMMYLOU HARRIS

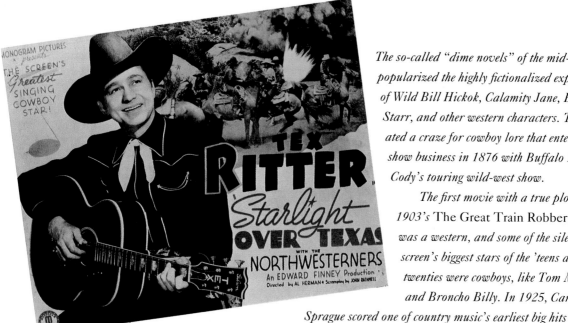

The so-called "dime novels" of the mid-1800s popularized the highly fictionalized exploits of Wild Bill Hickok, Calamity Jane, Belle Starr, and other western characters. They created a craze for cowboy lore that entered show business in 1876 with Buffalo Bill Cody's touring wild-west show.

The first movie with a true plot, 1903's The Great Train Robbery, was a western, and some of the silent screen's biggest stars of the 'teens and twenties were cowboys, like Tom Mix and Broncho Billy. In 1925, Carl T. Sprague scored one of country music's earliest big hits by singing the traditional cowboy favorite "When the Work's All Done This Fall." Jules Allen followed in 1928–29 with "Home on the Range," "Zebra Dun," "Little Joe the Wrangler," and other discs. With the coming of sound films, the Hollywood singing cowboy came to life as a full-blown American icon.

[**DOUG GREEN, OF RIDERS IN THE SKY**] The cowboy tradition started out as the songs that the cowboys sang about ranching and horses they'd ridden, and then, in the 1930s, there came a whole new crop of songwriters—to write for the movies. They were brilliant writers—still some of the best that this music's ever known—Bob Nolan, Tim Spencer, Stan Jones, Billy Hill.

[**DON EDWARDS**] Ken Maynard actually was the first singing cowboy in a motion picture, and, of course, Gene Autry was the guy that made it really famous.

[**SNUFF GARRETT**] Ken Maynard came from silent film. They credit Maynard with doing music, but he was such a horrible singer, and he played fiddle, and it was pretty miserable. But they brought a radio singer who was popular in Chicago, and his name was Gene Autry. He

Hollywood films made American icons of singing cowboys such as Tex Ritter (above) and Gene Autry (right). The image was so powerful that people used to refer to the entire country idiom as "country and western music."

was the first singing cowboy. A man named Nat Levine, who owned a picture company, invited Autry out to be in a Ken Maynard film called *In Old Santa Fe* in 1934, and he sang a song in it. Then Nat Levine decided he wanted to do a very successful serial with Gene called *Phantom Empire* (1935). Then they made the picture *Tumbling Tumbleweeds*, the first Autry film, and it was a monster success. That registered Gene as the first legitimate, starring, singing cowboy.

[**CLIFFIE STONE**] Gene was born in Oklahoma in a little bitty town, and when he was eight years old he got a job sweeping out the Bijou Theater. As a teen, he traveled as a singer with The Fields Brothers Marvelous Medicine Show. Then he took a course in telegraphy, you know da-da da-da-da da—telegrams. Will Rogers's sister had a ranch right close to this little town, so, once a year, Rogers would come to the town to see his sister. And he had a weekly column with the *Washington Post*, which he had to send in, and Gene Autry would send the story. Will saw this eight-dollar guitar that Gene had bought and says, "Whose guitar is that?" Gene says, "Well, that's mine." Will says, "You sing? Sing for me." So he sang. Will says, "Boy, you're pretty good. Tell you what, I want you to go to New York."

Encouraged by Will Rogers, Autry headed for Manhattan in 1927. After a stint in Tulsa on KVOO as "Oklahoma's Yodeling Cowboy," he began recording for RCA in 1929. He ascended to stardom at Art Satherley's American Record Company in 1932 with "That Silver Haired Daddy of Mine," plus star billing on Chicago's WLS National Barn Dance. Autry's radio and disc stardom of 1931–34 led to interest from Hollywood. By 1939, Autry was one of the biggest box office stars in filmdom. His Melody Ranch *was a nationwide radio show from 1939 to 1955. In 1950 he became the first movie star with his own TV series.*

[**GENE AUTRY, 1989**] I personally never considered myself a great actor, a great singer, or anything of that sort. But what the hell is my opinion against that of 250 million other people? I didn't deserve it, but I've had lumbago a few times, and I didn't deserve that either.

[**BILLY WALKER**] Gene Autry captured my heart when I was about thirteen years old, and I said, "I have to do what that guy's doin' on the screen."

GENE AUTRY
(1907–)

HOME AREA
Texas/Oklahoma

SIGNIFICANCE
The first Hollywood singing cowboy star. Image upgraded country culture.

POPULAR SONGS
"That Silver Haired Daddy of Mine" (1932), "The Yellow Rose of Texas" (1933), "Tumbling Tumbleweeds" (1935), "Mexicali Rose" (1936), "Back in the Saddle Again" (1939), "South of the Border" (1939), "You Are My Sunshine" (1941), "Jingle Jangle Jingle" (1942), "Don't Fence Me In" (1945), "Buttons and Bows" (1948), "Rudolph the Red-Nosed Reindeer" (1949), "Peter Cottontail" (1950), "Frosty the Snow Man" (1950)

INFLUENCED
Roy Rogers, the Sons of the Pioneers, Tex Ritter, Riders in the Sky

HONORS
Country Music Hall of Fame, 1969; Nashville Songwriters Hall of Fame, 1970; National Cowboy Hall of Fame, 1972; Academy of Country Music Pioneer Award, 1972; ASCAP Voice of Music Award, 1989; six stars on the Hollywood Walk of Fame; Berwyn, Oklahoma, renamed Gene Autry, Oklahoma

"We only go through this life once. I don't know anybody that's come back. There's only two things you have to worry about—if you're happy or unhappy. I've had an awful lot of fun. I've enjoyed every minute of everything I've done. I had to give the audience and the people who supported me the very best I could, from the bottom of my heart."

GENE AUTRY
1989

Gene Autry and Champion

[**CLIFFIE STONE**] I was doing a show called *Wake Up Ranch* in the morning, a DJ show from seven to nine, and I found sound effects of a rooster crowing. I'd say, "The time is 7:18," and the rooster would crow, "Cockadoodledoo!" People loved the rooster. The rooster's name we picked was Gene Off Key. And I got a call one morning, "Are you Cliffie Stone? I'm Gene Autry." You know at that point, that's kind of like hearing from Frank Sinatra. You're gonna be out of work the rest of your life, right? I mean, he was such a king. He said, "I been hearing about this Gene Off Key you've got down there. I'd like to come down and meet him." And so he did. I introduced him to the rooster on the radio, and he talked to the rooster. It was really, really a great, great moment. And that's how I met Gene.

They hired me to run his publishing companies. I wanna tell you, I have the deepest respect for the man for his business acumen. You know what Gene said to me once? He says, "You know, Cliffie, I can't sing. I can't play the guitar. I can't ride a horse. But I can make money."

Unquestionably one of the greatest American superstars of all time, Autry sold more than 40 million records, recorded more than 635 selections, and wrote some 200 songs. By the 1980s, he owned radio and TV stations, a luxury hotel, three song publishing companies, considerable California real estate, oil interests, and the California Angels baseball team.

Gene Autry's open honesty and just-folks sincerity became the model for an entire generation of silver-screen singing cowboys.

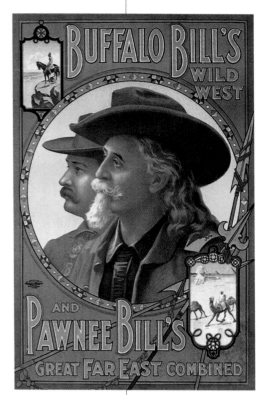

[**ROY ROGERS**] One day I was just practicin' at my sister's house. She says, "Why don't you go on the amateur show up in Inglewood and get on that? I hear 'em singin' every Saturday night." To this day, I don't remember what songs I sang. I was so scared. The funny part of it was, about three days later, I got a call from some guy who had a group called The Rocky Mountaineers. He said, "We've got a group. We'd like you to join." And that was the start in 1931.

Over a period of the next four or five years, I organized the Sons of the Pioneers. From the time I can remember, I could yodel, and so could Bob Nolan and Tim Spencer. We even did yodels in harmony. We were singin' on this radio station, and I was out to a little hat store in Glendale, waitin' for my hat they had cleaned. All of a sudden the door almost come off the hinges. The guy came in there and says, "Can you get a cowboy hat in here?" I said, "I don't know. I'm gettin' mine cleaned." He said, "I've gotta have a cowboy hat. I gotta be at Republic Pictures in the morning, eight o'clock. I'm gonna have a screen test, 'cause they're lookin' for a new

The appeal of the cowboy image was at its height in turn-of-the-century wild west shows, as advertised in the poster above, and in the music of singing cowboys like Gene Autry and Roy Rogers, who is pictured in the kiddie pull-toy below left.

ROY ROGERS

Leonard Slye (1 9 1 1 –   )

HOME AREA
southern Ohio; moved to California
at age eighteen

SIGNIFICANCE
"The King of the Cowboys," the most
handsome, flashy, and talented of the
singing buckaroos. Brilliant yodeler.
Founder of the Sons of the Pioneers.

POPULAR SONGS
"Hi-Yo Silver" (1938), "My Chicashay
Gal" (1947), "Blue Shadows on the
Trail" (1948), "Lovenworth" (1971),
"Hoppy Gene and Me" (1975)

INFLUENCED
The Sons of the Pioneers, Dale Evans,
Riders in the Sky, Randy Travis,
Clint Black, Suzy Bogguss, Holly Dunn

HONORS
The only star inducted twice into the
Country Music Hall of Fame: in 1980,
as Sons of the Pioneers member, and 1988,
as solo star; Academy of Country Music
Pioneer Award, 1975; National Cowboy
Hall of Fame, 1976 (with Dale Evans);
Music City News Living Legend Award,
1992; four stars on Hollywood Walk
of Fame; star of ninety-two feature
films (1935–76); own network TV series
(1951–57, 1962); All-star RCA
tribute album, 1991

singin' cowboy out there." And I said, "Well, I'll be darned."

Ridin' back to my house, I got to thinkin', "Maybe I'll go out there." But I couldn't get in. I didn't have any appointment or anything. So I waited around, and I went back and forth. Finally, lunchtime come and here come a whole bunch of extras back from lunch. I got right into the crowd, you know, and walked in. Just got inside the door and a hand fell on my shoulder, and I thought, "Oh Lord, they're gonna throw me out again." It was the producer of all the western pictures there at that time. And I said, "I heard you're lookin' for a singing cowboy, and I thought I'd just come out." He said, "I've seen you here with the Sons of the Pioneers a lot, but I never thought about you. When you walked through that gate, that's when it hit me. That's why I stopped you." I signed up there at Republic Pictures, October the thirteenth, 1937.

I had no lessons on anything. I've never had any singin' lessons, no guitar lessons, no acting lessons. I wondered what they were gonna do with me after they signed me up. But they gave me a script in about two months, and we got a horse, called him Trigger, and we started.

[**RUSTY RICHARDS, OF THE SONS OF THE PIONEERS**] Roy Rogers had been approached to join a singing group, and he thought it would be great if they could add another singer and do some harmony. So they ran an ad, and Bob Nolan answered the ad. And Bob Nolan knew Tim Spencer, and they got together and called themselves The Pioneer Trio. Then they realized that they needed more instrumentation, and there were two fellows who were wonderful jazz musicians. And that was of course the Farr Brothers, Hugh and Karl Farr.

They were being introduced on a program there, and the fellow said, "Here they are—the Sons of the Pioneers!" Well, they got a little hot about it. They went to the guy and said, "How come you didn't get our name right?" The guy said, "Well, I don't know, I looked at you, and you're too young to be pioneers, and you weren't a trio. There were five of ya. I don't know, it just fell out of my mouth." After they'd had time to think about it, they said, "You know, that isn't bad."

The Sons of the Pioneers have survived for more than sixty years as an American show-

business phenomenon. *Members have changed, but their romantic western style has endured.*

[**DALE EVANS**] I was friends with the Pioneers in Chicago, when I was on CBS there, and I made seven pictures at Republic Studios before I worked with Roy. Mr. Yates [Republic's executive] saw the musical *Oklahoma* in New York, and he decided that Roy's pictures should be like *Oklahoma*—with the girl's part built up, and that there would be more music, more horses. The chemistry was right between us, apparently, because after I made one picture, the exhibitors said, "Don't break the team up."

I'll tell you what attracted me to Roy. When I started working with him, he was the most natural person that I met in Hollywood. He was himself. He was like Popeye—"I am what I am, and that's all I am."

[**CLINT BLACK**] He is that person we all wanted to grow up to be. I got to see

The Sons of the Pioneers (above) are regarded as one of the greatest bands in the annals of country music. The 1946 lineup on the magazine cover pictured at left is (clockwise, from the top) Bob Nolan, Karl Farr, Lloyd Perryman, Tim Spencer, Hugh Farr, and Pat Brady.

the side of him that truly makes him a hero—the family man, the foster parent.

[**ROY ROGERS**] I always liked "Tumbling Tumbleweeds," but, as far as my personal favorite song, I like "Happy Trails." Dale wrote "Happy Trails," and it's meant so much. How she come to write it was, I used to sign my autographs, "Many Happy Trails, Trails of Happiness, Trails of Success—Roy Rogers & Trigger." And Dale got the idea of writin' a song and callin' it "Happy Trails."

Roy Rogers, Dale Evans, and Trigger (below) are second only to Walt Disney in merchandising their images. Hundreds of products have been marketed with their likenesses, including the lunchbox and thermos pictured at right.

[**DALE EVANS**] I used to dream of being a radio singer, and in Memphis, while I was working in this insurance office, I was trying to write songs all the time. I wrote a little song called "He's Mine, All Mine" and took it to a publisher that did sheet music. He said, "Well, it's pretty good. Let us think about it." Well, I never heard from him again, and I went into a dime store one day where they had a lot of sheet music. There was this song of mine! But changed just slightly. I didn't know anything about copyrights or plagiarism or anything like that. So I gave up. I thought, "Well, that's not for me." Then, when I got to Chicago on CBS, I had a program called *That Gal From Texas*, and I wrote a song called "My Heart Is Down Texas Way." When I came out here to Hollywood, I started doing lots of camp shows, singing "Will You Marry Me, Mr. Laramie" for the troops here.

I didn't try writing anymore until after Roy and I married. The first thing I wrote was a little song called "Happy Birthday, Gentle Savior" for Roy's little children to sing. Then I thought, "He should have a trail song. He needs a song that when you sing, you can see him ridin' across on Trigger." And I love the *Grand Canyon Suite* by Ferde Grofe, so I took that trombone slide—clip-clop slide—and it was done in three hours: "Happy Trails to You."

In addition to songwriting, Dale's other major contribution was the popularization of the cowgirl image. Teddy Roosevelt first used the term to describe rodeo champ Lucille Mulhall in 1905. Billie Maxwell, Kitty Lee, and Mommie Gray were cowgirls who recorded in 1928–29, but it wasn't until Gene Autry's radio contemporaries Louise Massey, The Girls of the Golden West, and Patsy Montana adopted the image at the National Barn Dance that the cowgirl became a permanent part of country music culture.

[**PATSY MONTANA**] I was born in Arkansas. When I was workin' in California at a station out there with Stuart Hamblin, I was with a trio of girls, and we worked with Monty Montana, world's champion roper. And they wanted us to go by the name Montana. My real name is Ruby, and it conflicted with the other girl's name, Ruthie, so Stuart Hamblin thought of the name Patsy. It just

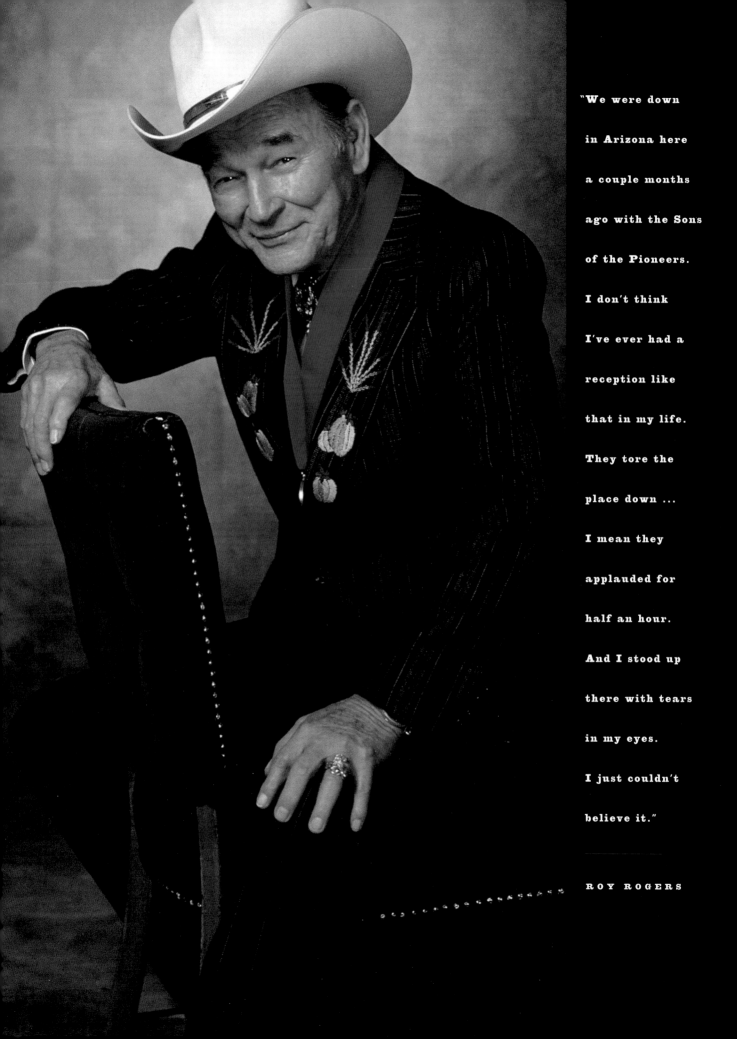

"We were down in Arizona here a couple months ago with the Sons of the Pioneers. I don't think I've ever had a reception like that in my life. They tore the place down ... I mean they applauded for half an hour. And I stood up there with tears in my eyes. I just couldn't believe it."

ROY ROGERS

Patsy Montana and the Prairie Ramblers rose to western-music fame on WLS's National Barn Dance. Patsy's "I Want to Be a Cowboy's Sweetheart" of 1935 is now a female country standard.

connected together—Patsy Montana. I know that name better than I do my own.

[GOVERNOR JIMMIE DAVIS] I was on the radio every Friday night in Shreveport, KWKH. Patsy came down there to see me and thought I could help her in some way. I said, "I don't know whether I can help you or not. I'm just tryin' to make it myself." But I had been up there, and I had recorded. I said, "You can play violin ... you can play the guitar and you can yodel.... But you need to get to New York." She said, "I don't know how I can get to New York." I said, "Well I'm goin' next week. My wife and a couple of musicians are goin' and we got room for you. You can go with us." Took her down to Victor Records. They listened to her. She had a song called "I Want to Be a Cowboy's Sweetheart," and Victor signed her up.

Today, 1935's "I Want to Be a Cowboy's Sweetheart" is regarded as the first big solo female country hit. Columbia Records executive Art Satherley believed it was the genre's first million seller by a woman.

The cowboys and cowgirls of the 1930s and 1940s were the single biggest influence on the generation of stars that followed. Western songs have been part of country music ever since.

[**HANK THOMPSON**] Tex Ritter was a big influence in my life and my career. I was just starting in the business. Tex brought me to the attention of Capitol Records. Tex had me appear on his program.

In addition to starring in dozens of movie westerns, Tex Ritter was one of the more successful cowboys on disc. "Green Grow the Lilacs," "Rye Whiskey," "High Noon," and "Hillbilly Heaven" are all associated with him. In later years, Tex became a member of the Grand Ole Opry and a Nashville political figure.

Golden-voiced Rex Allen became the last of the great singing cowboys. From his movie and TV fame of the early '50s, he built a recording career that included such hits as "Crying in the Chapel" (1953) and "Don't Go Near the Indians" (1962).

Gene, Roy and Dale, Tex, Patsy, and Rex were just a handful of the prominent singing western stars. At one time, the country music world was full of them. The genre was so pervasive that there was even a contingent of black singing cowboys, notably Mantan Moreland, The Four Tones, and Herb Jeffries.

[**HERB JEFFRIES**] I was working with Earl Hines's band, 1935. I was in Columbus, Ohio, working at a club there. In those days, they didn't have air conditioning, so when we did the dances, they'd go out into the alleyway to cool off, smoke their cigarettes, and take their break. That evening, there were a bunch of kids running down the alley. About seven or eight little white children and then one little black child following along behind them cryin'. The boys called him over and said, "What's the matter, did those kids hit you?" And he said, "No. They're playing cowboy, and they won't let me play."

So that struck me pretty hard and sort of stayed in my mind. When I was down South playing with Hines, I noticed that there were thousands of discriminated theaters. Black theaters—playing white cowboy pictures. I had done some research on some of the great cowboys that were in the pioneer days, and I said, "My goodness, why isn't somebody

SONS OF THE PIONEERS

ORIGINAL MEMBERS
Roy Rogers, Bob Nolan (1908–80), Tim Spencer (1908–76), Hugh Farr (1903–80), Karl Farr (1909–61).

OTHER ALUMNI
Lloyd Perryman, Pat Brady, Deuce Spriggins, Shug Fisher, Ken Curtis, Tommy Doss, Dale Warren.

HOME AREA
Los Angeles

SIGNIFICANCE
The wellspring of western harmony.

POPULAR SONGS
"Tumbling Tumbleweeds" (1934, 1948), "Cool Water" (1941, 1948), "Cigareetes, Whusky and Wild Women" (1947), "The Ballad of Davy Crockett" (1955), "How Great Thou Art" (1956)

INFLUENCED
Riders in the Sky, Sons of the San Joaquin

HONORS
Country Music Hall of Fame, 1980; Nashville Songwriters Hall of Fame (Spencer and Nolan), 1971; Hollywood Walk of Fame, 1976; Academy of Country Music Pioneer Award, 1977; National Cowboy Hall of Fame (Curtis), 1981; Gospel Music Hall of Fame (Spencer), 1985; Grammy Hall of Fame ("Cool Water"), 1986; Canadian Country Music Hall of Honor (Nolan), 1993

TEX RITTER

Maurice Woodward Ritter

(1907–1974)

HOME AREA
East Texas

SIGNIFICANCE
"America's Most Beloved Cowboy."
The most folk-oriented and scholarly
of the singing cowboys.

POPULAR SONGS
"There's a New Moon Over My
Shoulder" (1944), "Jealous Heart" (1945),
"You Two Timed Me One Time Too
Often" (1945), "Christmas Carols by the
Old Corral" (1945), "Rye Whiskey"
(1948), "Deck of Cards" (1948), "Rock
and Rye" (1948), "High Noon" (1952),
"I Dreamed of a Hillbilly Heaven" (1961),
"Just Beyond the Moon" (1967)

INFLUENCED
Ralph Emery, John Ritter,
Riders in the Sky

HONORS
First singing cowboy in Country Music
Hall of Fame, 1964; Academy of Country
Music Pioneer Award, 1970 (the organiza-
tion's movie-of-the-year honor is named
the Tex Ritter Award); National Cowboy
Hall of Fame, 1980; Hollywood
Walk of Fame; star of forty-six feature
films (1936–67); hosted TV's
Town Hall Party (1953–60)

playing black cowboy pictures?" Came out to California, and the deal was put together.

Neither the Opry nor Nashville ever completely abandoned western music. Like bluegrass and Cajun, it remained a major country sub-style through various decades and fads.

[**LYNN ANDERSON**] One of the most important western records was Marty Robbins's, when I was in school. And I just flipped. I knew every word to every song.

[**MICHAEL MARTIN MURPHEY**] Marty Robbins's grand-father was a Texas Ranger and an Arizona Ranger, a real Wild West character—shoulder-length hair, beard. Marty absorbed a lot of experiences of the really old-time trail period.

[**BILLY WALKER**] Marty and I had been accused of sounding a lot alike on the western ballads, and I would tell people, "Well, we both stole it from the Sons of the Pioneers and Gene Autry."

Rex Allen's wonder horse, Koko, watches his master make the transition from film to TV star of the 1950s.

Johnny Cash, Rex Allen Jr., Randy Travis, and dozens of others have continued to record cowboy songs in Music City. Another legacy of country's western branch is the enduring presence of Spanish-language material.

[**BUCK OWENS**] Mexican music has that longing, that yearning, that hurting, warming feeling. And I really think that's where I got some of my influences.

[**FREDDY FENDER**] I lost my father when I was about eight years old. We definitely were very poor in south Texas. We would migrate to northern Texas or west Texas to pick cotton, and by the time that the cotton was over in Texas, it was beginning in Arkansas. So we'd go to Arkansas. I think the impact of music besides Spanish hit me about the time that I was ten or eleven years old, while I was picking cotton in Arkansas. It was 1947 or '46, and we had some black people picking cotton with us. I just loved the way these guys were singing. It made me want to learn how to speak English well. The cultural aspect of the black person picking cotton and my music of the Mexican-American picking cotton combined, I think—somehow—to what I do now—what people call Tex-Mex.

[**JOHNNY RODRIGUEZ**] When I came to Nashville, I wanted to sing country music like

Tex Ritter, shown here in a movie still of the late 1930s, was the singing cowboy who sang the folk songs of the Old West. Arizona native Marty Robbins (below) took the tradition into the Nashville Sound era.

African American singing cowboy Herb Jeffries starred as "Herbert Jeffrey" in films of the 1930s, as these movie posters attest. In 1995, at age eighty-three, he issued a new collection of western songs.

Merle Haggard. And Tom T. Hall says, "Why don't you take a song and do it half English and half in Spanish?" He stopped to see Jerry Kennedy, who was producing him at that time. Told me to come along with him. So I went in there, and I sang him "I Can't Stop Loving You" in English and Spanish, and when I got to the middle of the song, he said, "I'm gonna sign you right there on the spot."

In 1992, Warner Bros. Records established a western-music division to promote the sounds of a new generation of cowboys—Don Edwards, the Sons of the San Joaquin, Waddie Mitchell, Red Steagall, Michael Martin Murphey, and Native American troubadour Bill Miller. And many of the original western stars are still "riding the range."

[**PATSY MONTANA**] A couple months ago in New Orleans, a little lady came up, grabbed me around the neck, and she was cryin'. I could feel the tears on my neck. She said, "Patsy, don't ever quit. You're the only one singin' these songs."

[**HERB JEFFRIES**] I'm not old, I'm vintage. I don't use the word *old*. I'm vintaged at eighty-three—not old. I'm not searching for any kind of superstardom. I'd like to be remembered as a guy who walked among kings and never lost the common touch.

[**BAXTER BLACK**] I think the cowboy image is so enduringly popular because it's still real. It's one thing to be talking about Knights of the Round Table and science-fiction astronauts, but cowboys are still out there. You just can't see 'em from the interstate very easy, but as long as people eat hamburgers, there'll be cows, and as long as there's cows, there'll be cowboys.

Western Swing (Ah-haa!)

bob wills and the texas playboys ~ pee wee king and the
golden west cowboys ~ hank
thompson ~ spade cooley
~ johnny lee wills ~ tex
williams ~ the aladdin laddies
~ milton brown and the musical brownies ~ the light crust
doughboys ~ cliff bruner ~

By the early 1940s, the cowboy craze was in full flower in American popular culture. Even pop performers were singing western tunes. Meanwhile, the increasingly sophisticated cowboy entertainers were borrowing from the big-band sounds of the day. The resulting fusion of jazz with country was dubbed "western swing."

[**RAY BENSON, OF ASLEEP AT THE WHEEL**] Western swing developed in the thirties, forties, and fifties in the Southwest and West. It's defined by its instrumentation: fiddles, steel guitars, electric guitars, a rhythm section (being drums and bass), usually a piano, and some horns and a fiddle section. It's dance music, also. Gotta be dance music.

[**DOUG GREEN**] Western swing sort of started when the cowboys got radios, and they could hear the dance bands. They put that dancing swing beat to the cowboy music. That was the heyday when electric instruments started to come in. They got the electric steel guitar, and they added the drums.

[**HANK THOMPSON**] The main thing was a beat. You could dance to it. And since they used the fiddles and guitars—as opposed to what an orchestra would use, reeds and brass—it was more "country" or western.

[**LEON RAUSCH, OF THE TEXAS PLAYBOYS**] It's quite a mixture. We got blues, country, swing, and just about anything you can imagine: the black culture and the Mexican culture. It's all mixed together.

[**DOLLY PARTON**] I've always loved listening to western swing, but I didn't really realize how hard it is to do western swing. First of all, you have to sing on the beat, moreso than with country music.

[**HANK THOMPSON**] Milton Brown was given the credit for bein' the first one to use the electric steel guitar and use the twin fiddles and really have the dance band as such.

Texan Milton Brown led the Musical Brownies, but his death in a 1936 car crash ended the days of this western-swing innovator. Parallel contributions by such acts as the Aladdin Laddies, the Light Crust Doughboys, Cliff Bruner, Adolf Hoffner, Bill Boyd, and Roy Newman added to the development of the new style. One name towers above all others in the history of western swing: Bob Wills.

[**RAY BENSON**] If you looked up in the dictionary "What is western swing," you'd see a picture of Bob Wills there.

[**RED STEAGALL**] Bob Wills came along at a time when people were all having the same problems. The wind was blowing the land away, we were in the middle of a Great Depression, there was talk of war in Europe, everything was unsettled. Bob brought a dance attitude that made people get together. In the early days, Bob was trying to create a band that was typical of the big bands on the East Coast. Instead of using woodwinds and brass as his dominant instruments, he used fiddles and steel guitars, which were indigenous to the culture in which he was working. He added lyrics that were indigenous to those people.

Bob Wills was the first massively popular country artist whose band members used electronic amplification, prefiguring the rise of rock 'n' roll by twenty years.

"Western Swing would have just been a footnote in American music if it weren't for Bob Wills, because Bob Wills was the Elvis Presley of his day."

———————

RAY BENSON
(ASLEEP AT THE WHEEL)

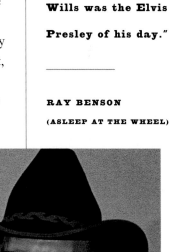

BOB WILLS

(1905–1975)

HOME AREA
Limestone County, Texas

SIGNIFICANCE
"The King of Western Swing." At twenty-two pieces in 1944, Bob Wills and the Texas Playboys was country's all-time largest band.

POPULAR SONGS
"Sittin' on Top of the World" (1935), "Steel Guitar Rag" (1936), "Ida Red" (1938), "San Antonio Rose" (1939), "Corrrine, Corrina" (1940), "New San Antonio Rose" (1940, 1944), "Texas Playboy Rag" (1945), "New Spanish Two-Step" (1946), "Bubbles in My Beer" (1948), "Faded Love" (1950)

INFLUENCED
Johnnie Lee Wills, Billy Jack Wills, Spade Cooley, Ray Price, Mel Tillis, Commander Cody, Asleep at the Wheel, Merle Haggard, Toby Keith, Riders in the Sky, Shelby Lynne, George Strait

HONORS
Country Music Hall of Fame, 1968; Academy of Country Music Pioneer Award, 1969; Nashville Songwriters Hall of Fame, 1970; ACM Touring Band of the Year (Texas Playboys), 1978

[**TOMMY ALLSUP, OF THE TEXAS PLAYBOYS**] Bob Wills started, you know, with just a fiddle and guitar, and he called it the Bob Wills Fiddle Band. He kept adding instruments. He just kept adding and kept adding. They started swinging back in the thirties, but to me, in 1945, when he recorded "Roly Poly" and "Stay All Night, Stay a Little Longer," using twin guitars to replace those horn sections, that's when it really started to be what we consider western swing now. Art Satherley, who was A&R director for Columbia Records, said, "Bob, your music is really swinging today. We need to put a name to it." Said, "Why don't we call it western swing?"

After apprenticing in his native Texas, Bob Wills ascended to stardom on KVOO in Tulsa, Oklahoma, in 1934. He and his Texas Playboys began recording a year later. By 1940 they were popular enough to be in singing-cowboy movies. Between 1940 and 1950, the band was consistently at the top of the country charts with tunes like "New San Antonio Rose," "Bubbles in My Beer," and "Faded Love."

[**GOVERNOR JIMMIE DAVIS**] Bob Wills had that hollerin' he did. When he'd sing he'd holler, "Ah-Haaa!" I don't know when he started that, but he was very good at it.

[**LEON RAUSCH**] Bob Wills did take a drink at different periods in his life. He had his own demons to deal with, so if it was a problem to him, that was the way it was. That's public information: he just liked his booze.

I started with Bob Wills's band in 1958. We started with a '47 Flex bus at that time. People would come on that bus and talk to Bob and say, "Bob, do you have air conditioning?" And he said, "Yeah, slide one of 'em open there. We got twenty." Our heater wasn't very good, either.

At his peak in California, during and immediately after World War II, Wills was packing eight thousand people a night into big dance halls, starring in cowboy movies, getting his songs recorded by Bing Crosby, and riding at the top of the country-music world. In 1949, he moved back to Oklahoma, but the big band era ended in the 1950s. Bob's last big western-swing adventure

was the creation of the Bob Wills Ranch House, now the legendary Longhorn Ballroom, in Dallas.

[**RAY BENSON**] The late fifties kind of signaled the demise of western swing as a big, big attraction. So this was Bob's "last stand," I'd say. Had a great band but lost the whole place in a couple-a three years. Wasn't the greatest businessman, I guess. But he had a great idea and built a cool place. Later on, it was taken over by a lot of colorful characters. The most notable name would be Jack Ruby. He ran it for a while. The longest resident of the place in terms of ownership and managership was Dewey Groom.

We came in 1975 to play a show, and I got out of the bus, and a guy from the AP comes over and says, "Did you hear Bob Wills died?" It was a really very emotional kind of night. The place filled up. It was jammed. People came out 'cause it got on the news.

During Bob's heyday in the 1940s, the styles of Al Clauser and His Oklahomans, Bill Boyd's Cowboy Ramblers, Al Dexter's troupe, Pee Wee King's Golden West Cowboys, the Hank Penny band, Spade Cooley, Tex Williams, Hank Thompson, and Bob's brothers Billy Jack Wills and Johnnie Lee Wills all owed a debt to the Texas Playboys to one degree or another.

[**PATTI PAGE**] The things I sang with Al Clauser and the Oklahomans were just the regular country music. We did country swing, the "San Antonio Rose."

[**EDDY ARNOLD**] When Pee Wee King hired me I was appearing in little clubs

Bob Wills and the Texas Playboys pause during a 1947 recording session (top). As the flyer above suggests, they were the hottest western-swing ensemble in history. Opposite are albums featuring Mel Tillis (1967), Merle Haggard (1970), and Asleep at the Wheel (1994) that illustrate Wills's enduring appeal.

Western swing spawned dozens of national hits, including "Detour" (1946) by Spade Cooley's band (above) and "Ragmop" (1950) by Johnnie Lee Wills and His Boys (below).

and joints and wherever I could to earn a half a dollar or a dollar or a dollar and a half. Pee Wee was a good showman.

[**HANK THOMPSON**] I kind of modified western swing by featuring more of my singing, since the honky-tonk music was becoming so popular on the jukeboxes. It was by necessity swing music if it was in honky-tonks, so ours became known more as the honky-tonk swing, a hybrid version of western swing.

We were the last ones to do the Light Crust Doughboy Show on radio, but that was not necessarily an endorsement deal. With Falstaff Beer, we actually were a representative. The band had some special shirts made with that Falstaff emblem on them. We were about the first to do that type of thing.

[**WANDA JACKSON**] My folks loved to dance and so they used to take me to the dances when I was a little girl—Tex Williams, Spade Cooley, Bob Wills, the big bands. They said they never had to worry about where I was. I was always right in front of the bandstand, lookin' straight up and listenin' to the music.

[**RAY BENSON**] In Texas, every little town had a dance hall that you bring your own bottle to, BYOB, and they would sell mixers and perhaps beer, and it was a great thing. It was a family thing.

By the 1960s, the revolutionary Bob Wills style was institutionalized in the country sound. Patsy Cline brought back "Faded Love"; Floyd Cramer revived "San Antonio Rose"; Barbara Mandrell picked the "Steel Guitar Rag." Ray Price issued a 1962 album of Wills favorites, and, in 1967, Mel Tillis recorded with the legend himself. Merle Haggard launched a major Wills revival with the 1970 LP A Tribute to the Best Damn Fiddle Player in the World *and joined the Playboys for the 1975 album* For the Last Time. *Today, western swing resonates through the work of such diverse acts as Shelby Lynne, Commander Cody, Riders in the Sky, George Strait, and, unmistakably, Asleep at the Wheel.*

[**MEL TILLIS**] I went over to the RCA studio one night, and, man, there he stood. Big as life. Had the white hat on, the big ole cigar. Bob said, "Would you like to sing a song with me?" I said, "Yes, sir." He said, "Well, which one? And I said, "Well, uh, I, I, here's one that I, you know, I've written." We did that song, and we ended up doing five or six more. And that's how I met Mr. Wills.

[**WAYLON JENNINGS**] "Bob Wills Is Still the King" is a

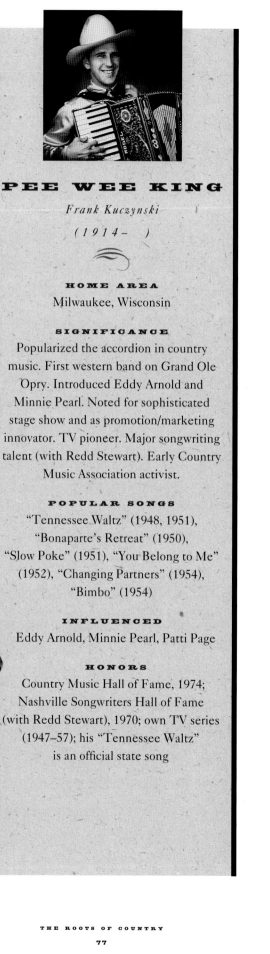

PEE WEE KING

Frank Kuczynski

(1914 –)

HOME AREA
Milwaukee, Wisconsin

SIGNIFICANCE
Popularized the accordion in country music. First western band on Grand Ole Opry. Introduced Eddy Arnold and Minnie Pearl. Noted for sophisticated stage show and as promotion/marketing innovator. TV pioneer. Major songwriting talent (with Redd Stewart). Early Country Music Association activist.

POPULAR SONGS
"Tennessee Waltz" (1948, 1951), "Bonaparte's Retreat" (1950), "Slow Poke" (1951), "You Belong to Me" (1952), "Changing Partners" (1954), "Bimbo" (1954)

INFLUENCED
Eddy Arnold, Minnie Pearl, Patti Page

HONORS
Country Music Hall of Fame, 1974; Nashville Songwriters Hall of Fame (with Redd Stewart), 1970; own TV series (1947–57); his "Tennessee Waltz" is an official state song

HANK THOMPSON

(1 9 2 5 –)

HOME AREA
Waco, Texas

SIGNIFICANCE
Regarded as major figure of both western swing and honky-tonk styles. First modern country act with corporate sponsorship (Falstaff Beer). Groundbreaking country act in Las Vegas. First to record a live LP.

POPULAR SONGS
"Humpty Dumpty Heart" (1948), "Green Light" (1948), "Whoa Sailor" (1949), "The Wild Side of Life" (1952), "Waiting in the Lobby of Your Heart" (1952), "Rub-a-Dub-Dub" (1953), "Honky Tonk Girl" (1954), "New Green Light" (1954), "Wildwood Flower" (1955), "The Blackboard of My Heart" (1955), "Squaws Along the Yukon" (1958), "A Six Pack to Go" (1960), "Oklahoma Hills" (1961), "Hangover Tavern" (1961), "On Tap, in the Can or in the Bottle" (1968), "Smoky the Bar" (1968), "The Older the Wine the Sweeter the Music" (1974), "Who Left the Door to Heaven Open" (1974)

INFLUENCED
George Strait, Reba McEntire, Wanda Jackson, Jean Shepard

HONORS
Country Music Hall of Fame, 1989; Hollywood Walk of Fame

After serving as Spade Cooley's lead vocalist, Tex Williams formed his own band, made Hollywood cowboy movies, ran his own California nightclub and scored hits like 1947's "Smoke! Smoke! Smoke! (That Cigarette)."

song that I wrote because, when you got right down to it, all of those Texas honky-tonks and all of those dance floors and stages of them honky-tonks were built for Bob Wills–type bands. And people still dance to your music as if you were Bob Wills.

[**SHELBY LYNNE**] Oh, my God—Bob Wills is probably my greatest country influence. Bob Wills was the king of western swing. And he still is.

[**TOMMY ALLSUP**] As long as I'm alive, and guys like Leon Rausch, there'll always be a Texas Playboys band.

[**LEE ROY PARNELL, 1989**] First time I ever sang professionally was with the Texas Playboys. I was, like, six years old. My dad held me up to the microphone on WBAP out of Ft. Worth, and I sang "San Antonio Rose." I changed keys three times, and the band changed with me. That's how good those guys were.

[**MERLE HAGGARD**] Bob Wills and the Texas Playboys were the group that was really hot for the ten years prior to, say, Lefty Frizzell and Hank Williams. Someone said that Lefty Frizzell came in and knocked Bob Wills out of the saddle and said Elvis came in and knocked the saddle off.

[**RED STEAGALL**] Bob Wills created a music that will live forever. It feels good; it's fun to dance to. "Lone Star Beer and Bob Wills Music."

hank williams ☞ johnny

and jack ☞ minnie pearl ☞

efty frizzell ☞ faron young

WSM

☞ webb pierce ☞ ray price ☞

Honky-Tonk Kings

and Queens ☞ kitty wells

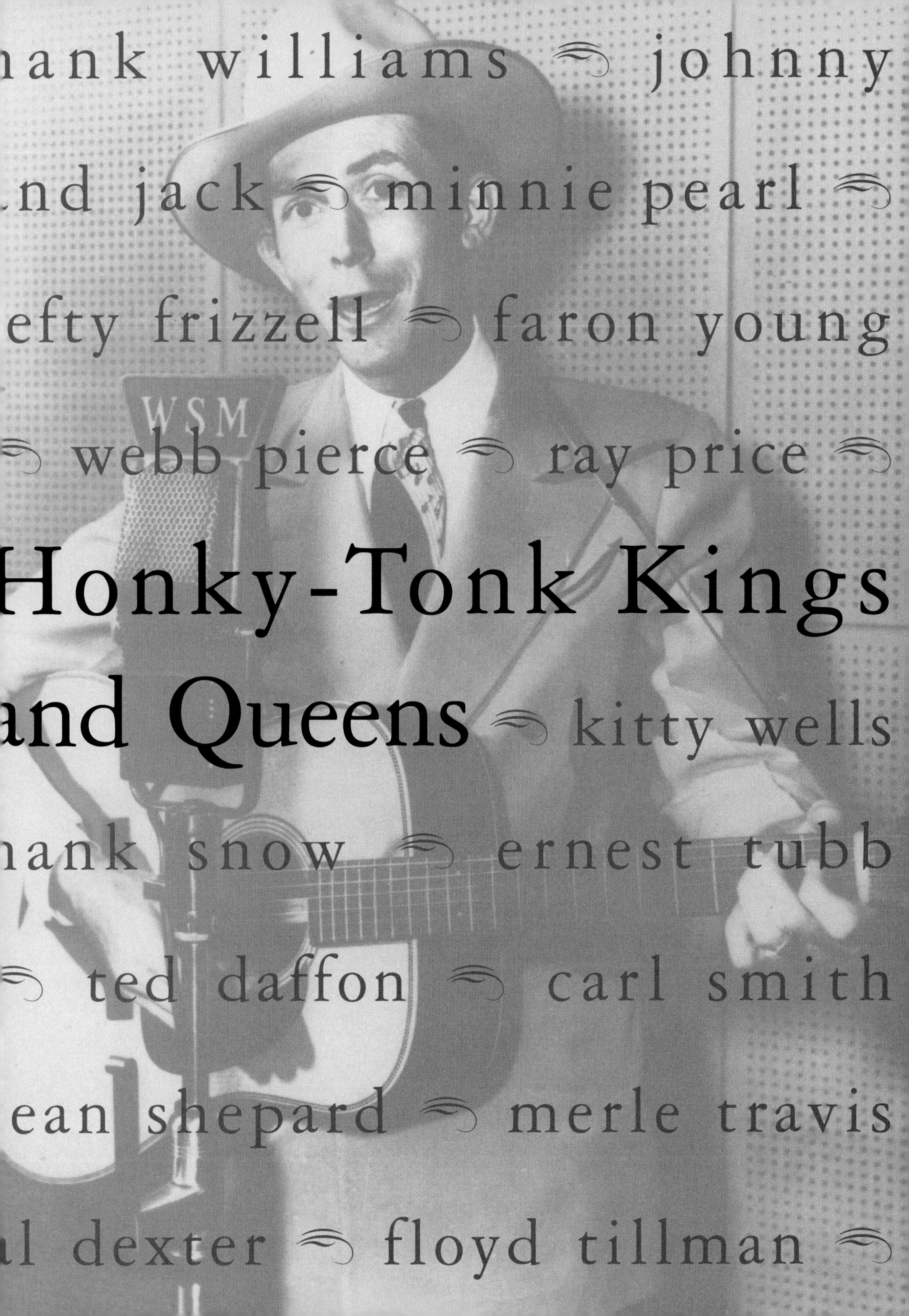

hank snow ☞ ernest tubb

☞ ted daffon ☞ carl smith

ean shepard ☞ merle travis

l dexter ☞ floyd tillman ☞

They say that America lost its innocence during World War II. So did country music. During the 1940s, country zoomed to national popularity and created its first modern superstars. At first, songs retained the sentiments of the old-time era. But as the decade wore on, country began to reflect the problems of the postwar years.

Loud, emotional, electrified, hard-hitting songs of "cheating" and drinking emerged, thudding from America's jukeboxes. Whether waving the flag in the early '40s, backing the square dance craze of the mid-'40s or reflecting the strained domestic climate of the late '40s, country caught the ears of the nation like never before.

———⟫◆⟪———

[**CLIFFIE STONE**] In those days, a lot of the Southerners came to Southern California. There was a song called "Dear Okie, If You See Arkie, Tell Him Tex Has Got a Job for Him Out in California." And that was a real big hit during the war years.

[**JERRY RIVERS, OF THE DRIFTING COWBOYS**] Some of the biggest hits came out of World War II. My friend Zeke Clements would stop the Grand Ole Opry with "Smoke on the water / On the land and the sea / When our Army and Navy/ Overtake the enemy." Then we had in later years "Filipino Baby" and "Fraulein."

[**HANK THOMPSON**] Right at the start of World War II my theme song was "There's a Star Spangled Banner Waving Somewhere," which was the big giant of a hit by Elton Britt back in those days.

The golden-voiced Britt sold a million copies of that war-themed tune in 1942. During this era, more country balladeers came to the fore, including Red Foley, George Morgan, Governor Jimmie Davis, and the massively popular Eddy Arnold.

[**GOVERNOR JIMMIE DAVIS**] "You Are My Sunshine"—I tried to get that song recorded somewhere, but nobody'd let me record it. Then it hit in 1940. Bing Crosby, Guy Lombardo, The Andrews Sisters, they all got to doing it.

[**MEL TILLIS**] Red Foley was my idol. He was the man that inspired me the most to get into the business. I remember when I went to Okinawa in the Air Force, I wrote him a letter. I believe it was in '52. And he wrote me back! Man, I took it all over the island and just showed it to everybody over there.

[**EDDY ARNOLD**] I never felt like I was a superstar. I guess I was too busy [in 1948, when he was Number One on the country charts for the entire year]. See, I was then doing a daily radio show, fifteen minutes a day on the Mutual network for the Ralston Purina Company, five days a week. And then you do public appearances in addition to that. I had to rehearse. I had to read scripts.

While Arnold, Foley, and their peers were redefining country stardom stateside, thousands of country boys were spreading the music among their fellow G.I.s overseas.

[**JERRY RIVERS**] During and after the war, writers like Hank Williams were discovering that most people had left the farm. They were in Detroit building cars or tanks or in Panama City building boats. They had heard about all they wanted

"A honky-tonk is a place where working people hang out. They come into there to dance, to listen to country music, and drink a lot of beer. Maybe a fight every now and then."

MARK CHESTNUTT

HANK WILLIAMS

(1923–1952)

HOME AREA
Alabama

SIGNIFICANCE
Regarded as the greatest singer-songwriter
in country music history.

POPULAR SONGS
"I Saw the Light" (1947), "Lovesick
Blues" (1949), "I'm So Lonesome I Could
Cry" (1949), "Long Gone Lonesome
Blues" (1950), "Cold, Cold Heart" (1951),
"I Can't Help It" (1951), "Hey, Good
Lookin'" (1951), "Jambalaya" (1952), "Your
Cheatin' Heart" (1953), "Kaw-Liga"
(1953), "Take These Chains from My
Heart" (1953), "There's a Tear in My
Beer" (with Hank Williams Jr., 1989)

INFLUENCED
Every country singer of modern times

HONORS
Country Music Hall of Fame, 1961;
Nashville Songwriters Hall of Fame, 1970;
Academy of Country Music Pioneer Award,
1973; Recording Academy Hall of Fame
("Your Cheatin' Heart"), 1983; NARAS
Lifetime Achievement, 1987; Rock 'n' Roll
Hall of Fame, 1987; Grammy Award
("There's a Tear in My Beer"), 1989; CMA
Award ("There's a Tear in My Beer"),
1989; *Music City News* Award ("There's
a Tear in My Beer"), 1990

to about the farm. Hank and a few others discovered that they wanted to hear about the everyday life of love and cheating and gettin' in trouble and the wife puttin' you in the dog house, gettin' a little drunk, and goin' out in the pickup truck—the things which are still prevalent in country music today.

[**HANK THOMPSON**] When the war was over, people said, well, this is great to have fun and feel fine and enjoy the music and the old dance halls—the honky-tonk thing.

The small taverns and roadhouses that sprang up in the 1940s couldn't afford big western-swing bands. The only thing that could be heard above the raucous din in these places was the bottom-heavy sound of the jukebox. So country music developed a new style. The sound featured the wails and slurs of the steel guitar, the thud of the upright bass, keening fiddle, piercing electric guitar, and sometimes a small drum kit. Singing became loud and histrionic, with hiccup, crying, nasal whining, vocal-break, and yodel effects to wring emotion out of every line. Lyrics treated such previously taboo subjects as infidelity ("cheating"), alcohol, and divorce. They named the style after its birthplace: honky-tonk.

[**MARTY STUART**] A honky-tonk is an establishment on the edge of town where you can go and hear good country music, hang out with some good country people, do some good country dancin' to some of your favorite country songs.

[**MAGGIE VAUGHN**] The jukebox was a poor man's psychiatrist. People would be in a barroom or a tavern or in a little

The G.I. with the guitar could be any one of the thousands of country boys who taught their fellow soldiers to love the sound of country music during World War II.

cafe, and maybe their mate just left them or something happened in their life—they caught their spouse cheating. And they'd drop a nickel into the jukebox, and someone would be singing about that.

[**MERLE HAGGARD**] Those people worked hard and they played hard. Those clubs that I grew up in were just kind of like the cotton fields that I grew up in. They were rough, thrown up on the edge of the peach orchard somewhere.

[**RICKY LYNN GREGG**] A honky-tonk is somethin' where, when you walk in the door and they frisk you to see if you have a gun, if you don't, they hand you one.

[**RAY BENSON**] Honky-tonks were the devil's playground, where man meets woman, woman meets man, people drink. Good things happen, bad things happen. Kissin' and killin'. I said to Merle Kilgore, "Merle, what do you do when the fights starts at a honky-tonk and you're playin'?" He said, "Play louder."

[**GLEN CAMPBELL**] I started with my uncle when I was sixteen. We was in the "joints." There was a fight every fifteen minutes, it seemed like. I remember settin' at the bar one time at the Hitchin' Post. I should have put a sign up saying,

▲

Hank Williams,
in the white hat,
poses in the WSM
studios for a 1951
radio show public-
ity shot promoting
Mother's Best
livestock feeds.

"Hank Williams was a combination of blues and bluegrass and gospel. Hank Williams laid the groundwork for everybody. George Jones idolized Hank. George modeled himself after Hank, and everybody modeled theirself after George."

ALAN JACKSON

Hank Williams on stage at the Grand Ole Opry

"Fightin' and dancin' to the music of Glen Campbell and the Western Wranglers." A guy was settin' at the bar, and a guy come in and said, "You ask my girl to dance one more time, and I'll shoot ya." He went over and said, "Can I have this dance?" And, bang, he shot the guy right there.

No place produced more honky-tonk musicians than Texas. Al Dexter ("Pistol Packin' Mama," 1943), Ted Daffan ("Born to Lose," 1942), Floyd Tillman ("Slipping Around," 1949), and most of the style's other pioneers worked there. So did the most influential and successful of all the early honky-tonk stars, Ernest Tubb.

[**JUSTIN TUBB**] My dad's contributions to country music are so many and so varied. There's the people that he's helped—Hank Williams, Hank Snow, Stonewall Jackson, the Louvin Brothers, Skeeter Davis, George Jones, the Wilburn Brothers, Loretta Lynn, Jack Greene, Cal Smith—and it goes on and on. But one of the basic things that he contributed was a change in style of music when he moved here from Texas. He brought the honky-tonk sound to the Grand Ole Opry and was the first to use an electric guitar.

[**STONEWALL JACKSON**] I was twenty-three and right off the sharecrop farm, and Ernest took me under his wing. I went out on the road with him and opened the show for him for about a year and a half before I got my first hit record. I learned a lot from Ernest. He helped me a lot monetarily. He helped me with my clothes and stuff like that. Never would let me pay him back.

[**LORETTA LYNN**] I learned a great deal from Ernest Tubb. He said to me, "Now, hon, I'm gonna tell you something in this business. Tomorrow you may not have a hit record." So every time I'd put out a record, I never looked for a hit. Every year I'd raise my garden and can. People from the Grand Ole Opry'd say, "Well, Loretta, why are you canning so much?" I said, "Hey, tomorrow I may not have a hit record."

For twenty-five years I kept looking for 'em to flop out of the charts, you know. So one day Ernest come up to me, and he said, "Well, honey, forget what I said to you."

[**JUSTIN TUBB**] The idea behind the Ernest Tubb Record Shop in the beginning was to provide a place where country fans could buy country records, because there was no place. There were very few record shops, and there was no big chain stores like there are now.

▲
Four-month-old Hank Williams Jr. gets his first guitar lesson from his superstar pop at home in Nashville in September 1949. As the ad at the top of the page indicates, Hank Sr. sang gospel as well as honky-tonk tunes.

ERNEST TUBB
(1914–1984)

HOME AREA
Texas

SIGNIFICANCE
Definitive honky-tonk pioneer.

POPULAR SONGS
"Walking the Floor Over You" (1941),
"Tomorrow Never Comes" (1945),
"Drivin' Nails in My Coffin" (1946), "You
Nearly Lose Your Mind" (1948), "Let's
Say Goodbye Like We Said Hello" (1948),
"Blue Christmas" (1949), "Letters Have
No Arms" (1950), "Goodnight, Irene"
(with Red Foley, 1950), "You Don't Have
to Be a Baby to Cry" (1950), "The Yellow
Rose of Texas" (1955), "Half a Mind"
(1958), "Thanks a Lot" (1963), "Waltz
Across Texas" (1965), "Sweet Thang"
(with Loretta Lynn, 1967)

INFLUENCED
Justin Tubb, Willie Nelson, Stonewall
Jackson, Loretta Lynn, Jack Greene,
Cal Smith, Conway Twitty

HONORS
Country Music Hall of Fame, 1965;
Nashville Songwriters Hall of Fame, 1970;
Academy of Country Music Pioneer
Award, 1980; *Music City News* Founders
Award, 1978, and Living Legend, 1984;
own syndicated TV series, five Hollywood
films, 1943–47; All-star tribute album, 1979

Today the Ernest Tubb Record Shop is the world's largest mail-order source for country music. Its Midnight Jamboree *remains one of the longest-running radio shows on earth. Both provided a launchpad for honky-tonk's kings and queens, including the man they call "The Hillbilly Shakespeare," Hank Williams.*

[**JERRY RIVERS**] Hank Williams was country music's first superstar.

[**WAYLON JENNINGS**] He was just pure soul, is what it amounted to.

[**JIMMY MARTIN**] The greatest man that ever sung a country song. That's about enough of that, ain't it?

[**HILLOUS BUTRUM, OF THE DRIFTING COWBOYS**] He was like most of us, just a plain old country boy. He was raised down in Montgomery, Alabama, and had quite a hard life; sold peanuts on the streets and shined shoes. He got a radio show at thirteen years old at WSFA there in Montgomery. Then he started playin' different clubs and what have you down there.

[**MERLE KILGORE**] I had heard of his coming. It sounds like a Biblical thing: *I had heard of his coming.* I was fourteen years old at the time, and I was just learning to play a guitar. The only way I could get into the studios was to carry instruments. The Bailes Brothers came from the Grand Ole Opry to start the Louisiana Hayride. They had talked about this young man from Montgomery, Alabama, who was absolutely stealing the shows away from Roy Acuff, the Bailes Brothers, and all the greats of that era. He had a little slight problem; that is, he liked to drink. He was a teenage drunk. We had heard these tales on him.

I was there waiting. I was wanting to carry his guitar and get next to him. I wanted to meet this guy—a teenage drunk—I'd never seen one of those. About five-thirty in the morning, here came an old car. It was a Chrysler or DeSoto town car. I heard the car before I saw it. Smoke was billowing down the

canyons of the city of Shreveport. This guy got out. He had a white suit on. I said, "This guy looks truly beautiful." Me and my buddy rushed over. I said, "You Hank Williams?" He said, "Who are you?" I said, "My name is Merle. The elevators don't work, and you have to carry your own instruments up. I know the Bailes Brothers. I work for them, and I can show you around the Hayride here." He looked at me and said, "Grab it, Hoss."

[**WAYLON JENNINGS**] His best friend in this world had to be Fred Rose. I think Fred helped him a lot in songwriting. I saw the original words of "Kaw-Liga," and if you'd see them, you'd wonder how it got over here. You can hear where he helped him. He was a great song doctor.

[**CHET ATKINS**] I met Hank when I first came down to Nashville in 1950, and he was hot as a firecracker. I remember I was impressed by how slender he was and how dark his eyes were. He had real dark eyes, brown eyes, and had on that western-type hat. In a few days he came to me and said, "Fred Rose says you write. We should get together and try to write one." And we did, but I was too awestruck by his stardom and everything and nothin' happened. He would say, "Hey, Hoss, listen to this." You could smell the bourbon on his breath, and he'd sing "Jambalaya" or one of those new songs he'd written.

▲

Ernest Tubb, his bus, his band, and his touring troupe (including Kitty Wells) pose on Broadway in Nashville, outside the renowned Ernest Tubb Record Shop, the site of radio's Midnight Jamboree every Saturday night. During each performance, Ernest would flip his guitar over and show the crowd his "Thanks" (opposite).

Honky-tonk king
Webb Pierce defined
the spangled style of the
'50s with his rhinestone
suits and silver
dollar–encrusted car
(top). The cover of
Webb's 1954 songbook
(above) hints at the
dozens of awards he
collected with more
than twenty chart-
topping hits.

[**HANK WILLIAMS JR**.] Daddy and his band partied big time. The man had fun. Loved his dogs. Loved hunting. Loved fishing. People have too much of this heartbroken image and they got to remember that he did have fun.

The legs. When he would do "Lovesick Blues," Minnie Pearl and a lot of people told me his legs were just rubber. It was *gyrating*—for 1950 and '51.

These legs are goin' all over the place. She told me that he would just drive women berserk.

[**RAY PRICE**] I met Hank Williams through a music publisher, Troy Martin, who was with Peer International. Troy got me a spot on Hank's radio show. When Hank and I met, it was one of those instant-friendship things. He took me to the Grand Ole Opry the next day, and then we went to Evansville, Indiana, and wrote "Weary Blues from Waitin'" together. We became very dear friends. He's the one that got me on the Grand Ole Opry.

[**JOHNNY WRIGHT**] I guess everybody knows that Hank Williams was let go off the Grand Ole Opry because he drank so much. I was out there when he got fired. Jim Denny called him and told him he was gonna have to leave. Hank told him, "Hell, you can't dismiss me. I'm already quit." I was getting ready to take him home. We loaded everything he had in the backseat. Kitty and I had a '51 model Chrysler limousine. We put the reclining chair in the back of the limousine, put Hank up in that chair, stretched him out, and took him to Montgomery, Alabama. On the way out of town with Hank's trailer, we stopped at a liquor store on 16th and Broad. Hank wanted to get that Opry check cashed and get him a fifth of whiskey, so we stopped there. The guy saw "Hank Williams The Drifting Cowboy" on the trailer, and he said, "Is ole Hank out there? I wanna see him!" So he went out to see Hank stretched out in that recliner.

Hank's mother ran a boarding house in Montgomery, so we took Hank there. His mother met us at the door, and we took him in, pulled his pants off, put his pajamas on, and put him to bed. The next time we saw Hank was back working on the Louisiana Hayride after that.

[**FARON YOUNG**] I got to know Hank real well. I was dating a girl from Shreveport named Billie Jones, and I brought her up to Nashville with me. And one night we went on a double date. Hank was with some girl. He was broke up with his wife then. So he started to flirting around with Billie. Well, I didn't care. Hank was God to me—"Whatever you want." Didn't matter to me. Two weeks later, they got married onstage in Birmingham, Alabama.

I had just went in the army when they got married. And I remember my company commander called me down, said, "Faron, why don't you take the day off? One of your good friends passed away last night." I said, "Who?" He said, "Hank Williams." I said, "That's two favors he's did for me. He got Billie Jones off my hands, and he got me a day off in the army."

[**JOHNNY WRIGHT**] He died on the way to Canton, Ohio.

Hank Williams's 1953 funeral was the biggest event in Montgomery, Alabama, since the death of Confederate President Jefferson Davis.

WEBB PIERCE
(1926–1991)

HOME AREA
Monroe, Louisiana

SIGNIFICANCE
The consummate honky-tonk vocalist, and the style's most prolific hit maker. The first to use pedal steel guitar on a record (1954's "Slowly"). Co-owner of Cedarwood Publishing, one of the founding firms of the Nashville music business. Colorful personal style defined country stardom of his era with coin-encrusted convertible, guitar-shaped swimming pool, rhinestone suits, diamond rings, etc.

POPULAR SONGS
"Wondering" (1952), "Back Street Affair" (1952), "There Stands the Glass" (1953), "Slowly" (1954), "More and More" (1954), "In the Jailhouse Now" (1955), "I Don't Care" (1955), "I'm Tired" (1957), "Honky Tonk Song" (1957), "Missing You" (1957), "Tupelo County Jail" (1958), "I Ain't Never" (1959), "No Love Have I" (1959), "Fallen Angel" (1960), "All My Love" (1962), "Fool, Fool, Fool" (1967)

INFLUENCED
Faron Young, Mel Tillis, Willie Nelson, Gail Davies

HONORS
Cast membership: Louisiana Hayride, Grand Ole Opry; three motion pictures

HANK SNOW

(1914–)

HOME AREA
Nova Scotia, Canada

SIGNIFICANCE
"The Singing Ranger." Enormous song repertoire, a living link to the dawn of commercial country music. Fine flattop guitar player. Considered one of the "pillars" of the Grand Ole Opry. Widely admired, highly individualistic, clipped vocal style.

POPULAR SONGS
"I'm Moving On" (1950), "The Rhumba Boogie" (1951), "Bluebird Island" (with Anita Carter, 1951), "The Gold Rush Is Over" (1952), "A Fool Such as I" (1953), "I Don't Hurt Anymore" (1954), "Let Me Go, Lover" (1955), "These Hands" (1956), "Miller's Cave" (1960), "I've Been Everywhere" (1962), "Ninety Miles an Hour" (1963), "Hello Love" (1974)

INFLUENCED
Willie Nelson, Elvis Presley, Jimmie Rodgers Snow, Opry stars

HONORS
Nashville Songwriters Hall of Fame, 1978; Country Music Hall of Fame, 1979; Canadian Country Music Hall of Honor, 1985; own career museum

They had a lot of people on that show, Johnnie and Jack, Kitty Wells, Ray Price, Webb Pierce, the Osborne Brothers, George Morgan, Little Jimmy Dickens, Homer & Jethro, Del Wood—just a bunch of them from the Opry. Hank was on the way there, and he passed away. Little Jimmy's manager introduced everybody onstage and told 'em that Hank had just passed away. A sold-out crowd. It was probably the saddest show we'd put on.

We went to the funeral, and it was probably the largest funeral I'd ever been to. Roy Acuff and myself, Red Foley, Webb Pierce, Little Jimmy Dickens and all had the ole Roy Acuff "Speckled Bird" plane, the one he used to charter all the time, a DC-3, two-propeller. And going down there, everybody was drinking pretty heavy, because it was so sad. I think Bill Monroe and myself were the only two on there that weren't drinking. From the auditorium in Montgomery, there were people lined up all the way out to the cemetery.

[**BRENDA LEE**] Gosh, Hank Williams, I mean what can you say about him? What a heart that guy had. "Jambalaya" was my very first record in 1956. It is just one of those songs that people just love the minute they hear it. It's infectious.

[**ALAN JACKSON**] I sing "Mind Your Own Business" in my live show all the time, and some of his other songs. Hank Williams laid the groundwork for everybody.

Ray Price went from being Hank Williams's roommate and understudy to wailing honky-tonk hits of his own such as "Crazy Arms" (1956) and "Release Me" (1954).

Hank's honky-tonk sound of the mid-1940s to the early 1950s was part of a nationwide country-music trend. Tennessee's Carl Smith, West Virginia's Jimmy Dickens, Louisiana's Webb Pierce and Faron Young, Canada's Hank Snow, California migrants Merle Travis, the Maddox Brothers and Rose, Tennessee Ernie Ford, and Tex Williams, plus Texans Hank Thompson, Ray Price, and Moon Mullican were all scoring at this time with the new hard-hitting style.

[**JERRY RIVERS**] While Hank Williams was still alive, The Drifting Cowboys, his band, had the opportunity to record with Ray Price, to play performances with him on the Grand Ole Opry and then to back him because he was sometimes an opening act for Hank Williams on the road. Hank and Ray were very close.

[**RAY PRICE**] The "Cherokee Cowboy" came in on me because, when Hank died, I had the Drifting Cowboys. One night in Colorado, we was out there playin', and a guy came to me and said, "Boy, you sound just like old Hank." And that wasn't what I wanted to sound like. So I hired a western-swing band that I had worked with in Texas, called the Western Cherokees. When I took the group into the Grand Ole Opry, the Solemn Old Judge, George D. Hay, said, "You gotta have a name for the band." So I took the last two names of both bands and called 'em the Cherokee Cowboys.

I found Roger Miller in the fire department in Amarillo, Texas. I needed a

▲

Canada's Hank Snow applied his distinctive vocal phrasing and crisp lead guitar picking to honky-tonk, rhumba, train, cowboy, folk, and romance songs as an Opry superstar.

"If you was ever around Lefty for any length of time, you would start copying him. He was the kind of guy that he didn't start talking like you, you started talking like him. He had one of the most magnetic personalities of anyone that I've ever been around, the kind of personality that just drew people to him."

DAVID
FRIZZELL

Lefty Frizzell was one of the most influential vocalists in country history.

front man at that time and I needed a fiddle player. So Roger came to try out. When he got through playin' the first tune, I asked him, could he sing and play a guitar, 'cause his fiddle playin' wasn't really all that great. He laughed. Roger came to work for me, and I recorded a song that he had written called "Invitation to the Blues" (1958), and it got Roger started. He was a real talent.

When I first heard "Night Life" (1963), Willie Nelson was in my band at the time. Willie sang it for me, and I thought it was a great blues song.

[WILLIE NELSON] When I was a songwriter at Pamper Music, Ray Price was an owner. I had a few songs that had gotten recorded. In the meantime, Ray was touring and Johnny Paycheck was playin' bass for Ray. And Ray called me from on the road and wanted to know if I knew a bass player, that Johnny was leaving. I said, "Sure." He said, "Who?" I said, "Me." I'd never played bass in my life, but I didn't figure Ray would notice for a while.

I've loved Hank Snow for a long, long time. Ever since "Brand On My Heart" (1946) was his first big hit in Texas.

[HANK SNOW, 1986] I did a lot of the old story songs, the tragic songs and novelty songs. I've always said I was deprived of a childhood. I only went to the fifth grade in school. But I feel that, through experience and through poverty and through learning to survive, I have a college education.

[CAROL LEE COOPER] I watch Hank Snow while we're working with him on the Opry. I try to memorize people like him and Bill Monroe. I remember seeing my dad in the wings watching Roy Acuff so intently, and I said, "Daddy, what are you doing?" And he said, "I'm learning."

[KRIS KRISTOFFERSON] Jimmy Dickens was one of the guys that, when I came along, would still hang out with the struggling songwriters. He would sit down with us after he'd just gotten in off the bus. He'd be exhausted, but he'd get down and start singin' these songs. He'd break your heart. The best kind of songwriters at the time were tryin' to make each other cry.

[JIMMY DICKENS] It was a dream, you know, for me to come to the Grand Ole Opry. I came in 1948. "Country Boy" (1949) was a song that I thought was perfect to follow up my first record with, "Take an Old Cold Tater and Wait."

I was the first artist to circle the globe on tour. That was

LEFTY FRIZZELL
(1928–1975)

HOME AREA
East Texas

SIGNIFICANCE
Enormously influential "singer's singer." Distinctive bent-note, curling-phrase vocal style the model for hundreds of honky-tonk stylists to come. Four songs simultaneously in the top-ten in 1951.

POPULAR SONGS
"If You've Got the Money, I've Got the Time" (1950), "I Love You a Thousand Ways" (1950), "I Want to Be with You Always" (1951), "Always Late" (1951), "Mom and Dad's Waltz" (1951), "Travelin' Blues" (1951), "Give Me More, More, More" (1951), "Run 'Em Off" (1954), "The Long Black Veil" (1959), "Saginaw, Michigan" (1964), "She's Gone, Gone, Gone" (1965), "I Never Go Around Mirrors" (1974), "That's the Way Love Goes" (1974)

INFLUENCED
David Frizzell, Allen Frizzell, Merle Haggard, Willie Nelson, George Jones, Johnny Rodriguez, John Anderson, Dwight Yoakam, Randy Travis, George Strait, Keith Whitley, many others

HONORS
Nashville Songwriters Hall of Fame, 1972; Country Music Hall of Fame, 1982

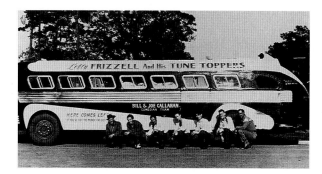

Country stars like Lefty Frizzell adopted tour buses during the honky-tonk era (above). Another legacy is vibrant costuming, sported by such acts as The Maddox Brothers and Rose (below), billed as "The Most Colorful Hillbilly Band in the Land."

quite a thing. It was all American military installations, all over the world. I was in Saigon at Christmastime, and I don't think I've ever seen a bunch of guys so happy to see an American entertainer. That was in 1967.

[**GAIL DAVIES**] Classic country music, to me, was people like Webb Pierce and Carl Smith. Carl Smith had that emotional content in his singing. I remember "It's a Lovely, Lovely World" (1952) made me so happy. I love the lines in it like, "My guitar stays a little better in tune / Stars shine bright and there's honey on the moon." It was a Felice and Boudleaux Bryant song. I cut the song as a duet with Emmylou Harris.

[**KRIS KRISTOFFERSON**] I can remember when every Number One record that was on was a Webb Pierce record. He had a string of 'em.

[**WILLIE NELSON**] I liked his swimmin' pool. It was shaped like a guitar. Remember when Ray Stevens got upset because there was so many people comin' by in tour buses lookin' at Webb Pierce's pool, buyin' "Webb Water" out of the pool and all that stuff? He was real hot about it, and Webb said, "Well, you shouldn't have moved next door to a star."

[**FLOYD CRAMER**] I graduated from high school in 1951, and I moved straight to Shreveport, and it was there I started with Webb Pierce, the first person that was on the Louisiana Hayride.

[**MERLE KILGORE**] I quit college in 1952 because a TV station in Monroe, Louisiana, was coming on the air, and the owner had heard me singing. He talked me into quitting college and becoming a TV star. I was called "The Tall Texan." Webb's hometown was West Monroe, Louisiana. Webb came home after having all the big success he had in Nashville. He waited for my show to come on that night. I wrote a song on the way to the studio called "More and More" (1954). I sang that song on the show, and when I came on, Webb said, "That's Merle Kilgore! He used to carry my guitar at the Louisiana Hayride!" Webb called me and said, "If you'll give me half of the song, I'll record it and make it Number One and make you famous." I said, "Go ahead." It opened the door for me in the music business.

[**FARON YOUNG**] Webb Pierce had a high, really country, corny sound. At that time, that's what country music was. I sang a little bit more mellow, but he was having hit records, and I wasn't—until I kind of really got to singing something like him and Hank Williams and whined it a little bit.

[**BILLY WALKER**] I worked with a lot of Hanks: Hank Thompson, Hank Williams, Hank Snow, and Hank Locklin. Hank Thompson helped me get my first record contract. I was doing live radio down in Waco, Texas, and doing a thing on the Big D Jamboree in Dallas. Hank came to me and he said, "I'm fixing to move to Dallas, and I'm starting a live radio program there, and I need some help. Would you like to come and be my opening act?" I said, "Man, yeah, let's do it." He said, "I told Lee Gillette about you on Capital Records, and he's coming in to town." Lee came into town, heard me, and gave me my first record contract. Hank Thompson was a big, big star.

[**WANDA JACKSON**] How would I describe Hank Thompson? Hank Thompson to me is like, maybe, the Perry Como or the Bing Crosby of western swing. His

MINNIE PEARL

Sarah Ophelia Colley
(1912–1996)

HOME AREA
Centerville, Tennessee

SIGNIFICANCE
The most popular country comic in history. Goodwill ambassador of the Grand Ole Opry. First major female Opry star.

POPULAR SONGS
"Jealous Hearted Me" (1954), "Papa Loves Mambo" (with Grandpa Jones, 1954), "How to Catch a Man" (1954), "Giddyup Go Answer" (1966)

INFLUENCED
Rod Brasfield, Hank Williams, Opry cast, Mel Tillis, the cast of *Hee Haw*, Chely Wright

HONORS
Country Music Hall of Fame, 1975; Academy of Country Music Pioneer Award, 1986; *Music City News* Minnie Pearl Award, 1988; own career museum

diction is always perfect. He has a way with words. He wrote almost everything that he recorded. His songs were different than the normal country songs that you hear. They were very poetic. He was always my idol. I was so thrilled when he became my mentor and friend.

Hank Williams was honky-tonk's messiah; Ray Price was the apostle; Webb Pierce and Hank Snow had the style's longest string of hits; Hank Thompson was its greatest bandleader, and Faron Young, Carl Smith, and Jimmy Dickens became its greatest showmen. But honky-tonk's most influential voice was Lefty Frizzell.

[**MERLE HAGGARD**] Lefty Frizzell was the first guy I ever heard sing with the "curls" of Bessie Smith, and I think one of the first to bring a certain kind of blues into country music.

[**DAVID FRIZZELL**] I used to imitate him right down to the way he put a jacket on, the way he used to walk if he'd had maybe three drinks. Because everything he did was so different from anybody else. He was the most original person I've ever been around.

[**MEL TILLIS**] Did we roar? Boy, I'm tellin' you! I remember one night we was out for three days. And he said, "Melvin, could you go home with me? Maybe then Alice won't get mad at me. She likes you." We went out there, and he said, "You better stay out here 'til I make peace." The next thing I knew, out come a big ole buffalo head. It came right by me and knocked off one of the horns. And in a minute he come out and said, "Melvin, I don't think you better come in. But you can have my buffalo head. She don't want it in the house anymore." And when I got home, Doris threw the head out and broke the other horn off. It took me forever to get back in the house. The buffalo head, it stayed out there two or three days. The dogs drug it off.

[**DAVID FRIZZELL**] Everybody drank. There wasn't so much of the other stuff going around in those days. It was just all booze. My brother Lefty was forty-seven when he died. That was July 19, 1975. After Lefty passed away, Willie Nelson did a tribute album to Lefty. I appreciated that.

The honky-tonk was a man's world. But, ironically, the same era produced

"'Minnie' will never grow old. When I first 'met' her, she was in her early flirties—that's young enough to flirt with men, but too old to have 'em flirt back. And she's stayed that way. She is ageless."

MINNIE PEARL, 1986

Sarah Ophelia Colley became Minnie Pearl, the most famous comic in country history.

▲

*Honky-tonk star
Carl Smith pauses in
the midst of his forty-
song hit streak of the
1950s to receive con-
gratulations on the
Grand Ole Opry stage.*

*Nashville's first big female stars. The earliest on the scene was come-
dienne Minnie Pearl, who arrived at the Opry in 1940.*

[**JOE TALBOT**] Minnie Pearl is possibly the most beloved
person that's ever been in the country music business.

[**VIC WILLIS, OF THE WILLIS BROTHERS**] She came
across as one of the audience. They knew that she didn't buy
that hat. They knew that that wasn't the way she dressed every day. But they accepted it, because there was someone in
that little town where they lived that reminded them of her.

[**MINNIE PEARL, 1986**] "Minnie" will never grow old.
When I first "met" her, she was in her early flirties—that's
young enough to flirt with men, but too old to have 'em flirt
back. And she's stayed that way. She is ageless.

[**JUNE CARTER CASH**] Minnie Pearl meant a lot to me.
She encouraged me as a comedienne. I must have been
about ten, and the Carter Family was workin' a date with
Minnie. I was talkin' to her in the dressin' room. She said,
"There's no two ways about it. You're gonna end up bein'
kind of a comedienne, so let me give you a little bit of
advice. Just be yourself."

[**MEL TILLIS**] Minnie Pearl hired me, and she hired my friend Roger Miller at
the same time. But she hired me first. Then she said, "I need a fiddle player." I
hurried on down to the coffee shop in that hotel. Roger was in there, and he had
on his little bellhop outfit. And I said, "Roger, you want a job with Minnie Pearl?"
He said, "Yeah!" I said, "Well you've got a job, ain't you? He said, "Yeah, but I'm
gonna give them my two-minute notice." And we went out on the road.

[**CONNIE SMITH**] There weren't very many women when I was first listening to
country music. Kitty Wells was the Queen, and she was going strong. Jean Shepard
was just as steady and strong as she is now in her singing. Rose Maddox was doing
great. And I knew a little bit about Molly O'Day and Goldie Hill.

[**ROSE MADDOX, 1989**] Prior to the war, we just worked in honky-tonks for
tips, mostly. After the war, we started getting paid for doing dances and stuff.
Everything we did, we did ourselves. We didn't have managers and publicists
and all such as that. I was one of the pioneers of country music, especially of the
women singers. I was always a honky-tonk singer. I think I've been singing for
two hundred years, in other lives.

[**HANK THOMPSON**] I think that "The Wild Side of Life" and its answer by
Kitty Wells, "It Wasn't God Who Made Honky-Tonk Angels," was really a turning
point in country music, in the thinking and the songs. Prior to Kitty's success in
recording that answer, it was dominated by male singers. The songs were written
with the male conception of things, the male being the one that gets out and does
the work, goes and has some drinks, and comes home and he finds his wife has

run off with somebody else, or he's got a girlfriend back there at the honky-tonk.

[**KITTY WELLS**] Back then they weren't writin' songs just for women, you know. I sang "May I Sleep in Your Barn Tonight Mister" and "Little Cathy Fiscus" and maybe "Matthew 24," a lot of gospel songs, "Amazin' Grace," and songs like that.

Freddy Rose, who ran Acuff-Rose Publications, gave me that title, The Queen of Country Music. That was back in 1953, I believe. I felt it was a great honor. You really had to be on your toes to live up to that title.

[**EMMYLOU HARRIS**] How do you explain Kitty Wells? You just have to have an emotional reaction to her. I always wanted that kind of voice. I'm always honoring the "ghost" of Kitty Wells. When I'm singing "Making Believe," there's a shadow of Kitty Wells in there.

[**LORETTA LYNN**] Everybody would tell me to quit sounding like Kitty Wells or I'd never make it. Yeah, I tried to sing like Kitty Wells. I'm not ashamed to say that. I was trying to sing like the best, wasn't I?

[**NORMA JEAN**] Kitty Wells had the biggest impact on me

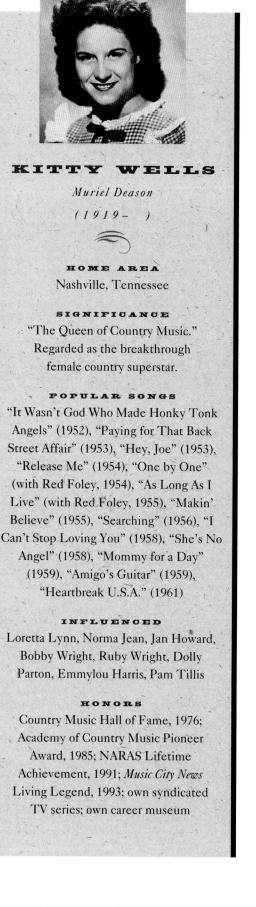

KITTY WELLS

Muriel Deason
(1 9 1 9 –)

HOME AREA
Nashville, Tennessee

SIGNIFICANCE
"The Queen of Country Music." Regarded as the breakthrough female country superstar.

POPULAR SONGS
"It Wasn't God Who Made Honky Tonk Angels" (1952), "Paying for That Back Street Affair" (1953), "Hey, Joe" (1953), "Release Me" (1954), "One by One" (with Red Foley, 1954), "As Long As I Live" (with Red Foley, 1955), "Makin' Believe" (1955), "Searching" (1956), "I Can't Stop Loving You" (1958), "She's No Angel" (1958), "Mommy for a Day" (1959), "Amigo's Guitar" (1959), "Heartbreak U.S.A." (1961)

INFLUENCED
Loretta Lynn, Norma Jean, Jan Howard, Bobby Wright, Ruby Wright, Dolly Parton, Emmylou Harris, Pam Tillis

HONORS
Country Music Hall of Fame, 1976; Academy of Country Music Pioneer Award, 1985; NARAS Lifetime Achievement, 1991; *Music City News* Living Legend, 1993; own syndicated TV series; own career museum

Kitty Wells has reigned as The Queen of Country Music since 1952.

JEAN SHEPARD

(1933–)

HOME AREA
Oklahoma

SIGNIFICANCE
Long chart career, 1953–78. Recorded country's first "concept" album, *Songs of a Love Affair*. Major activist in keeping country "country" in the face of pop influences of the '70s. Matriarch to younger female acts at Grand Ole Opry.

POPULAR SONGS
"A Dear John Letter" (with Ferlin Husky, 1953), "A Satisfied Mind" (1955), "Second Fiddle" (1964), "Then He Touched Me" (1970), "Slippin' Away" (1973), "At the Time" (1974)

INFLUENCED
Jeannie Seely, Connie Smith, Lorrie Morgan, Jeanne Pruett, Ray Pillow, Skeeter Davis

HONORS
Cast membership: Ozark Jubilee, Grand Ole Opry

of anybody. She was the first woman to have the really big hits.

[**DOLLY PARTON**] I can't think of a nicer person to look up to than Kitty Wells. I did a tribute album to her, years ago. When I did the *Honky Tonk Angels* album with Tammy Wynette and Loretta Lynn, I said, "We gotta have Kitty. She's just got to come and sing on this."

[**BOBBY WRIGHT**] My dad, Johnny Wright, doesn't get the credit he deserves. If it had not been for him, there wouldn't be a Kitty Wells, because he was largely responsible for promoting Kitty Wells. She's the Queen of Country Music, and he made her what she is today because he picked out all her material.

[**JOHNNY WRIGHT**] I've learned that whenever Kitty tells me something, I do it.

[**HANK THOMPSON**] We were playin' a little town, Hanford, California. The nightclub manager told us, "You know, we have an all-girl band." And I said, "I've heard they're very good." He said, "Yeah, and the girl that sings with it, Jeannie Shepard, is here tonight."

[**JEAN SHEPARD**] It was called the Melody Ranch Girls. One night, Hank Thompson come into this place where we played, and I had the pleasure of getting up and singing with Hank Thompson. He said, "Young lady, would you like to have a recording contract?" I think I was seventeen or eighteen years old. I said, "Yes, sir, I sure would!" He got me a recording contract with Capitol Records.

[**JOE TALBOT**] I would like to mention something about how it was back then; and we're talking the '40s and the '50s. There was no money. Those of us who were in the business were in because we loved it and because we had to do it. It was an obsession. As I recall, union scale to go on the road and play a one-nighter was ten dollars a day, and out of that we had to buy our food and clothes. There were no interstates, no buses. We rode in Cadillacs, which I thought was a pretty big deal. It was kinda uncomfortable, with the bass laying across the top of the seat. In fact, Jean Shepard says that's why she walks this way to this day. She was the smallest one, and they scrunched her under the bass. But it didn't make any difference. We wanted to do it.

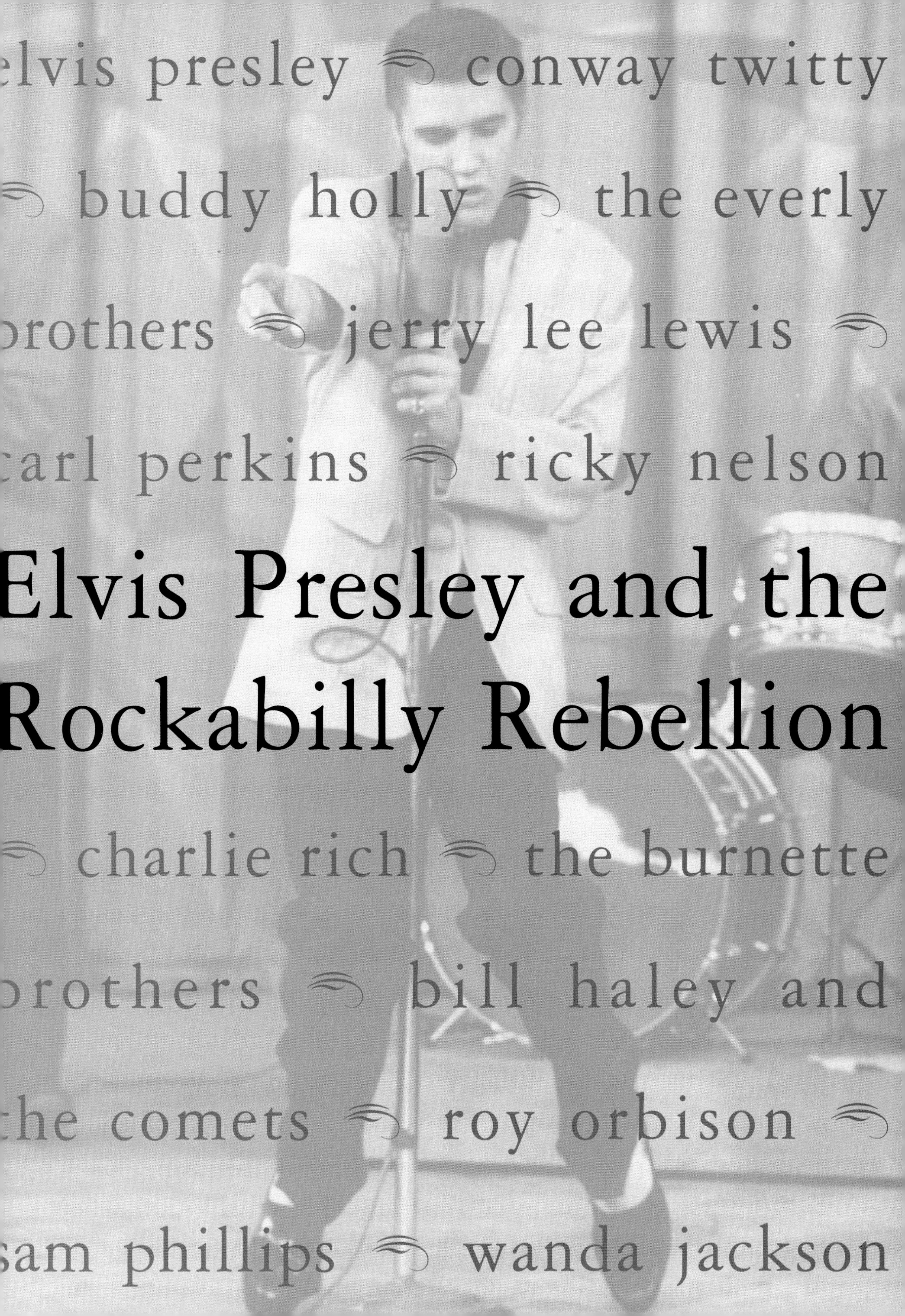

elvis presley ∾ conway twitty
∾ buddy holly ∾ the everly
brothers ∾ jerry lee lewis ∾
carl perkins ∾ ricky nelson

Elvis Presley and the Rockabilly Rebellion

∾ charlie rich ∾ the burnette
brothers ∾ bill haley and
the comets ∾ roy orbison ∾
sam phillips ∾ wanda jackson

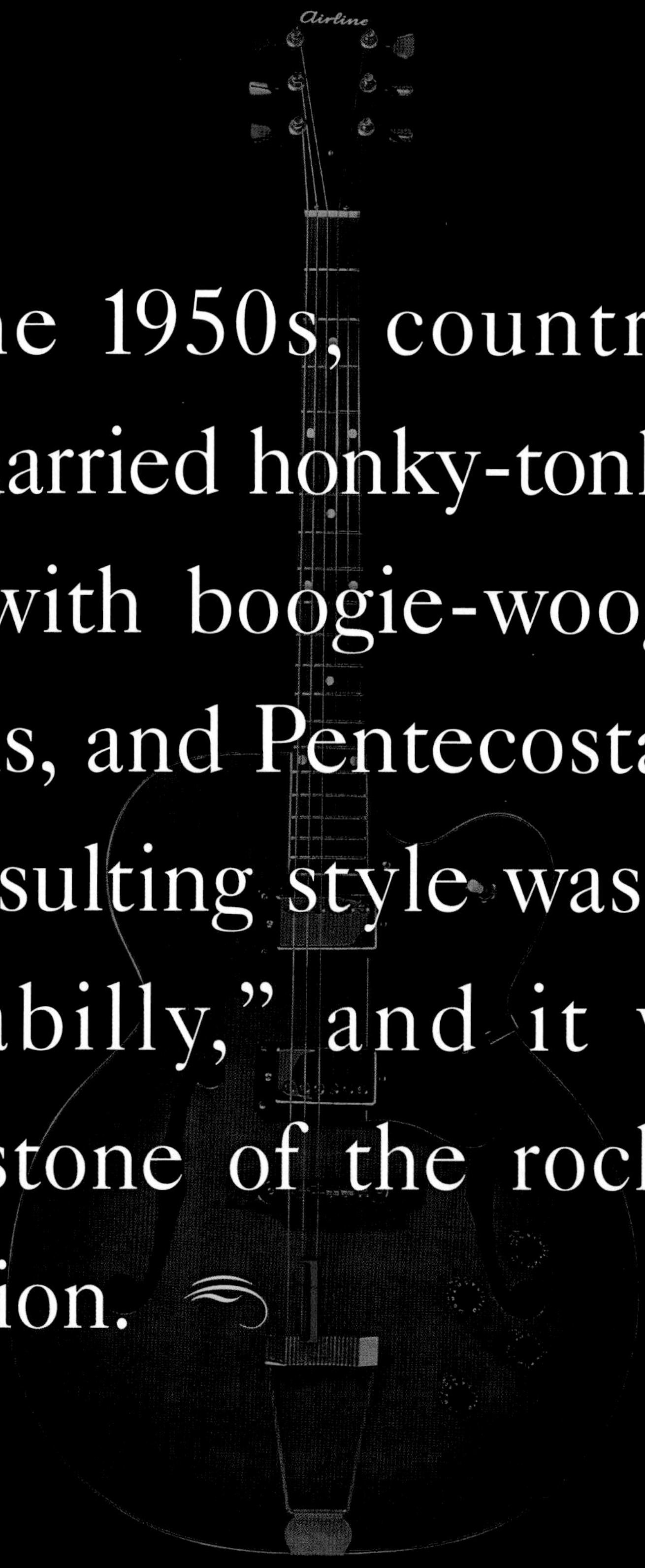

In the 1950s, country musicians married honky-tonk "jump" tunes with boogie-woogie, r&b rhythms, and Pentecostal fervor. The resulting style was dubbed "rockabilly," and it was the cornerstone of the rock 'n' roll revolution. ⌇

Despite segregation laws, black and white musical interaction has always been intense in the South. A. P. Carter was accompanied on his Appalachian song searches by black musician Leslie Riddles. Jimmie Davis worked with black sidemen Oscar Woods and Ed Schaffer. Bill Monroe learned guitar from a black string-band player named Arnold Shultz. Hank Williams was taught by street singer Rufus "Teetot" Payne. The styles of Jimmie Rodgers and Bob Wills were heavily laced with blues. So it was a long-simmering pot that boiled over when hillbillies began to rock.

⟻⟼◆⟻⟼

[**RAY STEVENS**] The kids really were tired of the old Tin Pan Alley production, the slick everything. They gravitated towards something more earthy, more real.

[**CHARLIE DANIELS**] Black music was called rhythm and blues. Back in the fifties, a lot of white kids started listening to that and started really liking it.

[**BRENDA LEE**] When I was singing rockabilly I didn't know what I was singing. It was just a style of singing that I started out doing that came from within. That's the only way that I can explain it. Elvis was singing the same kind of stuff. A lot of us were. It wasn't country, and it certainly wasn't rock, because rock 'n' roll was not invented at that time. I did start listening to a lot of rhythm and blues 'cause I always loved the black artists. I always thought that they had a handle on guts and feeling, maybe, that we hadn't caught on to yet.

[**ROSE MADDOX, 1989**] When I was doin' what they're callin' rockabilly now, I thought it was hillbilly music. I had got my songs in rhythm and blues, from the colored people's records. But I turned 'em around and did 'em my way.

[**MERLE HAGGARD**] The Maddox Brothers and Rose were almost rock-a-hillbilly in the early 1950s. They didn't know how to play music. Music was the farthest thing from their mind. But they could entertain.

Rockabilly experimentation was done by the Maddoxes in L.A., by Bill Haley in New York, by the Davis Sisters in Nashville, and by acts in Texas, Louisiana, and elsewhere. But rockabilly's true birthplace was Memphis, the home of the Burnette brothers, Johnny and Dorsey, as well as of the scrappy independent label Sun Records.

[**BILLY BURNETTE**] My dad and uncle were the true rebels. You had to be tough to play that kind of music back then. There's even a story that goes back. Rocky's my cousin, Johnny's son. And I'm Billy. So they dedicated a song to us one night, "to our sons Rocky and Billy," and they wrote "Rock Billy Boogie" (1956) after that. They say they've traced the name "rockabilly" back as far as that.

The Burnettes began their Memphis band in 1953. Johnny worked at Crown Electric, as did truck driver Elvis Presley, who attended their rockabilly shows.

"Country music is innovative, and country music is the thing that produced Elvis Presley."

———

MERLE HAGGARD

Sun Records's "million-dollar quartet" gathered in the label's Memphis studio in December 1956. Surrounding Elvis Presley at the piano are, from left, Jerry Lee Lewis, Carl Perkins, and Johnny Cash. Label founder Sam Phillips (right) was a visionary in bringing together black and white musical traditions.

[**SAM PHILLIPS**] Elvis Presley had heard about Sun Records at Memphis Recording Service. But Elvis didn't know how to get up the courage to come in and ask for a free audition. So he concocted this wild story he wanted to make a record for his mother. That's how it happened. It was that casual.

We were talkin' about, you know, maybe he could get an audition to get on Sun Records. I said, "Look, Elvis, I'm goin' to Nashville, leavin' in the mornin', and goin' to the prison and record The Prisonaires. And I understand that there's a guy over there that writes real good songs. He's a prisoner, and I wanna check him out. If there's anything there, I'll call you up, and we'll see if anything comes of it." Listen, all of a sudden there was just a look. This man was bubblin' inside."

This guy looked different. Real different. This guy had sideburns down to here. It's hard for younger people to believe this, but with sideburns that long back then, old people hated ya. After we'd talked and I heard him do "That's When Your Heartaches Begin," I said, "Hell, we're gonna do somethin' with this guy or bust

a big gut tryin'." We tried, and you know what? Damn, if I don't believe we made it.

After about six months we were in the studio, and I told 'im, "We're gonna have to come back another day." And I heard this three-chord vamp, "That's All Right, Mama." Scotty was pickin' a little bit. Elvis was floggin' his guitar. Bill Black was in a notion to chime in, too. I said, "What in the hell are you-all doin'?" "We don't know." I said, "Well, I don't know either, but let's do some more of it now. We been messin' around here for six months. It's time for us to get off of our cans and do something."

When I came along with Presley, here he was doin' Arthur "Big Boy" Crudup's "That's All Right, Mama" (1954), and on the other side, I was so stupid I didn't have more sense than to put "Blue Moon of Kentucky" by Bill Monroe. And I can tell you at that point, I just didn't believe that we were gonna have a real big problem of finding acceptance for Elvis Presley. But I got news for ya. I did find some problems. And a lot of them. But you had to keep drivin', man. Had we have given up at Sun Records because we had been told by radio stations, "We can't play this," we wouldn't have been worth our bread. I wasn't the only one. There was some crusadin' goin' on for rhythm and blues, for that combination of southern country music that we're talkin' about—the roots. Now I wanna tell you somethin', folks. It came out of the soil of the South. It came out of desperation and it came out of exhilaration.

[**FARON YOUNG**] When Elvis Presley was just starting, I'd carry Elvis on my show, and he'd open the shows for me, and them little girls would just squeal and holler. All the girls wanted to tear my clothes off, too. They didn't care nothing about seeing Faron Young; they just knew I was on the show with Elvis Presley, so they're gonna tear all my clothes off. I remember the last day that I worked with him was in Amarillo, Texas. I had a brand-new Cadillac limousine, and those kids dissected that car. They took the hubcaps, the headlights, scratched their names into it, completely wrecked it.

[**SAM PHILLIPS**] I tell you who gave us the first opportunity was Ernest Tubb, when he got Elvis on that radio show at Ernest Tubb's Record Shop on Broadway after the Grand Ole Opry at midnight.

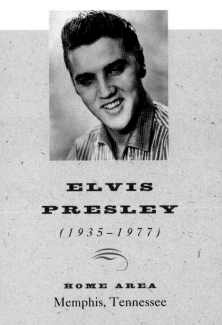

ELVIS PRESLEY
(1935–1977)

HOME AREA
Memphis, Tennessee

SIGNIFICANCE
"The King of Rock 'n' Roll." The most popular solo recording artist in history.

POPULAR SONGS
"Heartbreak Hotel" (1956), "Hound Dog," (1956), "Love Me Tender" (1956), "All Shook Up" (1957), "Jailhouse Rock" (1957), "Are You Lonesome Tonight" (1960), "Can't Help Falling in Love" (1961), "Return to Sender" (1962), "Crying in the Chapel" (1965), "Kentucky Rain" (1970), "Burning Love" (1972), "Moody Blue" (1976), "My Way" (1977)

INFLUENCED
Conway Twitty, Merle Haggard, Ronnie Milsap, Jerry Reed, Eddie Rabbitt, hundreds of others

HONORS
Grammy Award, 1967 (*How Great Thou Art*); Grammy, 1972 (*He Touched Me*); Grammy, 1974 ("How Great Thou Art"); NARAS Lifetime Achievement, 1971; Grammy Hall of Fame, 1988 ("Hound Dog"); Rock 'n' Roll Hall of Fame, 1986; more than ninety Gold and Platinum record awards; two stars on Hollywood Walk of Fame

"He had charisma like nobody I've ever seen. It was him and a three-piece band and they were awesome. I'll never forget that night."

GLEN
CAMPBELL

Elvis Presley barnstormed the South and Southwest in 1954–56, touring with Faron Young, Ferlin Husky, The Carter Sisters, Hank Snow, Martha Carson, the Duke of Paducah, Marty Robbins, Jimmie Rodgers Snow, Tommy Collins, Wanda Jackson, Porter Wagoner, Johnny Cash, The Louvin Brothers, Justin Tubb, Minnie Pearl, and other country stars on "package" shows. During the next twenty-five years, "The King of Rock 'n' Roll" would place more than eighty singles on the country popularity charts.

Phillips sold Elvis's contract to RCA Records. "The Hillbilly Cat" recorded his first national hit, "Heartbreak Hotel," in Nashville in 1956.

[**CHET ATKINS**] When Elvis Presley came to town, we all knew he was gonna be a star.

[**K. T. OSLIN**] I saw Elvis in 1956 when I was fourteen. It was in Houston, and he was just starting to be a ball of flame. Everybody was talking about it.

[**BRENDA LEE**] Elvis and I performed on the Grand Ole Opry for the first time in 1957, December. It was his first and my first time. We became friends and stayed friends throughout his life.

[**CAROL LEE COOPER**] I got to meet him at the old Ryman Auditorium. I was fifteen at the time and I thought, "Don't care if it is Elvis Presley; I'm not passing out." Daddy and Mother and I were rehearsing, and he stood there and listened. Then Bill Monroe rehearsed a little while, and while Bill was rehearsing, he grabbed my hand and said, "Come on, Carol, let's dance." He went over to my dad, Stoney Cooper, and said, "Can I take her home? I'll take good care of her." And my eyes are going, "Say yes, *please.*" Later, he took home Priscilla. I think he was looking for someone to take home.

[**BILL MONROE**] He come up to the Opry on a Saturday night. I had never met him, but I said, "Well, if 'Blue Moon of Kentucky' helped give you your start, why, I'm for you 100 percent."

[**JERRY REED**] Elvis had heard "Guitar Man" off my album (1967) and wanted to record it. He called me to come down and play on the song, and I went right through the roof. I couldn't believe it. As soon as I kicked it off, you could see Elvis's face light up. Then Pete Drake said, "Sing him 'U.S. Male.'" I sung him "U.S. Male" and, blame, if he didn't like that, and we cut it that night. He later on cut "Talk About the Good Times" and "A Thing Called Love." But, boy, what a night! And what a great looking dude. He made me feel like I was born wrong or something.

[**MERLE HAGGARD**] Elvis is written all over me. I grew up doin' Elvis's music. He was two years older than me. He was nineteen years old, hottest thing in the world, and I was seventeen years old, coldest thing in the world. But I was havin' to make a livin', and if you didn't know how to play Elvis Presley songs, you might as well go home.

[**JOHNNY CASH**] Elvis, of course, was the one that opened the door for all of us, singin' the old country songs with a black feel.

[**SAM PHILLIPS**] Carl Perkins always said, "Mr. Phillips, I can't compete with

▲

Roy Orbison began his rockabilly career singing "Ooby Dooby" and "Rockhouse" at Sun Records in 1956. In the '60s he created throbbing, operatic teen anthems in Nashville.

CONWAY TWITTY

Harold Jenkins

(1933–1993)

HOME AREA
Friar's Point, Mississippi

SIGNIFICANCE
"The High Priest of Country Music"

POPULAR SONGS
"Rockhouse" (1956), "It's Only Make
Believe" (1958), "Fifteen Years Ago"
(1970), "You've Never Been This Far
Before" (1973), "Louisiana Woman,
Mississippi Man" (with Loretta Lynn,
1973), "There's a Honky Tonk Angel"
(1974), "I'd Love to Lay You Down"
(1980), "Crazy in Love" (1990), "Rainy
Night in Georgia" (with Sam Moore, 1994)

INFLUENCED
Ronnie McDowell, Vince Gill

HONORS
Grammy Award, 1971 ("After the Fire
Is Gone," with Loretta Lynn); CMA Duo
of the Year, 1972–75 (all with Loretta
Lynn); *Music City News* Male Vocalist
1974–77; Duet of the Year, 1972–78,
1980–81 (all with Loretta Lynn); Song of
the Year, 1970 and 1974 ("Hello Darlin',"
"You've Never Been This Far Before");
Living Legend, 1988; ACM Male Vocalist,
1975; Duet of the Year, 1971, '72, '74–76
(all with Loretta Lynn); Album of the
Year, 1975 (*Feelin's*, with Loretta Lynn);
Nashville Songwriters Hall of Fame, 1993

Elvis. He is a good lookin' young cat. I look like an old mule lookin' over a whitewashed fence." But I felt that Carl did have a very unusual style on the guitar. And I knew that there wasn't really any great point in attemptin' to follow along the lines of Nashville in strictly country. I knew if I could bargain between that and rhythm and blues, Carl Perkins could kick that around pretty good. So we put the blue suede shoes on him. Met him in Dallas at the Sportatorium for the Big D Jamboree. I bought some blue suede shoes in a store in downtown Houston. I found me some glitter, and I got me some glue, and I glued 'em all on there. About the time he was ready to kick off "Blue Suede Shoes" (1956), "Carl! You gotta wait just a minute!" I walked up on the stage with the shoes, put those things on that cat, and he blew the Sportatorium away.

[**BRENDA LEE**] What do I like about Carl Perkins? He's real. He's honest with his music. He doesn't compromise. He's just a good guy.

[**SAM PHILLIPS**] Charlie Rich has been always one of my favorite all-time people in or out of the music business. Charlie came to the studio about 1957. He was farmin' somewhere over there in the Delta, workin', I believe, for his uncle. He is such a combination of all of the elements that we are talkin' about here: rhythm and blues, the pure old blues. He can tear a country song all to pieces and is a great jazz artist.

Charlie Rich began his career with the Phillips-recorded "Lonely Weekends" (1960). By then, the Sun studio was a magnet for experimental rockabilly stylists. Among them were two others who, like Rich, later achieved pop and country glory, Roy Orbison and Conway Twitty.

[**PHIL EVERLY, OF THE EVERLY BROTHERS**] We met Roy up in Hammond, Indiana. Roy had "Ooby Dooby" (1956) as his first record out. We asked Roy if he had any songs. He played us "Claudette" backstage. "Claudette" went on the backside of "All I Have to Do Is Dream." When we decided we were gonna do "Claudette," Wesley Rose of Acuff-Rose Publishing went to Sun Records and brought Roy to Nashville. That's how Roy wound up in Nashville on Monument Records.

[**JEAN SHEPARD**] Roy Orbison loved country music better than anything in the world. He always wanted to sing country

music. He said, "I just don't have the voice." I said, "Goodness gracious, alive, he could sing anything he wanted to."

[**CONWAY TWITTY**, 1982] Friar's Point is a little riverport town sittin' right on the banks of the Mississippi, about seventy or eighty miles south of Memphis. About five hundred people lived there and about three hundred and fifty of 'em were black. On Saturday nights it was the Grand Ole Opry. Listened to it every Saturday night for years. Then, as I learned to play a little bit, the black man next door would teach me a little more. Went to Japan in the army. The first thing I heard when I came back was Elvis Presley. That was a new kind of music—Carl Perkins's "Blue Suede Shoes," Bill Haley's "Rock Around the Clock." I headed straight for Memphis.

Conway didn't strike gold at Sun Records, but when he began recording in Nashville, he became a teen idol with "It's Only Make Believe" (1958), "Lonely Blue Boy" (1960), and other hits. He switched to country recording in 1965 and became an even bigger star with more number-one country records than anyone in history.

[**JOHNNY CASH**] And then came Jerry Lee Lewis, the biggest soul man of all, from Ferriday, Louisiana. He came in one day at a Carl Perkins session. We asked

▲

Producer Owen Bradley (left) confers with Conway Twitty during the early days of the star's conversion from teen idol to honky-tonk singer. Twitty recorded both rockabilly and country in Nashville.

him to set down at the piano and sing one for us. And I knew that Sam had found another one.

[**JACK CLEMENT**] Basically, he was just singing country when I first heard him. I asked him if he knew any rock 'n' roll, and he said, "Nah, I hadn't got into that." About three weeks later, he came back, and he had come up with a version of the old Gene Autry song "You're the Only Star in My Blue Heaven." He goes, "baump, baump, baump" and had me right off the bat then.

[**JERRY LEE LEWIS, 1988**] I was ready, way ahead of the game. I knew that. I never practiced. I was good. All I wanted to do was get somebody to release a record on me. Once I did get it done, I knew it was a hit. I don't like to upset people, but I like to keep 'em on the ball. I get a kick out of anything I do, if I do it right. I'm livin'; I'm breathin'; I'm still rockin', brother. And I did it my way.

[**JOHNNY CASH**] Elvis and Carl and Jerry Lee, all of us had roughly the same background. We lived within one hundred miles of the Memphis radio stations, grew up within one hundred miles of the Mississippi. And there were programs on the air like Dewey Phillips's "Red Hot and Blue," which they called "race music" at the time. There were also black gospel programs, featuring artists like Sister Rosetta Tharpe. There were also live country-jamboree shows that I listened to faithfully. I listened. And so did Elvis, and so did Carl. We grew up on that.

[**SAM PHILLIPS**] Johnny came in and apologized: "Mr. Phillips, hi, I'm John Cash. I sure would like to audition for ya." I said, "We can arrange that, I'm sure." He said, "I got a couple boys who work down here at the Desoto/Plymouth auto sales on Union, just a few doors down here, Mr. Phillips. And I can get them to come in."

He came in—he and Luther Perkins and Marshall Grant—and he apologized for not havin' more people. I listened a little while, and I said, "John, that sounds pretty good to me. It's different." He was singing all religious songs that he had written. I said, "Johnny, as much as I love religion myself and spirituals of all sorts, black and white, I can't peddle that stuff yet. I'm havin' a hard time keepin' my doors open as it is." He was back in a couple weeks, and I believe we cut "Cry Cry Cry" and "Hey, Porter." Wasn't bad for beginners, was it?

Nashville resisted the new sound at first, fearing that it would drown out traditional country music, but within months of Presley's Nashville-recorded "Heartbreak Hotel," the city was developing its own stable of teen stylists.

[**CHET ATKINS**] The Everly Brothers were friends of mine. I met them when they were just kids. They were workin' in Knoxville with Cas Walker on the radio show with their dad and mother. I suppose they were about fourteen and sixteen, somethin' like that. Don and Phil had one of the best producers that ever came to town. His name was Archie Bleyer. The way he did it was he would take the records he cut in Nashville back to New York, and he would let his daughter, who was about sixteen, have parties and play the records. Whatever they played the most, that's what he would release. He was no dummy.

[**PHIL EVERLY**] Don and I were listening to Hank Williams and Hank Snow and George Morgan and all of the country acts that were popular. But we were also listening to LaVern Baker and to Bo Diddley and Clyde McPhatter. Move up to about 1955—rock 'n' roll was happening in pockets all across the country. And then you have Elvis Presley come on the scene.

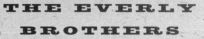

THE EVERLY BROTHERS

MEMBERS
Don Everly, born 1937;
Phil Everly, born 1939

HOME AREA
Central Kentucky

SIGNIFICANCE
One of the purest duet sounds in country music history. Highly influential in both rock and country contexts. Major song-writing talents. International ambassadors with huge popularity in Great Britain.

POPULAR SONGS
"Bye Bye Love" (1957), "Wake Up, Little Susie" (1957), "All I Have to Do Is Dream" (1958), "Bird Dog" (1958), "Devoted to You" (1958), "Let it Be Me" (1960), "Cathy's Clown" (1960), "When Will I Be Loved" (1960), "Walk Right Back" (1961), "Crying in the Rain" (1962)

INFLUENCED
Connie Smith, the Beatles, the Hollies, Peter & Gordon, Foster & Lloyd, Stacy Dean Campbell, Linda Ronstadt, Reba McEntire

HONORS
Grand Ole Opry cast membership, 1957; own TV series, 1970; Rock 'n' Roll Hall of Fame, 1986

Phil (left) and Don Everly took wing in 1957–58 with Nashville rockabilly titles like "Bye Bye Love," "Bird Dog," "Problems," and "Wake Up, Little Susie," as well as with sweet ballads like "All I Have to Do Is Dream."

[**OWEN BRADLEY**] With an Ernest Tubb or Red Foley you don't experiment with rockabilly that much. But we had Bobby Helms. "Fraulein" (1957) was a real strange record because it had country fiddle and rock 'n' roll piano, and he's singin' a song about a German girl. And then he had "You Are My Special Angel" (1957). That sold a lot of records. And we had "Jingle Bell Rock" (1957) with Bobby. In the meantime, Don Law was just doin' great with Columbia Records with Johnny Horton, "The Battle of New Orleans" (1959). "Gone" (1957) by Ferlin Husky was one that Ken Nelson had on Capitol Records. Seemed like everybody was having a nice little run.

[**BRENDA LEE**] I came to Nashville in 1956, at the age of eleven, and I started recording. At twelve years old, I was having hits with "One Step at a Time" and

"Dynamite." Nobody told me I was a star. I went to regular high school. I was a cheerleader; I was on my school newspaper; I was on the debating team. I only worked on the weekends.

The other major female rockabilly artist was West Coast stylist Wanda Jackson.

[**WANDA JACKSON**] When I'm asked about rockabilly and how did I move from country music into rockabilly, I have to say, "I kinda backed into it." I had worked with Elvis, and he had encouraged me to do this kind of music. Finally, I got the nerve to sing some on some of my shows. The ones that I listened to and that were influential in my style of singing were Elvis, Little Richard, Carl Perkins, and Jerry Lee Lewis. When you blend them all together, I guess it came out with Wanda Jackson.

[**BOBBY BARE**] If Eddie Cochran had lived, he would have been a major rock 'n' roll star, because he was coming on like Elvis with 1958's "Summertime Blues" and 1959's "Somethin' Else." When I first met the Cochran brothers, they had their collars turned up. They had suede shoes.

[**JIMMY BOWEN**] Down at Memphis there was Carl Perkins and Jerry Lee Lewis. Out where we were, in Clovis, New Mexico, was Buddy Holly and Buddy Knox [1957's "Party Doll"] and myself [1957's "I'm Stickin' with You"].

[**SHERRY HOLLEY, BUDDY HOLLY'S NIECE**] Buddy went out to Clovis, New Mexico, and did a recording at the Norman Petty Studio there, "That'll Be the Day" (1957). He was workin' for my father in the tile business. Buddy was real depressed one day, and my dad said, "Well, Buddy, what's wrong?" Buddy says, "I finished this recording about two months ago, and they're supposed to be doin' something with it in New York." My dad said, "Well, why don't you call New York and see if something's happenin' with it?" He stopped right in the middle of that tile job and made a phone call to New York. The man that he talked to said they were playin' his song all over the streets. My dad lost his helper right then.

[**SNUFF GARRETT**] I left Lubbock and moved to Wichita Falls and had a television show in the afternoons, sort of the local Dick Clark. And Buddy used to come down and stay with me; and then we'd go do the show. If Buddy had lived, he would have been

Wanda Jackson (above) had the most ferocious vocal attack of all the female rockabilly artists. Despite his untimely death in 1959, Buddy Holly (below) and the Crickets became one of the most influential rockabilly acts of all, inspiring the names of both the Beatles and the Hollies, launching Waylon Jennings and Sonny Curtis, and providing songs that later became hits for Linda Rondstadt and Mickey Gilley.

BUDDY HOLLY

Charles Hardin Holley

(1936–1959)

HOME AREA
Lubbock, Texas

SIGNIFICANCE
The biggest of the Texas rockabillies.
Influential singer-songwriter, particularly
in England, where he remains legendary.

POPULAR SONGS
"That'll Be the Day" (1957), "Peggy Sue"
(1957), "Oh Boy" (1957), "Maybe Baby"
(1958), "Rave On" (1958), "Heartbeat"
(1958), "It Doesn't Matter Anymore"
(1959), "Raining in My Heart" (1959),
"True Love Ways" (1959)

INFLUENCED
The Crickets, Sonny Curtis, Bobby Vee,
Peter & Gordon, the Hollies, the Beatles,
Waylon Jennings, Linda Ronstadt,
Elvis Costello

HONORS
Rock 'n' Roll Hall of Fame, 1986;
biographical film, 1980; biographical
musical, 1988; Nashville Songwriters
Hall of Fame, 1994; All-star country
tribute album, 1996

just an absolute giant, because he had it all. He had all of the things that make magic.

In one of the music world's most famous tragedies, Buddy Holly, Richie Valens, and the Big Bopper were killed in a plane crash on February 3, 1959, "The Day the Music Died."

[**SKEETER DAVIS**] I loved Buddy Holly. I always said I wanted to do a tribute to him. I had to fight to do that [1967's *Skeeter Davis Sings Buddy Holly*]. Waylon Jennings played guitar, and Buddy's family came to the recording sessions.

One by one, Nashville's stars lined up to sing the new teen sounds.

[**RONNIE ROBBINS**] Marty Robbins's first big hit was "Singing the Blues" (1956). It had a little bit of Memphis rockabilly in it. A guy by the name of Guy Mitchell, who was big at the time in pop, covered it, and it sold about two million records. That was a little bit upsetting to Daddy, because he felt like he cut it just as well. To kind of appease him a little bit, the next session he did, they cut in New York, and one of those sides was "A White Sport Coat and a Pink Carnation" (1957). That was a complete departure from his earlier sounds, a total New York production. It was a Number One in country, and it was Number Two in pop, so it was kind of a victory for Daddy.

[**BOBBY BARE**] The first hit I had was in 1958, under rock 'n' roll. They called it "The All American Boy" [credited to "Bill Parsons"]. Everybody thought it was about Elvis getting drafted into the army, but it was about me. I went into the army two days after I recorded it.

[**FARON YOUNG**] Rock 'n' roll killed country music; the rockers knocked it down for about two years. People like Jerry Lee Lewis and those guys coming in, they didn't care what they did to us. They were just looking out for their ownself. I was making a quarter of a million a year, and the next year I made fifty thousand.

The country industry didn't falter long. By the early '60s it was back with a new style called the Nashville Sound. And most of the surviving rockabillies "returned to the fold" as country stars in decades to come.

[**HANK WILLIAMS JR.**] I watched those men walk out there and just tear an audience to pieces. Don't ever count country music out, especially if you've got a little of that rockabilly image.

eddy arnold ❧ jim reeves ❧

red foley ❧ owen bradley ❧

fred rose ❧ patti page ❧ the

ordanaires ❧ brenda lee ❧

rances preston ❧ patsy cline

The Nashville Sound

skeeter davis ❧ jo walker

meader ❧ johnny horton ❧

floyd cramer ❧ ralph emery

immy dean ❧ chet atkins ❧

[If there is one name that is interchangeable with "country" the world over, the name is "Nashville." During the 1950s the city rose to become the unchallenged headquarters of this music style, and it has retained its reputation as country's mecca ever since. To this day, this is where the stars live their lives, write their songs, and record their hits.]

Nashville was not always the capital of country music. Its rise to preeminence in the industry did not occur until the aftermath of World War II. Prior to that, the Grand Ole Opry was merely one of dozens of similarly sized radio barn dance shows. But during the 1940s, the Opry went on a major talent drive and became a nationally broadcast program. This was the first step on Nashville's road to renown. At the time, the Opry controlled tours, merchandising, and all other aspects of its cast's professional life. That began to change in December 1942, when the show's superstar, Roy Acuff, formed a song publishing company with Tin Pan Alley veteran Fred Rose.

━━━◆◆◆◆◆━━━

[**ROY ACUFF, 1988**] When I first came here, I began to realize the value of a song. I never thought a song would be worth a hundred dollars. But I found out that some of the little simple songs that I wrote back in those days, why, they'd came in here from New York and Chicago, California, and offered me $1,000, $1,200 for a song. I thought, "My goodness, is a song worth that much now?" So I just kept my songs, and I wouldn't sell 'em.

I went to Harry Stone, the manager of WSM at that time, and I said, "Is there any way that I can get a program on the air and sell my songs?" He said, "Well, if you want to take the chance on it, we'll sell you fifteen minutes after eight o'clock." I think it was eighty-five dollars that it would cost me. And I figured I had enough money to gamble eighty-five dollars in selling songbooks. So I put my songbooks on the air for sale for twenty-five cents. That was on Saturday night. By Wednesday, it scared WSM so bad they hired six girls to come out and get my mail and open it and take the quarters out of 'em. It was ten thousand letters the first week—and quarters. That's how I accumulated enough money to start the music publishing business. A lot of people have followed in my footsteps.

[**WAYLON JENNINGS**] Fred Rose was was not what you'd call a country boy at all. Fred Rose was a great songwriter. I think he was from vaudeville and had written songs up in New York. And then he and Roy Acuff got together and started Acuff-Rose; and he's the one who discovered Hank Williams.

The concentration of talent at the Opry made it convenient for the record companies to begin making records in Nashville. At first, the WSM radio studios were rented for sessions. In December 1944, Eddy Arnold sang "Cattle Call" into the WSM microphones. This launched the modern Nashville recording industry.

Nashville's first million-selling hit was 1947's "Near You" by the Frances Craig Orchestra. It sold so well that it spawned the city's first record pressing plant (1948). In 1950, WSM disc jockey David Cobb ad-libbed the term "Music City," and the moniker stuck. That same year, Acuff-Rose had the city's first major country/pop crossover success, "The

"Nashville, Tennessee, is the mecca. It's a melting pot of musicians, songwriters, and people who love the music business. We all congregate here."

———————

RONNIE MILSAP

OWEN BRADLEY

(1 9 1 5 –   )

HOME AREA
Middle Tennessee

SIGNIFICANCE
Architect of the Nashville Sound. Built first music enterprise on Music Row (The Quonset Hut/Bradley Studio). First permanent record-company representative in Nashville (Decca, 1947). Produced Kitty Wells, Bill Monroe, Ernest Tubb, Patsy Cline, Conway Twitty, Brenda Lee, Red Foley, k.d. lang, Webb Pierce, Goldie Hill, Justin Tubb, Bobby Helms, Bill Anderson, Burl Ives, The Wilburn Brothers, and Loretta Lynn. Performed on Nashville's first ad-jingle session (1946) and first TV broadcast (1950). The only Nashville producer to be nominated for an Oscar (*Coal Miner's Daughter*, 1980).

POPULAR SONGS
"Blues Stay Away from Me" (1949), "The Third Man Theme" (1950), "White Silver Sands" (1957), "Big Guitar" (1958)

INFLUENCED
Chet Atkins, Jerry Bradley, Jim Foglesong, Harold Bradley, Don Law, Frank Jones, and all subsequent Nashville producers and label executives

HONORS
Billboard Man of the Year, 1961; Country Music Hall of Fame, 1974; Academy of Country Music Pioneer Award, 1976

Tennessee Waltz." Patti Page's version of the tune remains the largest-selling female single hit in history.

[**PATTI PAGE**] It was put on the recording session as just a fifth song. We had no arrangement for it. They put it on the other side of a Christmas song called "Boogie Woogie Santa Claus." So here comes "The Tennessee Waltz" out, and it took off. I was appearing at the Copacabana in New York. One night, someone said to me, "Sing the waltz," and I really didn't know what they were talking about. Within the six weeks, before the end of the year, I had sold almost two million records of "The Tennessee Waltz."

The phenomenal success of Acuff-Rose with "The Tennessee Waltz" and with Hank Williams songs created a climate for more publishers in Nashville, notably Tree International (1951) and Cedarwood (1954). To handle their royalty distribution, Frances Preston opened a Broadcast Music, Inc. (BMI) office in 1955, and the industry spread like wildfire. With publishing and recording in place, the next

Two pioneering Nashville music ambassadors reminisce, the multimillion-selling Eddy Arnold and Patti Page.

step was the concentration of the live-performance booking business in Nashville. Hubert
Long blazed the trail (1953), followed by Jim Denny (1954).

[**BILL DENNY**] My dad, Jim Denny, became the manager of the Grand Ole
Opry. He kind of established the major booking agency for the Grand Ole Opry,
creating a market for country music artists all over the country. He formed a publishing company called Cedarwood that was in partnership with Webb Pierce. He
also had a small publishing company called Driftwood Music, which was a partnership with Carl Smith. He also had an artist bureau, the Jim Denny Talent Agency.
He combined booking artists and managing artists all in one.

In 1950, Capitol Records became the first national label to open a Nashville office. Mercury's
outpost became the first permanent label headquarters there in 1952. RCA (1955),
Decca/MCA (1958), and Columbia (1962) laid the rest of the building blocks. Decca's Owen
Bradley built a studio on 16th Avenue South in 1954. Three years later, RCA's Chet Atkins

▲

*Tin Pan Alley tune-
smith Fred Rose
(left) teamed up
with Grand Ole
Opry superstar
Roy Acuff in 1944
to found Nashville's
first independent
song publishing
business.*

*built Studio B two blocks away on 17th Avenue South. During the next decade, that area
became known as Music Row.*

[**KRIS KRISTOFFERSON**] At the quonset hut that was Bradley's studio, I was a
janitor. But I got to listen to Bob Dylan doin' "Blonde on Blonde." I got to know
Johnny Cash. I sat through every one of his sessions. And Lefty Frizzell, my God,
he was such a hero to me. Songwriters, at that time anyway, were at the very bottom
of the scale in Music City. They didn't want 'em around. They called us "bugs." You
weren't allowed into the sessions, because you'd pester 'em to death, wantin' 'em to
do your song. And I became one of them guards. I kept out those nasty songwriters
that were tryin' to get in.

[**CHET ATKINS**] RCA recorded at 1525 McGavock. I made a couple hits in there.
We made "Oh Lonesome Me" with Don Gibson, "I Can't Stop Lovin' You," Jim
Reeves's "Four Walls," "Heartbreak Hotel." And all of a sudden, RCA is rakin' in all
this money. I worked for RCA Victor at first as just helpmate to executive Steve
Sholes. He paid me seventy-five dollars a week to hire musicians for him when he
couldn't come down from New York. I went on the payroll at RCA in 1957—$7,500
a year, I believe it was. No royalties from the records or anything. We were just

company employees. I don't remember havin' a title. After I made a lot of hits, I told 'em I had to have $30,000 a year. They came down and talked to me and said, "Well, it's been nice workin' with you." I knew they'd pay me and they did. They made me a vice president.

[**SKEETER DAVIS**] Chet Atkins is so close to me as a friend. All through my career he's been there. Don Gibson and myself were the first two artists that Chet produced. After a session, instead of taking me to the hotel, he'd call Leona, his wife, and say, "Fix some more cornbread, Leona, I'm bringing Skeeter home," and I went to spend the night. I love Chet.

[**PHIL EVERLY**] He is the one responsible for us coming to Nashville. It was his support, his belief in us, that allowed us cut that first record.

As the community came together on Music Row, a distinctive style of recording began to emerge. Traditional country music had become highly unfashionable during the early rock 'n' roll era. In response, Nashville's producers and pickers began recording country songs with smooth, pop-influenced arrangements featuring backup voices and strings. Sessions became imaginative brainstorming events in which frequent collaborators invented ear-catching sonic gimmicks to sell heartache laments, folk lyrics, rockabilly tunes, pop ballads, and honky-tonk songs. Bradley, Atkins, guitarist Grady Martin, producer Don Law, pianist Floyd Cramer, arranger Anita Kerr and her vocal group, and the Jordanaires quartet were among the architects of this new style, dubbed the Nashville Sound.

[**GORDON STOKER, OF THE JORDANAIRES**] The Jordanaires was organized in the late '40s. We sang black spirituals with a beat. We were the first white group that sang that type of music. But then before we knew it, we started recording with everybody in the world and singing other types of music, too.

[**EDDY ARNOLD**] The Nashville Sound was a very, very important thing to our kind of music. Chet Atkins was a tremendous force in that. So was Owen Bradley. He and Owen really did the Nashville Sound. That brought the music out of the hills and brought it uptown.

The Nashville Sound made national noise with a string of discs that not only topped the country charts but "crossed over" to become pop

CHET ATKINS
(1 9 2 4 –   )

HOME AREA
East Tennessee region Appalachia

SIGNIFICANCE
"Mr. Guitar." The most recorded solo instrumentalist in music history (more than one hundred albums). Architect of the Nashville Sound. Opened first record company office on Music Row and built Studio B.

POPULAR SONGS
Galloping on the Guitar" (1949), "Country Gentleman" (1953), "Mr. Sandman" (1955), "Silver Bell" (with Hank Snow, 1955), "Yakety Axe" (1965), "I Can Hear Kentucky Calling Me" (1980), "Poor Boy Blues" (with Mark Knopfler, 1990)

INFLUENCED
Steve Wariner, Vince Gill, Mark Knopfler, George Benson, Earl Klugh, Duane Eddy, George Harrison, The Ventures, Eddie Cochran, Jerry Reed

HONORS
Country Music Hall of Fame, 1973; nine CMA Instrumentalist of the Year awards; eleven Grammy awards (more than any other country entertainer); four *Playboy* Jazz Poll honors; NARAS Lifetime Achievement Award, 1993; NARAS Governors Award, 1994

hits as well. Don Gibson's double-sided hit "Oh Lonesome Me"/"I Can't Stop Loving You" of 1958 is sometimes cited as the first Nashville Sound record.

[**REX ALLEN**] I was in Nashville gettin' ready to do a session. There was a local record down in Dallas, a kid named Darrell Glenn. And it was gettin' a lot of play in Dallas on some little small label, Valley Records. So we recorded it. "Crying in the Chapel" (1953) became one of my biggest records.

[**CHET ATKINS**] The Browns had several hits that went pop, and their one really big hit was "The Three Bells." I've always had an ear, I think, for good melodies. I used to hear that on *The Ed Sullivan Show.* There was a French group he'd have on there every once in awhile. They were called the Companions of Song, and they'd sing this. I said, "Oh, what a melody!" I searched around and found it. We took that song and we edited it way down and made it a three-minute record. When they'd go into the chorus, "All the chapel bells were ringing," what a smash that was!

[**FLOYD CRAMER**] I'd signed with RCA in 1959 and had a release called "Flip Flop and Bop," kind of a '50s rock hit. Chet said, "Why don't you try to write something?" I made a song up, and we recorded it, and I didn't even have the title. We said, "What would be a good title for it? Everybody can relate to their 'Last Date.'"

▲

The Opry trio The Browns had the first Nashville Sound record to become a number-one pop hit, 1959's "The Three Bells."

"Last Date" (1960) became the biggest instrumental hit of the Nashville Sound era.

[**STONEWALL JACKSON**] They brought me "Waterloo" (1959), and it didn't make my hair stand up on the back of my head, but some of my management talked me into it. Once I did it and heard it on the session, I said, "I believe we've got something here." They put it out in the pop field, and it was number one in just a few weeks.

[**CHARLIE McCOY**] Roy Orbison was a great artist and turned out to be a very good friend. I must say the recording of "Candy Man" (1961) is very special and dear to my heart because it was the first real big hit that I ever played on. It kind of opened the door for me to be a studio musician in Nashville.

[**FARON YOUNG**] The way I found "Sweet Dreams" (1956) is Webb Pierce had heard Don Gibson's record of it. And Don had not been heard of yet. Webb called me and said, "You need to record this song. It's a hit." So when I cut this thing, it went immediately to number one. Then, years later (1963), Patsy Cline cut it, and it went to number one again. Then Emmylou Harris cut it (1976), and it went to number one. Don Gibson redid it again (1980); it went to number one. Now when I go out and do a show and sing "Sweet

Dreams," some of those younger kids will come up and say, "Boy, you sure do a heck of a job on that Patsy Cline song."

[**JIMMY DEAN**] "Big Bad John" was a huge crossover thing. It was the number one record in 1961. They say that necessity is the mother of invention. I was on the way to Nashville from New York to record, and I had three sides, and I needed another side, 'cause we tried to go for four sides in a session in those days. I had worked in summer stock in a play called *Destry Rides Again* with a fellow named John Mento, who was six-foot-five. John was the only guy that I had to look up to, so around the dressing room I used to call him "Big John." On the way to Nashville, I took out a pencil and wrote "Big Bad John."

I just put John Mento in a mine and killed him is all.

[**RAY CHARLES**] When I went over to ABC Records, they basically got me over there

Frances Preston (right) signs Kris Kristofferson as a BMI songwriter, beginning a new era of country song craftsmanship. The Jordanaires (below) sang on more than one thousand Nashville Sound recordings.

▲

*Nashville Sound
star Jimmy Dean
took his troupe to
CBS-TV as a trail-
blazing country
TV personality
in 1957.*

because they wanted an R&B artist. That was when I came up with this idea, "I really wanna do this country music." Initially, they thought maybe I had kind of lost it, you know?

Ray Charles released Modern Sounds in Country & Western Music *in 1962, which brought "I Can't Stop Loving You," "Born to Lose," and "You Don't Know Me" onto the pop hit parade. With considerably more enthusiasm, the label issued a second such collection in 1963 that included "Take These Chains From My Heart," "You Are My Sunshine," and "Your Cheating Heart."*

[**CHET ATKINS**] Eddy Arnold didn't record with me at first when I took over. He wanted to record in New York. Then, finally, I started recording him, and we had "Make the World Go Away" (1965) as our first big hit.

[**RAY PRICE**] I decided to change my sound after I had so many records. So when Clive Davis gave me permission to do "Danny Boy" (1967), we used forty-six pieces from the Nashville Symphony, and it was a big hit for me.

[**GLEN CAMPBELL**] When I first heard "By the Time I Get to Phoenix" (1967), it made me real homesick. It was on a Johnny Rivers album. The song was just so haunting, it made me cry. That song has been recorded like six hundred times. "Wichita Lineman" (1968) was just an incredible melody. That longing is in there.

The electrifying voice of Johnny Horton made him one of the biggest pop-crossover Nashville stars. He exploded on the charts with "The Battle of New Orleans" (1959), "Sink the Bismarck" (1960), and "North to Alaska" (1961). Tragically, Horton died in a car crash in late 1960—after having played the same Texas venue where Hank Williams had done his last show. Others took up the torch. Country's conquest of the pop charts of 1956–65 made idols of vocal titans Jim Reeves and Marty Robbins.

[**TOM PERRYMAN**] Jim Reeves cut "Mexican Joe" in the studio after hours at KWKH in Shreveport. It was the record of the year in 1953. That was the era that I call the "Webb Pierce era," where everything was high-tone nasal. But Jim Reeves was a ballad singer, and not until he came up to Nashville with RCA in about '55 did they come up with that particular mike with that "close" sound with "Four Walls" (1957), "He'll Have to Go" (1959), and "Am I Losing You" (1960). Jim Reeves died in '64 in a plane crash, and for twenty consecutive years after that, Jim Reeves had singles in the charts, many in the top ten. Nobody else has ever done that.

[**RONNIE ROBBINS**] My father, Marty Robbins, was working in a night club in Phoenix in the late '40s and early '50s after he got out of the navy. He heard this cowboy singer on this radio station and thought he could do a better job, so he strapped his guitar on his back and rode his motorcycle down to the station, walked up to the station manager, and asked him for a job. The station manager said, "We've already got a singer." And Daddy said, "Yeah, I know, but he's not very good." That station eventually turned into a TV station, and so that radio spot turned into a TV spot.

Little Jimmy Dickens was comin' through town on a Grand Ole Opry package show and heard Daddy singing.

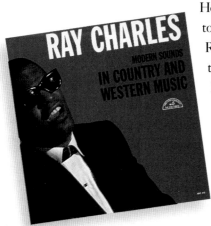

He liked what he heard and went on to Los Angeles and told Columbia Records chief Art Satherley about this kid in Phoenix. Then Fred Rose from Acuff-Rose Publishing in Nashville got wind of him, signed him to a writer contract, and through that, got an appearance on the Grand Ole Opry.

[**MARTY STUART**] I think if

MARTY ROBBINS
(1925–1982)

HOME AREA
Central Arizona desert country

SIGNIFICANCE
The greatest showman of his era.

POPULAR SONGS
"I'll Go On Alone" (1953), "That's All Right" (1955), "Maybelline" (1955) "El Paso" (1959), "Don't Worry" (1961), "Devil Woman" (1962), "Ruby Ann" (1963), "You Gave Me a Mountain" (1966), "My Woman, My Woman, My Wife" (1970), "Walking Piece of Heaven" (1973), "Love Me" (1973), "El Paso City" (1976), "Some Memories Just Won't Die" (1982), "Honkytonk Man" (1983).

INFLUENCED
Johnny Rodriguez, The Mavericks, Tompall & the Glaser Brothers, Jeanne Pruett, Ronnie Robbins, Michael Martin Murphey

HONORS
Nashville Songwriters Hall of Fame, 1975; Country Music Hall of Fame, 1982; two Grammy Awards, 1960 and 1970; seven feature films; star on Hollywood Walk of Fame; Gold Record awards, 1965 and 1982; Platinum Record award, 1986; four *Billboard* awards, 1956–63; twenty-five BMI Awards, 1957–83; Western Heritage Award, 1979; seven *Music City News* awards, 1980–83

JIM REEVES

(1 9 2 4 – 1 9 6 4)

HOME AREA
East Texas

SIGNIFICANCE
"Gentleman Jim." The definitive male
Nashville Sound singer.

POPULAR SONGS
"Mexican Joe" (1953), "Bimbo" (1954),
"According to My Heart" (1956), "Am I
Losing You" (1957, revived 1960), "Four
Walls" (1957), "Anna Marie" (1958), "Blue
Boy" (1958), "Billy Bayou" (1958), "He'll
Have to Go" (1960), "Adios Amigo" (1962),
"Guilty" (1963), "Welcome to My World"
(1964), "I Love You Because" (1964,
revived 1976), "Love Is No Excuse" (with
Dottie West, 1964), "Distant Drums"
(1966), "Blue Side of Lonesome" (1966),
"When Two Worlds Collide" (1969),
"Missing You" (1972), "Am I That Easy to
Forget" (1973), "Don't Let Me Cross
Over" (with Deborah Allen, 1979), "Oh
How I Miss You Tonight" (with Deborah
Allen, 1979), "Have You Ever Been
Lonely" (with Patsy Cline, 1981)

INFLUENCED
Ronnie Milsap, Deborah Allen, Bud Logan

HONORS
Country Music Hall of Fame, 1967;
cast membership, Louisiana Hayride,
Grand Ole Opry; own career museum;
two feature films; Gold Record
awards, 1964 and 1966

you went around town asking people who was the best singer we ever had around here, everybody would pretty much say, "The rest of us are just tryin'. It's Marty Robbins."

Robbins, Reeves, and the rest of the Nashville Sound singers brought country music unprecedented popularity. But today when people think of that style, one name towers above all others: Patsy Cline.

[**JIMMY DEAN**] I started Patsy Cline in the business. She was down there in Winchester, Virginia, and she used to come out to some of the dives that we worked and started doing some local radio and some local television with us. She was kind of a bawdy gal, but she could flat sing, and she knew it.

[**FARON YOUNG**] I think I loved everything about her. I loved her 'cause she was tough.

[**HAROLD BRADLEY**] I think the most magic record that I've ever done is the one with Patsy Cline, "Crazy" (1961). It took four hours. She'd been in the automobile wreck, and she couldn't hold the notes out. She had broken ribs. I think it was magic because in that four hours my brother, Owen Bradley, defined a distinctive Nashville Sound.

[**OWEN BRADLEY**] I pitched "I Fall to Pieces" (1961) to about six people, and everybody turned it down. Patsy finally said okay. After it was a hit, and she had had her accident, she stuck her head in the door and said, "I'm never gonna record anymore." I said, "Why?" She said, "I'm just gonna enjoy this one for the rest of my life. You know, I didn't like that old song, anyway." She only did it to please me.

[**GEORGE HAMILTON IV**] Patsy was larger than life, a '90s lady in the '50s. She didn't open the doors for ladies in country music, she kicked 'em down.

[**BRENDA LEE**] Patsy Cline had a heart as big as all outdoors. I met her when I was twelve years old; we were on a tour together. We were out somewhere in Texas, and the promoter ran off with the money. My mother and I were stuck. Patsy said, "Oh come on, ride back home with me. I'll pay all the expenses." She fed us, she got us back to Tennessee, and she was like a big sister to me.

[**KITTY WELLS**] It was really a great loss when Patsy got killed in the airplane crash. There was four of them right there together that was killed—Cowboy Copas, Hawkshaw Hawkins, and Randy Hughes, the one that was flying the plane. That was March 5, 1963. On March 7, they were having

the funeral service for Patsy and all of them. Jack Anglin, who was my husband's partner [in Johnnie and Jack], had started to the funeral services. His car turned over and killed him. So that was another one, right along about the same time. It was really a sad time for all of us.

[**JEAN SHEPARD**] Hawkshaw and I were only married just around two years when he got killed in the plane crash with Patsy and Cowboy Copas. I had a fifteen-month-old son, and I was eight months pregnant.

What Patsy started, her little buddy Brenda finished. By the time she was "sweet sixteen," Brenda Lee had taken the Nashville Sound worldwide and was the hottest-selling female vocalist on earth.

[**SHELBY LYNNE**] Brenda Lee's still singing today, 'cause she can still nail it, nail it to the wall.

[**BRENDA LEE**] Well, they tell me that I've sold one hundred million records. If I have, I think that's great, and I'm very grateful. I've performed in seventy-five

▲

Carl and Pearl Butler, famed for "Don't Let Me Cross Over," harmonize in the Quonset Hut at a Columbia Records session of 1963 featuring steel guitarist Pete Drake.

"Patsy Cline was a trooper. She was strong minded, strong willed; and if that's tough, yeah, she was tough."

WILLIE NELSON

Patsy Cline radiates "heart" from the Grand Ole Opry stage during a broadcast in May 1962.

foreign countries. I've performed for the Queen of England, the presidents of Mexico and South America, for some of our own presidents here in the United States.

Patsy and Brenda opened the door. A generation of female stylists entered country music because of their Nashville Sound breakthroughs, women such as Wilma Burgess, Marion Worth, Margie Bowes, and Jeannie Seely.

[TRISHA YEARWOOD] People ask me today, "Do you face obstacles, and isn't it harder for a woman in this business?" I think what they had to go through was ten times harder than any of the things that I face as a woman in this business.

[DOTTIE WEST, 1983] I came home to Nashville for vacation from Cleveland. We would come home when we'd have two weeks off from the TV show we were doing up there. In 1959, Bill and I were headed back to Cleveland, going north on Dickerson Road. I said when we got to the Starday Records building, "Just pull right in here. I'm going in there, and I hope they're gonna listen to me." I took my guitar in there and said, "I really am gonna make hit records. I am gonna be a singer in Nashville. And this is the only thing I have to show you, and it's a scrapbook from the TV show that I do."

It worked. I don't even think I realized how tough it might be. When you're that young, you're not afraid. I had absolutely no doubt that I could be a top singer. I was just "goin' for it." That's all.

[CONNIE SMITH] When I came to Nashville, I never really had the desire to be a star. I just wanted to sing. I found out before long that we were treated in the business as a product. It was up to me to sell Connie Smith, and I didn't like that. The third song that I sang on my very first recording session was a song called "Once a Day." We recorded it July 16, 1964. It went to number one and stayed there for about two and a half months. I thought, "Well, I might give this business a shot."

[JEAN SHEPARD] Back then what we called the Disc Jockey Convention, or what they call the CMA Awards Week now, was held in November instead of October. I became a member of the Grand Ole Opry in 1955. Jim Denny got up at this meeting with a bunch of the old disc jockeys and said, "We would like to welcome the newest member of the

PATSY CLINE
Virginia Patterson Hensley
(1932–1963)

HOME AREA
Winchester, Virginia

SIGNIFICANCE
The most influential female vocalist in country history. Her records defined the Nashville Sound.

POPULAR SONGS
"Walkin' After Midnight" (1957), "I Fall to Pieces" (1961), "Crazy" (1961), "She's Got You" (1962), "When I Get Through with You" (1962), "So Wrong" (1962), "Leavin' on Your Mind" (1963), "Sweet Dreams" (1963), "Faded Love" (1963), "He Called Me Baby" (1964), "Always" (1980), "Have You Ever Been Lonely" (with Jim Reeves, 1981)

INFLUENCED
Dottie West, Loretta Lynn, Jan Howard, Brenda Lee, k.d. lang, Barbara Mandrell, Reba McEntire, K. T. Oslin, Shelby Lynne, Mandy Barnett

HONORS
Country Music Hall of Fame, 1973; Gold Record awards, 1967 and 1985; biographical film: 1985's *Sweet Dreams*; Patsy's *Greatest Hits* album is the largest-selling female country album in history

BRENDA LEE

Brenda Mae Tarpley

(1 9 4 4 –)

HOME AREA
Central Georgia

SIGNIFICANCE
"Little Miss Dynamite." Biggest female pop act of the '60s, said to be the largest-selling female vocalist in history.

POPULAR SONGS
"Jambalaya" (1956), "Dynamite" (1957), "Rockin' Around the Christmas Tree" (1958), "Sweet Nothin's" (1959), "I'm Sorry" (1960), "I Want to Be Wanted" (1960), "Emotions" (1961), "Dum Dum" (1961), "Fool #1" (1961), "Break It to Me Gently" (1962), "All Alone Am I" (1962), "As Usual" (1963), "Thanks a Lot"/"The Crying Game" (1965), "Coming On Strong" (1966), "Johnny One Time" (1969), "Always on My Mind" (1972), "Nobody Wins" (1973), "Big Four Poster Bed" (1974), "He's My Rock" (1975), "Tell Me What It's Like" (1979), "Broken Trust" (1980), "Hallelujah I Love You So" (with George Jones, 1985)

INFLUENCED
Dolly Parton, Crystal Gayle, Lynn Anderson, Barbara Mandrell, Juice Newton, Cyndi Lauper, Shelby Lynne

HONORS
Four Grammy nominations; two feature films; NARAS Governors Award, 1984

Grand Ole Opry, Jean Shepard!" And he said, "Happy Birthday, Jean!" I can never, ever forget that day, November 21. It's my birthday, it's my anniversary at the Grand Ole Opry, and now it's also my wedding anniversary to Benny Birchfield [a guitarist for Roy Orbison], whom I married twenty-five years ago.

[**JOE TALBOT**] The Disc Jockey Convention was the beginning of what I call the cohesiveness of the people in this business. The whole world was trying to kill us. If we didn't get together and do something, we were going to get wiped out.

The Country Music Association established the Country Music Hall of Fame in 1961, and the Country Music Foundation was chartered to operate it in 1964. The museum opened in 1967, the same year the CMA decided to begin giving annual awards. Since then, the CMA Awards has become the centerpiece of the glittering Country Music Week festivities. No other music form has this, because no other music form has demonstrated such unity of purpose, respect for heritage, or cooperation among competitors.

The family that plays together stays together. There were only sixty-one full-time country radio stations in the U.S. at the dawn of the 1960s. Thanks to the CMA and Nashville's strong sense of mission, there are now more than two thousand, more than any other musical format.

When the Country Music Association opened in 1958, it was a one-person office. Jo Walker-Meador guided the CMA for the next thirty-three years.

Not the least of the CMA's accomplishments is that in 1968 it staged the first music awards program on national television. But Nashville was actually rather slow from the starting gate in television production. Philadelphia's Hayloft Hoedown (1948, ABC), New York's Saturday Night Jamboree (1948–49, NBC) and Village Barn (1948–50, NBC), Chicago's ABC Barn Dance (1949, ABC) and Cincinnati's Midwestern Hayride (1951–59, NBC) were on the air before any noticeable TV activity in Nashville, as were such stars as The Pickard Family (Sunday Night at Home, 1949, NBC), Patti Page (Music Hall, 1952, CBS), Eddy Arnold (The Eddy Arnold Show, 1952, NBC), Pee Wee King (Old American Barn Dance, 1953, DuMont, and The Pee Wee King Show, 1955, ABC) and Red Foley (Ozark Jubilee, 1955–60, ABC).

Largely barred from prime time and shunned by urban marketers, country created its own TV universe in syndication. Town and Country Time, Stars of the Grand Ole Opry, and Western Ranch Party were early syndicated ventures done by non-Nashville producers. Reasoning that they knew best how to market that kind of entertainment, Music City's executives began developing their own syndicated TV shows in the '60s. Porter Wagoner launched his in 1960. The Wilburn Brothers Show began in 1963; Bill Anderson's syndicated program came along in 1965. Ernest Tubb, Flatt and Scruggs, Del Reeves, Billy Walker, Buck Owens, Marty Robbins, Bobby Lord, Jim & Jesse, Kitty Wells, Hugh X. Lewis, Stu Phillips, Red Foley, The Stonemans, Tom T. Hall, Jim Stafford, Kenny Rogers, Ralph

▲
Known as "Little Miss Dynamite," Brenda Lee is said to be the world's largest-selling female vocalist.

Emery, Rex Allen Jr., Bobby Goldsboro, Dolly Parton, and Donna Fargo all tried country TV syndication at one time or another in the '60s and '70s.

[**RICKY LYNN GREGG**] My mom would put me right in front of that television every Saturday to watch *The Wilburn Brothers Show* and to watch *The Porter Wagoner Show*. Every Saturday I would always be lookin' for Del Reeves. He was country, but the beats were rock beats, like "Girl on a Billboard" (1965), and I thought he was a great character.

Networks might have resisted the music, but a boom in rural situation comedies occurred, beginning with The Real McCoys *(1957–62, ABC) and* The Andy Griffith Show *(1960–68, CBS) and cresting with the number-one rated* Beverly Hillbillies *(1962–71, CBS), plus its spin-offs* Petticoat Junction *(1963–70) and* Green Acres *(1965–71). A network return to country music seemed logical.* The Roy Rogers and Dale Evans Show *was on ABC in 1962. Next came the blockbusters.* Hee Haw *went on CBS in 1969–71, then thrived for the next twenty-five years as the most successful syndicated series in history. CBS also launched* The Johnny Cash Show *(1969–71) and* The Glen Campbell Goodtime Hour *(1969–72).*

[**CHARLIE McCOY**] I think that *Hee Haw* was one of the most important things that happened to Nashville. It was the first time that a network, I think, looked at country music seriously.

[**JOHNNY CASH**] The networks had all these rules. I heard they did, but I had my own. I said, "If I host a show, I want some real American artists on there. Some people with some backbone, with some grit, that really mean somethin' so far as the songs of this country are concerned. I liked The Weavers' songs, so I'd like to have Pete Seeger." Well, they made a big deal out of that for a while, but they finally said okay. I said I would like to ask for Bob Dylan to be on the first show. And of course they agreed to that. But there were so many other people—Neil Diamond, Mahalia Jackson, The Who, Kenny Rogers and the First Edition, Creedence Clearwater Revival, Linda Ronstadt. She was on our show four times—her first network TV appearances. We hired Kris Kristofferson, too.

[**STEVE WARINER**] Glen Campbell definitely was an influence on me. I remember watchin' his *Goodtime Hour*. The part I loved the most was when he would bring in the players and the musicians, and they'd all sit around. It was just off-the-cuff and spontaneous.

[**JIM FOGLESONG**] Roy Clark is a consummate entertainer. A lot of the country entertainers at that time had difficulty getting on network television. Roy really opened the doors for country music on network television back in those days. Roy was the ambassador.

[**WANDA JACKSON**] I knew Roy Clark long before *Hee Haw*. When I began working Las Vegas, The Golden Nugget, I put a band together. In Vegas, the shows were like forty minutes on, twenty minutes off—five of them, back to back. I knew a lot of songs, but I didn't think I could handle the whole thing and keep an audience. I remembered a fellow that I'd seen in Washington, D.C., in a club, Roy Clark, a fantastic entertainer, and he could help carry the load. He was glad to come and join. Roy Clark would have been found eventually, I'm sure. But I'm glad it was through my efforts.

[**HANK THOMPSON**] I was not the first artist to ever appear in Las Vegas. Other artists had appeared there—Eddy Arnold, Jimmy Wakley, people like that. But they had only appeared there as a part of an established show format—the big orchestra and that type of thing. We came in with the same show that we would have done had we been in Peoria, Illinois, or

EDDY ARNOLD
(1918–)

HOME AREA
East Tennessee region Appalachia

SIGNIFICANCE
"The Tennessee Plowboy."

POPULAR SONGS
"Cattle Call" (1945), "It's a Sin"/"I Couldn't Believe It Was True" (1947), "Anytime" (1948), "Bouquet of Roses"/"Texarkana Baby" (1948), "Take Me in Your Arms and Hold Me" (1950), "Kentucky Waltz" (1951), "I Wanna Play House with You" (1951), "I Really Don't Want to Know" (1954), "You Don't Know Me" (1956), "Tennessee Stud" (1959), "Make the World Go Away" (1965), "The Last Word in Lonesome Is Me" (1966), "The Tip of My Fingers" (1966), "Misty Blue" (1967), "Let's Get It While the Gettin's Good" (1980)

INFLUENCED
Faron Young, Elvis Presley

HONORS
Country Music Hall of Fame, 1966; CMA's first Entertainer of the Year, 1967; Academy of Country Music Pioneer Award, 1983; Songwriters' Guild President's Award, 1987; two feature films; star on Hollywood Walk of Fame; Gold Records, 1966 and 1968

RED FOLEY

Clyde Julian Foley

(1 9 1 0 – 1 9 6 8)

HOME AREA
Berea, Kentucky

SIGNIFICANCE
More than twenty-five million records sold.

POPULAR SONGS
"Old Shep" (1941), "Smoke on the Water" (1944), "New Jolie Blonde" (1947), "Freight Train Boogie" (1947), "Tennessee Saturday Night" (1948), "Tennessee Border" (1949), "Chattanoogie Shoe Shine Boy"/"Sugarfoot Rag" (1950), "Steal Away" (1950), "Birmingham Bounce" (1950), "Just a Closer Walk with Thee" (1950), "Goodnight Irene" (with Ernest Tubb, 1950), "My Heart Cries for You" (with Evelyn Knight, 1951), "Peace in the Valley" (1951), "Alabama Jubilee" (1951), "Too Old to Cut the Mustard" (with Ernest Tubb, 1952), "Don't Let the Stars Get in Your Eyes" (1953), "One by One" (with Kitty Wells, 1954), "As Long as I Live" (with Kitty Wells, 1955), "Satisfied Mind" (with Betty Foley, 1955)

INFLUENCED
Elvis Presley, Brenda Lee, Jean Shepard, Porter Wagoner, Wanda Jackson, Norma Jean, Hank Garland

HONORS
Country Music Hall of Fame, 1967; two feature films; two stars on Hollywood Walk of Fame

Dottie West signs on as a Grand Ole Opry cast member, June 24, 1964, while Opry manager Ott Devine looks on.

Ocala, Florida. We were the first ones to take an all-country music show into a showroom.

[**JIMMY DEAN**] I remember when I went into Vegas and things started really happening and doing really well for us. It's kind of funny, because I thought that $65,000 a week was all the money in the world. They've got lounge acts that make a lot more than that now. But I've told people on stage, "I wish I could give back to you what you give me up here." Because it's a wonderful thing to be paid so well for doing something that you have such a ball doing. Don't you think?

Network TV, the Las Vegas showrooms, and the nation's radio stations and major coliseums all opened their arms to the Nashville Sound. And as the word spread, so did audiences around the world.

[**SKEETER DAVIS**] International acceptance has been so amazing to me that it's almost unexplainable. On my trip to Kenya, Africa, I had 14,300 people at the concert. They told me I was selling more records than Elvis or anybody else. Jim Reeves was big, too. I was there in '64 and again in '74. All these wonderful African people just embraced me. I was in Korea, Singapore, Malaysia, Indonesia. I've already been to Ireland, New Zealand, Jamaica, and all those places. In 1964 my record of "Silver Threads and Golden Needles" was number one in Indonesia. I thought, "Where is Indonesia?"

johnny cash ⁌ tennessee ernie

ford ⁌ burl ives ⁌ woody

guthrie ⁌ harlan howard ⁌

bob dylan ⁌ joan baez

roger miller ⁌ merle travis

The Folk Revival

anne murray ⁌ john denver

⁌ tom t. hall ⁌ janis ian ⁌

bobby bare ⁌ don williams

boudleaux & felice bryant ⁌

During the 1950s and 1960s old-time country music got a new lease on life. Collegiate music fans picked up banjos and guitars and began to sing the songs of our ancestors. This folk-revival movement created a new climate for acoustic music, reacquainted millions with the sounds of Appalachia, and spawned a generation of songwriting troubadours.

Commercial country music has gradually moved its folk-music heritage aside, but periodic revivals of interest in antique Americana have benefited traditional country acts throughout the genre's history. Folk-song collecting from rural people began around the turn of the century. In the 1920s, Henry Ford sponsored old-time fiddle contests, and country musician Bascom Lamar Lunsford launched the Mountain Dance and Folk Festival at Asheville, North Carolina (1928). The American Folksong Festival was an annual event near Ashland, Kentucky from 1932 to 1972 and in 1938 drew twenty thousand fans. The administration of President Franklin D. Roosevelt promoted folk culture extensively in the '30s and '40s.

⟹◆⟸

[**WILMA LEE COOPER**] The National Folk Festival was started in '37. They had a contest where Eleanor Roosevelt wanted representatives from every state. They had Indian people from the different Indian reservations, all kinds of people, and it was really a big thing there in Washington. We were there representing the state of West Virginia.

[**MERLE HAGGARD**] Woody Guthrie was like Jimmie Rodgers, raw. He sounds like he's unrehearsed and doesn't come from the same school that everybody else comes from. An individual, something original.

[**JEAN RITCHIE**] The first time I ever met Woody Guthrie was when I did that contemporary music festival. He wasn't on the program, but he came into the back room where we all were. He came jumping into the room, blowing into each micro-phone, going, "Woosh, woosh, woosh, woosh," all over the place. I said, "Who is that crazy fellow?" Alan Lomax said, "Why, that's ole Woody," and he took me over and introduced me. He was a zany person, but could just start playing the guitar and singing, and everybody would rally around and listen. He had a magnetism about him.

Woody Guthrie and Jean Ritchie were part of a circle of folk-song popularizers of the 1940s that also included Pete Seeger, Leadbelly, Burl Ives, the Weavers, Josh White, Ramblin' Jack Elliott, and the Lomaxes. As Burl Ives was popularizing "Blue Tail Fly" (1948) and "Lavender Blue" (1949), and the Weavers were making it big, a square-dance craze erupted. The country industry published its first national popularity charts as "Juke Box Folk Records" from 1944 to 1957. Several country stars did "folk" discs, notably Merle Travis and Tennessee Ernie Ford.

[**CLIFFIE STONE**] I had *Hometown Jamboree* on Saturday nights on television and I had Merle Travis on the show. He wrote "Sixteen Tons." He taught the song to Tennessee Ernie to do on *Hometown Jamboree*. They did a few times as a duet. All

"I didn't think about whether coming from a folk background would be seen as revolutionary. It was just who I was. I played folk music; I got into bluegrass; I got into country. And it felt very natural."

———————

KATHY MATTEA

right, now we fade out, fade in: We're on NBC-TV five days a week (1955). We need five songs on every half-hour show. We had a music meeting, and Ernie says, "Why don't I do 'Sixteen Tons' sometime?" We all thought, "Well, okay, go ahead, an old hillbilly song, who cares?" So he did it. The whole world exploded. In the first month they sold over a million records.

Three years later the folk boom detonated even louder with the Kingston Trio's hit reworking of the Appalachian murder ballad "Tom Dooley" (1958). The Brothers Four (1960's "Greenfields"), the Highwaymen (1961's "Michael Row the Boat Ashore"), the Four Preps (1958's "26 Miles"), the Rooftop Singers (1963's "Walk Right In"), the New Christy Minstrels (1963's "Green Green") and Peter, Paul and Mary's hit streak of 1962–63 confirmed the folk fad.

Joan Baez, Bob Dylan, Judy Collins, Ian & Sylvia, Buffy Sainte-Marie, Donovan, Odetta, Eric Andersen, Tom Rush, Dave Van Ronk, Arlo Guthrie, Phil Ochs, the Smothers Brothers, the Serendipity Singers, and the Limeliters all emerged as stars. Most of them per-formed original "folk" songs as well as old-time country melodies. This was also the mix at the event that crystalized the new scene, the Newport Folk Festival.

[**JEAN RITCHIE**] The Newport Folk Festival was started in 1959. Seven of us were the first trustees. We all got together and planned the festival. I met Joan Baez at the 1959 first Newport Festival when she sang and swept everybody off their feet. Then we decided to have a lot of country people who were not known, so that people would be educated by this festival. They would come to hear the name performers and they would stay to hear the people they had never heard before. People like Bill Monroe, Roscoe Holcombe, Clarence Ashley, Doc Watson, Fiddlin'

Arthur Smith, Sam and Kirk McGee, Jimmie Driftwood, Earl Scruggs, Dorsey Dixon, and Roy Acuff appeared. I first met Mother Maybelle and Sara and all of those people at Newport.

[**DONNA STONEMAN**] We were going to "go underground" so we could get more money, you know. Leave the country scene a little bit. I ironed my hair, put a leather band around my head, and had a real short leather skirt with brown tights on. We were out there and cookin' it. I mean, they loved it. But Roni said, "My gosh, Donna, look behind ya at the light show." I looked behind me, and there was a movie runnin' of naked people.

[**RONI STONEMAN**] Strobe lighting is not good for people with epilepsy, like Jimmy [Stoneman]. I mean, that's a known fact. And they're squirrelly out there in that "blue smoke" that was kinda thick. I said, "Jimmy, take care of yourself, now." He was up there playin'. I heard immediately that he had a problem. The guy came up with this real fluffy hairdo and said, "He's groovin'." I said, "Wait a minute. He's not groovin'. He's havin' a seizure." He said, "That's a gas, man." He got a standing ovation for his seizure. For twenty minutes he couldn't get off the stage 'cause they loved him.

[**JIMMY STONEMAN**] I hit the floor slappin' that bass. The sound man gets the microphone and runs down to put it down there. My manager says, "What are you doing? He's in a seizure!" And he said, "Groovy, man, groovy. Keep it in the act."

[**WAYLON JENNINGS**] I think that folk music was one of the main influences to bring country music back from what had happened to it as a result of rock 'n' roll.

[**K. T. OSLIN**] I started singing folk music in 1962. I would sing the only song that I knew, which was "Barbara Allen." I got it off of the Joan Baez album.

[**JOHNNY CASH**] You know, on airplanes, these airsickness bags you get out of the back of the seat in front of you? I'd heard Bob Dylan, and I took one of those bags and wrote him a letter, wrapped it up, put a stamp on that air sickness bag and mailed it to him. Told him I liked his records. I got a letter right back from him. So we started the correspondence that led up to our meeting in Newport. That's where we met Bob and Joan and the whole bunch.

[**BILL MILLER**] I grew up listening to story tellers on an

WOODY GUTHRIE
(1912–1967)

HOME AREA
Oklahoma

SIGNIFICANCE
The prototype of the rambling folk poet of the common man. Father figure to the folk-revival generation, particularly Bob Dylan. Major songwriter.

POPULAR SONGS WRITTEN
"Do-Re-Mi" (1940), "Oklahoma Hills" (1945), "This Land Is Your Land" (1947), "So Long It's Been Good to Know Ya" (1951), "Philadelphia Lawyer" (1951), "Grand Coulie Dam" (1958)

INFLUENCED
Arlo Guthrie, Bob Dylan, Jack Guthrie, Pete Seeger, Leadbelly, the Weavers, Burl Ives, Ramblin' Jack Elliott, Cisco Houston, the Maddox Brothers & Rose, Johnny Cash, Merle Haggard

HONORS
Nashville Songwriters Hall of Fame, 1977; Grammy Hall of Fame ("This Land Is Your Land"), 1989; biographical film (*Bound for Glory*, 1976)

Indian Reservation, so the old tradition is really strong. My first experience of hearing a story song was listening to Bob Dylan, "Blowing in the Wind."

[**EMMYLOU HARRIS**] It was an exciting time. The singer-songwriter was really happening. Bob Dylan was an enormous influence on me. He was like God to us.

[**CHARLIE McCOY**] The producer of Bob Dylan was a guy named Bob Johnston. He had been trying to talk Nashville up to Bob Dylan, and Bob had resisted. Things went so easy during a session I did with Dylan in New York that Johnston said to him, "Now see? That's how easy it is in Nashville. Why don't you come down there?" He came, and we did what I think is a landmark album for Nashville, *Blonde on Blonde* (1966). People in the business really knew that this was going to have a very large impact on Nashville.

[**CHARLIE DANIELS**] Doing a Bob Dylan session was a dream to me, because I was a really big fan. I asked Bob Johnston, "Can I do *one* Bob Dylan session?" He said "Yeah, I'll put you on the six o'clock session." I was working in a club at the time. I went down, did the six o'clock session, and I started packing up and leaving. Dylan said, "Where's Charlie going?" He said, "Well, we've got another guitar player coming." Dylan said, "I don't want another guitar player; I want him." Well, that put me up about twenty feet walking off the floor.

The composers of the folk revival provided country music with major hits during this period. In addition to "500 Miles," Bobby Bare scaled the charts with Buffy Sainte-Marie's "The Piney Wood Hills" (1967) and Ian Tyson's "Four Strong Winds" (1964). Gordon Lightfoot's "Ribbon of Darkness" (Marty Robbins, 1965) and "That's What You Get For Lovin' Me" (Waylon Jennings, 1966), Tom Paxton's "The Last Thing on My Mind" (Porter Wagoner and Dolly Parton, 1967), Pete Seeger's "If I Had a Hammer" (Wanda Jackson, 1969), Tom Springfield's "I'll Never Find Another You" (Sonny James, 1967), John Denver's "Leaving on a Jet Plane" (The Kendalls, 1970), Joni Mitchell's "Urge for Going" (George Hamilton IV, 1967), Bob Dylan's "Like a Rolling Stone" (Flatt and Scruggs, 1968) and Gene MacLellan's "Snowbird" (Anne

Burl Ives (right) popularized American folk songs in the 1940s, then became a Nashville recording artist in the 1960s with tunes like "A Little Bitty Tear." Merle Travis (below) put his Kentucky background into songs like "Nine Pound Hammer," "Dark As a Dungeon," and "Sixteen Tons."

Murray, 1970) were just a few of the songs by folkies that made the country hit parade.
Traditional tunes like "Frankie and Johnny," "Fair and Tender Ladies," and "Knoxville
Girl" made the country charts for the first time in history.

[**GLEN CAMPBELL**] I played on all the Kingston Trio stuff, doin' sessions that
were so marvelous. Capitol Records executive Voyle Gilmore said, "What do you
wanna do, Glen?" I said, "I just wanna sing what I wanna sing. I haven't got to do
that, and I've been at Capitol for five years now." That was '67. I'd heard John
Hartford's "Gentle on My Mind" on the radio, and that was the first thing I did.
Leon Russell was playin' piano; Doug Dillard was playin' banjo; Joe Osbourne,
bass; Richie Frost, drums. That was it. We just did it with a rough track, and I was
singin' loosely. I was gonna put my voice on later. Voyle Gilmore heard that and he
released it the next week. I went, "*What?* I haven't even finished that yet." Well,

▲

Woody Guthrie's
common-folks
"ramblin' man"
persona was the
model for all
subsequent
folk singers.

▶

*Ernest Jennings
Ford was a native
of the Volunteer
State who found
national fame in the
1950s as Tennessee
Ernie, "the ol'
pea-picker."*

Voyle probably knew what he was doin'. Had I finished it, it probably
wouldn't have been the record that it was. It's just raw, settin' down
and playin', and it was a first take.

[**JOHNNY CASH**] Tim Hardin wrote "If I Were a Carpenter," a hit
for me and June Carter in 1970, but Ramblin' Jack Elliot had a very unique
performance of it. He liked to take his guitar in the cafes and walk right up to your
table and play in your face and sing "If I Were a Carpenter."

[**BOBBY BARE**] When I got through Phoenix in 1964, I heard this record on
the radio called "Just to Satisfy You," and I thought, "Boy, that's a good singer." It
turned out that it was Waylon Jennings. It blew me away. I called Chet Atkins up

on the phone. I said, "Waylon Jennings is a magnificent talent. I know that he and I will be doing the same kind of songs, because we have the same taste in material, and I know that it's going to hurt my career, but man, he deserves to be on a major label." I gave him Waylon's telephone number. Waylon came to Nashville and recorded and stayed out at my house. To this day, I think he is one of the greatest ballad singers ever.

At first, some in the country community reacted to the politically progressive folkies in their midst with mistrust and hostility. Whatever their political persuasions, however, Nashville's entrepreneurs were quick to cash in on the folk boom. Folkies flocked to their recording studios; folk festivals welcomed country's traditional performers; and folk stars' compositions were translated into country favorites. Just as significant, Music Row instantly imitated the folkies by turning out dozens of hits in that style. Dubbed "saga songs," many became huge pop crossover successes. Among the best known were Johnny Horton's "Battle of New Orleans" (1959), Hank Snow's "Miller's Cave" (1960), Lefty Frizzell's "Long Black Veil" (1959), Bobby Bare's "Detroit City" (1963), The Browns' "Scarlet Ribbons" (1960), Marty Robbins's "El Paso" (1959), Eddy Arnold's "Tennessee Stud" (1959), Jimmy Dean's "Big Bad John" (1961), and Johnny Cash's "I Got Stripes" (1959), "Five Feet High and Rising" (1959), and "The Rebel—Johnny Yuma" (1961).

The Nashville star who reached out to the folkies most was unquestionably Cash. He took a stand on social-justice issues as few of his country contemporaries did. His towering, from-the-soil image made him a massively popular icon to the alienated, idealistic youth of the era. He championed folk music to the country community, hitting with Bob Dylan's "It Ain't Me Babe" (1965), Pete Seeger's "If I Had a Hammer" (1972), and Tim Hardin's "The Lady Came from Baltimore" (1975) and "If I Were a Carpenter" (1970). Cash's "Understand Your Man" (1964) shares a melody with Dylan's "Don't Think Twice," and he duetted with the folk superstar in 1969. His Nashville home became a troubadour's mecca.

[**JOHNNY CASH**] A lot of people asked me for years why I wore black. I had my own reasons, but I never really had said anything. But then we were well into the Vietnam War, and the loss of American lives was, at the time I wrote "The Man in Black," one hundred a week. I got to thinkin' about the questions about why I wore black, and I answered a lot of

TENNESSEE ERNIE FORD
(1919–1991)

HOME AREA
Bristol, Tennessee

SIGNIFICANCE
"The Old Pea Picker." Major network TV star of the '50s and '60s. Folk/country fusion breakthrough act. The first country star to headline at the London Palladium. First to earn a Gold Record for gospel music. First to take a country troupe to tour the USSR

POPULAR SONGS
"Tennessee Border" (1949), "Mule Train"/"Anticipation Blues" (1949), "I'll Never Be Free" (with Kay Starr, 1950), "The Shot Gun Boogie" (1951), "Mr. and Mississippi" (1951), "River of No Return" (1954), "Ballad of Davy Crockett" (1955), "Sixteen Tons" (1955)

INFLUENCED
Cliffie Stone, Deborah Allen, Buck Ford

HONORS
Country Music Hall of Fame, 1990; Gospel Music Hall of Fame, 1993; Medal of Freedom, 1984; four Gold Record awards (all gospel), 1956-59; Grammy Award (*Great Gospel Songs*), 1964; own TV series; two feature films; three stars on Hollywood Walk of Fame

other questions when I wrote "Man in Black." That's what folk or country music is all about, givin' a voice to the people who have no voice.

[**HAROLD REID, OF THE STATLER BROTHERS**] We learned more from Johnny Cash than you can learn from any other one single person. It was our higher education in the music business.

[**MERLE HAGGARD**] Johnny Cash, he's like President Lincoln or somethin'. I was in the prison band when I first saw him in San Quentin. I was impressed with his ability to take five thousand convicts and steal the show away from a bunch of strippers. That's pretty hard to do.

[**DOLLY PARTON**] When I first met him, I was probably twelve or thirteen years old. He was just pilled to the gills, doped up and hyper and had all that nervous energy, but even still, he had that charm, that magic. I had never really known what true sex appeal really was, bein' a young girl, and I guess I had raging hormones at the time. I don't know how much is to Johnny's credit and how much was to my just bein' horny, but when I first came to Nashville, I saw Johnny Cash on stage, and I felt everything in the world that a girl could feel.

[**KRIS KRISTOFFERSON**] Well, he's sort of like the Father of Our Country, maybe God? John is a great person. He's got a big heart.

The folk revival's lasting legacy to country music lies in Nashville's songwriting community. The bonds of brotherhood among tunesmiths were just beginning when the folkies hit in the early '60s. The city's first full-time professional songwriters were Boudleaux and Felice Bryant, who had arrived in 1950. By the end of the decade they'd been joined by Marijohn Wilkin, John D. Loudermilk, Dallas Frazier, and a cluster of others hoping to catch the ears of the big stars on the Grand Ole Opry.

[**JOHNNY PAYCHECK**] I signed with Tree Publishing Company when they had just started. Buddy Killen and Jack Stapp had just opened the office. I think all they had was Roger Miller and Bill Anderson and me.

[**BUDDY KILLEN**] Tree Publishing was just a word. It had no office, nothing. It was just something that Jack Stapp was sorta doing out of his office at WSM. He gave me thirty-five dollars a week. Everywhere I'd hear about a songwriter or song, I'd go get the guy to sing a solo on that little tape recorder. Then I would learn it. In 1956

The Johnny Cash road show hit the stage in 1968, when the superstar was at his peak. Rockabilly guitar great Carl Perkins and the folk-singing Carter Sisters were part of Cash's troupe during this period.

"Johnny Cash is the reason I play country music. He was different. Cash was bigger than life. He knows how to fill up a room. Elvis Presley had it. Bob Dylan has it. Geronimo probably had it. Jesus Christ had it. Johnny Cash has it."

——————

MARTY STUART

The name "Johnny Cash"
means "country music"
throughout the world.

JOHNNY CASH

(1 9 3 2 –)

HOME AREA
Dyess, Arkansas, in the Mississippi Delta

SIGNIFICANCE
"The Man in Black."

POPULAR SONGS
"Folsom Prison Blues" (1956), "I Walk the Line" (1956), "The Rebel—Johnny Yuma" (1961), "Busted" (1963), "Ring of Fire" (1963), "Understand Your Man" (1964), "Jackson" (with June Carter, 1967), "A Boy Named Sue" (1969), "If I Were a Carpenter" (with June Carter, 1970), "Man in Black" (1971), "A Thing Called Love" (1972), "Highwayman" (with Waylon Jennings, Willie Nelson, and Kris Kristofferson, 1985)

INFLUENCED
Rosanne Cash, Rodney Crowell, Marty Stuart, The Mavericks, Bob Dylan, Kris Kristofferson, Hank Williams Jr.

HONORS
Country Music Hall of Fame, 1980; Rock 'n' Roll Hall of Fame, 1992; Nashville Songwriters Hall of Fame, 1977; seven Grammy Awards; Academy of Country Music Pioneer Award, 1990; TNN/*Music City News* Living Legend Award, 1989; Grammy Legend award, 1990; six CMA Awards; four American Music Awards; gospel music Dove Award, 1972; sixteen Gold and/or Platinum Record awards; star on Hollywood Walk of Fame

we had "Heartbreak Hotel," and in 1957 I signed Roger Miller; in 1958 Bill Anderson, and then Dottie West and Joe Tex; and from there Tree just became an unbelievable company.

[**BILL ANDERSON**] Roger Miller had to be the closest thing to a genius that I ever knew. He only had an eighth-grade education, but he could come up with things right off the top of his head—songs, funny sayings, lines, bits of wisdom, philosophy, that were just absolutely incredible.

[**ROGER MILLER, 1985**] That's kind of how the beginnings were here. I got a job about that time, 1957, as a bellhop at the Andrew Jackson Hotel. Oh, I would plug songs to anybody. I would sing songs for Tex Ritter, taking him up in the elevator. Bill Monroe used to call me into his dressing room at the Opry and tell his band, "Hey boys, listen to this kid." I'd play my songs, and he'd say, "Ain't that great?"

[**KRIS KRISTOFFERSON**] Roger was, when I came to town, the hottest thing in the music business. He had just gotten five Grammys and he broke open a lot of the doors. He took me and Mickey Newbury out to California right before he cut his 1969 album—flew us out first class. We spent three days waitin' for Roger to listen to our material. And he never did. He'd come home tired from appearing on TV and fall asleep. Then he says, "Hey, we gotta go home. Today we're gonna do this album. How 'bout that song you got, 'Me and Bobby McGee'? Mickey tells me it's a good song." So I sang it to him, and he says, "Okay. I'll do it."

[**JIMMY DEAN**] I have a wonderful award, the only one of its kind in the world, from Roger Miller. It's called the Gold Doorknob Award, and it's in my den. It is very simply a gold doorknob on a piece of mahogany, with a little plaque down at the bottom. The little plaque says, "To Jimmy Dean, for a million doors you opened for me. I'm forever grateful. Roger Miller." 'Cause we introduced "King of the Road" on our television show. It kind of chokes me. I miss him.

[**BILL ANDERSON**] I remember writing the song "Still" (1963), although at the time I really had no idea that this song was going to have the impact that it had. I thought it was a very "vanilla" song, as opposed to maybe "City Lights" (1958) or something which I thought had a lot more depth to it. I think that kinda points up something that Owen Bradley, the great producer, said many times: "Baskin Robbins has thirty-one flavors of ice cream, but vanilla still outsells them all."

Make it plain, make it simple, make it "vanilla," and it touches more people.

[**HARLAN HOWARD**] I got to Nashville in June of 1960 and immediately went out to a little company in Goodlettsville called Pamper Music, which had gotten me my first two hit records. I went out there and a young man named Hank Cochran had been there about six months. I think they were giving him about fifty bucks a week to be their song plugger. Hank would bring me down to Music Row, and that's where I met Chet Atkins, this wonderful producer, and also Owen Bradley, Columbia's Don Law, and Capitol's Ken Nelson. So I had these four great producers all listening to my songs.

I never had a good job in my life. I was a flunky. I've pumped gas and drove trucks. My last job was driving a forklift truck. I had three hits and suddenly all this money came to me, and, boy, I was gone to Nashville in a heartbeat. I had the fear of the devil, which was going back to the factory, so I wrote day and night.

[**BILL ANDERSON**] I won the *Music City News* Songwriter of the Year Award about four years during the '60s. One year, I wrote five songs that won BMI Awards. I thought that was pretty good, until I got to the BMI dinner and Harlan Howard won ten.

[**JOHNNY RODRIGUEZ**] Willie Nelson told me one time, "All you gotta do is be honest and make it rhyme."

[**FARON YOUNG**] Willie Nelson came to Nashville without a penny in his pocket. I think the only money he had was because he'd written one song

Opry star George Hamilton IV (above) championed the songs of Joni Mitchell, Gordon Lightfoot, and other folkies. Mother Maybelle and the Carter Sisters (below) became idols on the folk-festival circuit.

called "Family Bible" he sold for fifty dollars. I was down at Tootsie's Orchid Lounge, where me and all the guys always hung out. Willie had a crew cut and everything, all young, didn't have all this shaggy beard and all that back in those days. He says, "I've got a couple of songs I want to sing to you." He sang me "Hello Walls" and another thing called "Congratulations." I says, "I'm recording in a couple of weeks. I'll take 'em both." So we get in the studio, and everybody started making fun of the song, you know, "Hello walls, hello guitar, hello microphone." I said, "Y'all go ahead and make fun; I think it's a hit record." [In 1961, Young's version of the tune became Nelson's first Number One hit as a songwriter.]

[**BILLY WALKER**] I knew Willie in Texas. I was on radio in Waco, and he came from Abbott, right outside of there. And sometimes he used to come and watch me perform live on the radio. Then I was a member of the Ozark Jubilee, and Willie came to Springfield, Missouri, and I was tryin' to get him a job up there. I came to Nashville; Willie Nelson came to Nashville. I said, "What are you doing here?" He said "Well, there's nobody buyin' songs in Ft. Worth, so I came here to see what I could do." I said, "Where are you living?" And he said, "Out there in that old 1950-model gray Buick." I said, "Well, get your gear and come on out to the house," and he lived out there with me for about three months. Livin' with me, he wrote "Funny How Time Slips Away" and several other songs that came to be standards.

I took Willie Nelson around, tryin' to get him a songwriting job. In the meantime, he had written "Crazy," and I cut a demo on it over at Starday Studio, tryin' to show the guy what kind of songs Willie Nelson was writing. This guy said, "I don't think that song'll ever sell." I had "Funny How Time Slips Away" as a hit in 1961. Hank Cochran came to me and said, "Owen wants to cut 'Crazy' on Patsy Cline. Would you let go of it?" I really didn't want to, but Hank promised me that he would find me another song, which he did, which sold a million records for me, "Charlie's Shoes" (1962).

[**BOBBY BARE**] Kris Kristofferson was the first songwriter to come along to really "put you there." He knew how to write. The writers before that were mostly making up the crap as they went along. Kris knew what he was doing. I had two number-one records of Kris's songs, 1970's "Come Sundown" and 1971's "Please Don't Tell Me How the Story Ends." He got so hot as a writer that the disc jockeys would say "Well, here's another Kristofferson song," and play my record. They didn't say, "Here's Bobby Bare's latest hit." He changed Nashville forever, because he made the hippies and the long-hair, funky people acceptable.

[**JOHNNY CASH**] Kristofferson was a janitor at Columbia Records when he first came to town. I was always comin' in to record at the studio. He was writin' all these songs, and rather

Bob Dylan recorded Blonde On Blonde, Self Portrait, New Morning, Nashville Skyline *and other albums on Music Row in the 1960s.*

ROGER MILLER

(1936–1992)

HOME AREA
Erick, Oklahoma

SIGNIFICANCE
Major pop-crossover country star.

POPULAR SONGS
"Dang Me" (1964), "King of the Road" (1965), "Engine Engine #9" (1965), "England Swings" (1965), "Walkin' in the Sunshine" (1967), "Little Green Apples" (1968), "Me and Bobby McGee" (1969)

POPULAR SONGS WRITTEN
"Half a Mind" (1958), "The Last Word in Lonesome Is Me" (1966), "When Two Worlds Collide" (1969), "Lock Stock and Teardrops" (1988), "Walkin' Talkin' Cryin' Barely Beatin' Broken Heart" (1990), "Tall Tall Trees" (1995)

INFLUENCED
Bill Anderson, Glen Campbell, Justin Tubb, Billy Burnette, Dean Miller, Kris Kristofferson, Dwight Yoakam, Marty Stuart

HONORS
Country Music Hall of Fame, 1995; Nashville Songwriters Hall of Fame, 1973; Academy of Country Music Pioneer Award, 1987; eleven Grammy Awards in 1964–65; seven Tony Awards (*Big River*), 1985; ACM Single of the Year ("Little Green Apples"), 1968; four Gold Record awards, 1965–66

than take a chance on gettin' fired by bringing the songs directly to me—which they told him they'd do if he bothered me—he would slip the songs to June, and she'd put 'em in her purse. After we'd get home, she would hand 'em to me. Kris was determined that I was gonna listen to his songs. So one Sunday afternoon during the middle of all that, he landed a helicopter in our yard. I was asleep, and June came in and woke me up, says, "Some fool has landed a helicopter in your yard!" Went out, and it was Kris. He fell out of the helicopter with a tape in one hand and a beer in the other. I said, "Anybody that would go this far, I'm gonna listen to your song." It was "Sunday Morning Coming Down" (1970).

Kristofferson and hundreds like him are the sons and daughters of Bob Dylan and Joan Baez, who eventually came to Music City to ply their trade in acoustic-music nightspots, in the kitchens and living rooms of fellow composers, in the writer rooms of Music Row's song publishing companies, and sometimes on stage as country stars, themselves. In recent years the Bluebird Cafe, opened in 1982, has become the troubadours' mecca, continuing the tradition of songwriting brotherhood that was born in Tootsie's Orchid Lounge thirty-five years ago.

If there was a single event that cemented the connection between

Canada's Anne Murray graduated from barefoot folkie to country superstar in the 1970s, thanks to hits like "Snowbird" and "Danny's Song."

◀

*Willie Nelson was
a Nashville song-
writing troubadour
for fifteen years before
he found fame as
a country renegade.
He first hit the charts
in 1962 and joined
the Opry in 1964.*

folk and country, it was the recording of Will the Circle Be Unbroken *in 1972. Spearheaded
by the long-haired California folk-rock act the Nitty Gritty Dirt Band, the three-LP set of
old-time country songs sold more than a million copies and acquainted an entire generation
of pop fans with the music of country's pioneers.*

[**JOHN McEUEN, FORMERLY OF THE NITTY GRITTY DIRT BAND**] The folk
music thing that happened, there was something real about it. It draws you into the
stories of the songs, draws you into the people and their backgrounds. When my
brother put together the *Circle Be Unbroken* album, it was a fairly quick process.
We came to Nashville, and Earl Scruggs, who was the glue that held the album
together, put us in touch with people like Maybelle Carter, Jimmy Martin, Junior
Huskey, and Vasser Clements. One of the newspapers said, "What is the band
doing, recording with a bunch of old dinosaurs?" They didn't understand that they
were sitting in the middle of this great form of music that they'd been overlooking.
I was tired of people coming up to me at Dirt Band concerts and saying, "How'd

▶

In 1990 the Nitty Gritty Dirt Band reprised their Will the Circle Be Unbroken *concept with a second all-star album with that same title. Among those pictured with the band here are Earl Scruggs, Roy Acuff, Brother Oswald, and Marty Stuart.*

you learn how to play the banjo?" I said, "You ever heard of Earl Scruggs?" "No." They were college kids, and they were younger, and they hadn't reached back anywhere.

Merle Travis was just a real gentleman. When we first went into his living room to play, he took his guitar out of the closet and said, "I haven't played this thing for about a year," and he started fumbling around, trying to make a chord. We're sitting there going, "agh." He looks up at us and rips right into something. You know, he really put one over on us.

Acuff was very precise in what he wanted to do. He went through this lecture of what he had done and where it had taken him and all that. He listened to what we were doing. He looks at my brother, who has hair down to here, and goes, "What kind of music do you call that?" There is dead silence in the control room, and Bill's goin', "Well, it's Appalachian kind of bluegrassy traditional folky . . . " And Acuff goes, "Son, that's just country music. Let's go make some more." Everybody just went like, "Yahoo!"

Working with Maybelle Carter was like working with what you hoped your mother would be, or something. She's sitting there getting ready to record "Wildwood Flower," and she says, "Now if you all don't mind, I'd like to do it in the key of F, if that's okay." I wanted to say, "You're asking *us* if it's okay?" Working with her was like working with an angel, in attitude and delivery. It was just a magical thing. She never knew the impact she had on the music business.

[**GEORGE HAMILTON IV**] The folk music impact on Nashville is very evident today in the recordings of Kathy Mattea, of Vince Gill, of Nanci Griffith especially. I hear a lot of echoes of the '60s, of Ian and Sylvia, of Gordon Lightfoot. I think Kris Kristofferson would tell you in a hurry that he was very influenced by the folkies in his early days. As were Bobby Bare and lots of us. It was wonderful music. It was fresh, it was something new.

bill monroe ~ lester flatt &
earl scruggs ~ the stanley
brothers ~ mac wiseman
the louvin brothers ~ the
stonemans ~ jimmy martin

Bluegrass

im & jesse ~ alison krauss
aurie lewis ~ the nashville
bluegrass band ~ osborne
brothers ~ marty stuart

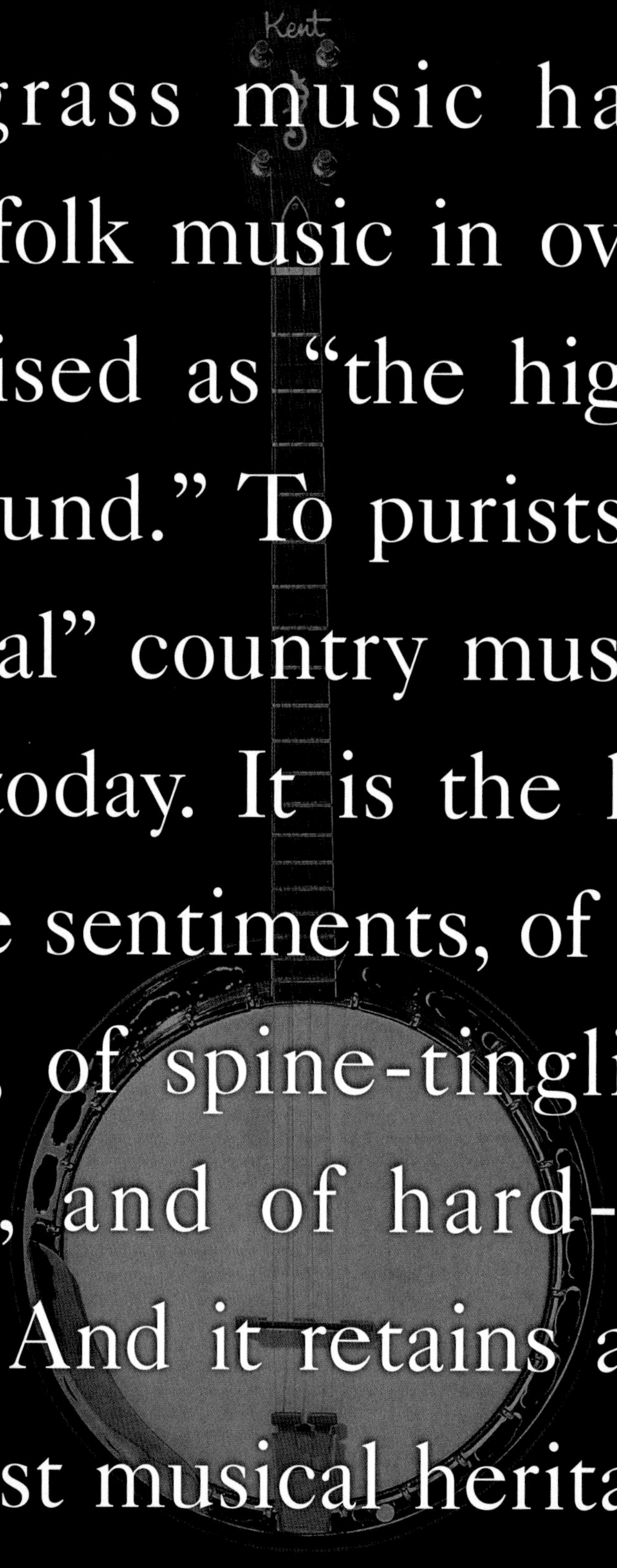

Bluegrass music has been called "folk music in overdrive" and praised as "the high, lonesome sound." To purists, it's the only "real" country music being played today. It is the home of old-time sentiments, of virtuoso picking, of spine-tingling harmonies, and of hard-driving rhythm. And it retains a link to our oldest musical heritage.

One of the most important results of the folk revival was a surge in popularity for bluegrass music. Bluegrass festivals, an outgrowth of the big outdoor folk gatherings, became fixtures of the country scene beginning in the 1960s. The dazzling, acoustic bluegrass instrumentation drew thousands of new pickers to the country sound.

——————⋗◆⋖——————

[**DOLLY PARTON**] I'm not so sure what it is I love so much about bluegrass music, but I always have. I love those rich harmonies, and I really appreciate the true voices that come out of bluegrass music. It's a style of emotion that really is just somethin' great. It's also like a religion, that world of bluegrass music.

[**EMMYLOU HARRIS**] There's a real melody there and a real intensity. There's a real passion. It's got real good, deep words that usually are about pretty dark subjects. It's kind of an interesting juxtaposition: It sounds like it's real happy music, but if you really go in deep and listen to the songs, they're incredibly sad. They deal with death and having your heart not just broken but just sort of wrenched out of you.

[**KATHY MATTEA**] Bluegrass harmonies are real clear. There's not a lot of vibrato; it's real straight toned. So you get this thing happening where there's a tension between the harmonies, and overtones start to happen. You can feel it when it's happening. It's like glue or like a magnet that happens between the singers.

[**CHARLIE DANIELS**] I cut my teeth on bluegrass. I was a bluegrass purist at one time; if it wasn't Bill Monroe or Flatt and Scruggs, I didn't want to hear it.

[**CHRIS HILLMAN**] Bluegrass is the foundation of country music. If you're going to have a career in country music, you should go to "bluegrass school."

[**LAURIE LEWIS**] My definition of bluegrass music might be a little bit controversial. I see it as having been, of course, started by Bill Monroe, who can be easily defined as a singer-songwriter with a string band. I think that's what Bill Monroe did. I mean, he's really a singer-songwriter with a string band. And that's what I do. I'm a singer-songwriter with a string band.

Bill Monroe was a Kentuckian who was surrounded by old-time mountain music as a boy. His parents died before he was out of his teens, so Bill went to live with his uncle Pendelton Vandiver, immortalized in his classic "Uncle Pen."

[**BILL MONROE**] He was a fine man. He was a good, decent man. He didn't cuss and all that stuff. He never drank. He was just a wonderful uncle. And lots of times he'd come down where we lived in Kentucky and bring his fiddle along. My mother, she would have supper for us, and then later on that night he'd get the fiddle out, and we'd listen to him fiddle. He could play a lot of old-time numbers that was mighty good.

"Bluegrass music is basically a back porch music. It's music that you play to entertain yourself, your fiddle and your banjo. It's a beautiful art form, the purest music that we have in America."

————

MARTY STUART

▲

Bill Monroe (stand-
ing) hits the road
with the band that
defined the bluegrass
sound—Chubby
Wise, Lester Flatt,
Earl Scruggs, and
Cedric Rainwater.

That's where I got that number "Jenny Lind," from him.

I had two brothers that I played with. And one of them, he wanted to be the fiddle player, and the other one, he wanted to play the guitar and be the lead singer. So I had to take the mandolin and sing tenor to be in the group. And now I'm glad that I took the mandolin.

You see, the Monroes, most of 'em come from Scotland. So I wrote that number, "Scotland." I don't know if you know it or not, but I have wrote a lot of instrumental numbers. I'm not bragging about this, but I can write an instrumental number in a half a minute or a minute. Now, that's pretty fast. I just hear a lot of sounds and things that I would like to come out with, and tie 'em together and make 'em into a good number.

After apprenticing in local string bands and at the National Barn Dance as square dancers,
Bill and his brother Charlie Monroe formed a 1934–38 duet act. After the breakup, Bill

formed his own *Blue Grass Boys* group. In 1939 they auditioned at the Grand Ole Opry and were hired.

After several editions of the group, Monroe hired guitarist/singer Lester Flatt and banjo player Earl Scruggs in 1945. This version of the Blue Grass Boys defined the emerging style, which took its name from the band. Dozens of bluegrass music's most important figures have subsequently been trained in Monroe's group.

[**BILL MONROE**] I like for bandmembers to be true and honest with me, you see, and play the bluegrass, play it right. Be sure that you take care of that part of it. And I don't allow nobody to say any bad, filthy words to anybody that comes to the show. I don't cuss, and I don't drink, so I want the Blue Grass Boys to go along the same way.

[**PETER ROWAN**] Bill Monroe was on tour, and when he came to Boston, he didn't have a band. I'd been listening to his stuff and thinking this was The Sound. I walked up to him, and I said, "I know this song." So we sang "Can't You Hear Me Calling," and a couple of his older songs. I went to work for Bill Monroe up there in Boston. I came down to Nashville and stayed with him for two years, from 1964 through '66.

Life as a Blue Grass Boy was—if Bill needed some help out on the farm, you helped. We wouldn't have too many idle moments around town. There was always something to be done out there. As soon as you enter the world of Bill

Bill Monroe is "daddy bluegrass," the patriarch of an art form, a true American icon.

BILL MONROE
(1911–   )

HOME AREA
Central Kentucky

SIGNIFICANCE
"The Father of Bluegrass Music."

POPULAR SONGS
"What Would You Give in Exchange" (The Monroe Brothers, 1936), "New Mule Skinner Blues" (1940), "Orange Blossom Special" (1941), "Kentucky Waltz" (1946), "Blue Moon of Kentucky" (1946), "Little Cabin Home on the Hill" (1947), "Molly and Tenbrooks" (1947), "Sweetheart You Done Me Wrong" (1948), "Wicked Path of Sin" (1948), "Toy Heart" (1949), "Uncle Pen" (1950), "My Little Georgia Rose" (1950), "Christmas Time's A-Coming" (1951), "In the Pines" (1952), "Scotland" (1958), "Gotta Travel On" (1959), "Walk Softly on This Heart of Mine" (1969)

INFLUENCED
Flatt and Scruggs, the Stanley Brothers, Jimmy Martin, Mac Wiseman, James Monroe, Ricky Skaggs, Emmylou Harris, Marty Stuart, the Nashville Bluegrass Band

HONORS
Country Music Hall of Fame, 1970; Nashville Songwriters Hall of Fame, 1971; Grammy Award, 1988; IBMA Hall of Honor, 1991; Grammy Lifetime Achievement Award, 1993; *Music City News* Best Bluegrass Act, 1980, 1981

Monroe, you enter the world of taking care of animals, speaking to animals, touching animals, listening to all the sounds of nature.

[**DOUG GREEN**] Bill Monroe is just an incredibly unique character. I was lucky enough in 1967 and again in 1969 to be a member of the Blue Grass Boys. At his eighty-third birthday party, he leaned over to me, and he said, "You made a good bluegrass man." What more can I say? That's the pinnacle. I'd been blessed by the Pope. He's one of the guys on Mount Rushmore.

[**BILL MONROE**] Now here's something I'd like to tell you. I don't know if you know it or not, but I have played in every state that's here in the United States. I'm proud of that. I've worked for the last four presidents, and I'm proud of that. Seems like when they come in office, they'll get in touch with me and want me to come and play for 'em, or to be on a show with 'em.

Flatt and Scruggs departed the Blue Grass Boys in 1948 and formed bluegrass music's second influential act, the Foggy Mountain Boys. This was the group that popularized bluegrass at folk festivals, on college campuses, in movie soundtracks, and on national television.

John Hartford's love of bluegrass led him to study banjo history, the origins of fiddle tunes, and other aspects of traditional American music.

▼

[**EARL SCRUGGS, 1995**] Maybelle Carter influenced me. The guitar playing of Maybelle really fulfilled a lot of happiness in my life. I used to hear her back when they were on radio in Texas years ago, and then at WBT in Charlotte, close to where I was.

My father died when I was four, and I don't remember him that well, but my mother never did anything to discourage; she left me alone when I was trying to learn music, unless I had a chore to do. You have got to love music to fool with it, or I don't think it is gonna work out that well.

[**JOHN McEUEN**] Earl Scruggs was able to take an instrument, the five-string banjo, and make it go to a developed state. He not only played it hard and fast, which was exciting, but he played it precise and clean. And on top of that, he played something mystical. He played notes that moved people. He took the five-string banjo and really made it "sing."

[**JOSH GRAVES**] Flatt and Scruggs, to me, was one of the greatest outfits that ever come along, or ever will. They set a pattern for younger people, but the old hard core still go back to the Flatt and Scruggs time: Cousin Jake on bass and Curly Seckler on the mandolin, Lester Flatt on the guitar, Paul Warren with the fiddle, Earl Scruggs with the banjo, and me on the dobro.

[**GLENN SNODDY**] I remember doing an album for Flatt and Scruggs in three hours. They were first-take artists. They could only do it one way, and that was the way they wanted to do it, and the way they wanted to be remembered.

After hitting the charts with "The Ballad of Jed Clampett" (1962), "Petticoat Junction" (1964), and "Foggy Mountain Breakdown" (the theme from Bonnie and Clyde, 1968), and starring in their own TV series, Flatt and Scruggs broke up in 1969. Flatt stayed in bluegrass as the leader of Nashville Grass. Scruggs formed a group with his sons, which explored country's connections to rock, jazz, folk, and pop.

[**ROLAND WHITE**, **OF THE NASHVILLE BLUEGRASS BAND**] Lester Flatt's my hero. He woke up in the morning laughing. He'd go to bed laughing.

[**MARTY STUART**] The very first weekend I was on the road with Lester Flatt was in Dover, Delaware. He said, "Come here. I wanna show you something." There were two real elderly people walkin' toward the bus. He said, "You see those people? I wanna tell you about country fans. Those people been followin' me and Earl Scruggs since we was with Bill Monroe and his band in 1945. And they're still here today. If you treat 'em right, that's what country fans'll do for you. They'll stick."

[**EARL SCRUGGS, 1995**] I toured with my sons in the Earl Scruggs Revue for

▲

Bill Monroe's annual Bean Blossom festival in Indiana was one of the best known of bluegrass music's many outdoor summertime events.

"The sound of Flatt and Scruggs just transported me. I never saw or heard anything like it, before or since. It was just amazing. Even today when I listen to those old tapes, that's just the best band that ever was, period, to my ear."

JOHN HARTFORD

By singing the praises of their longtime sponsor, Martha White Flour, Flatt and Scruggs turned a jingle into a bluegrass standard.

ten years, 1970 through 1980. We would play a jazz festival, a bluegrass festival, or a rock festival, with anyone from Billy Joel to Dave Brubeck.

[**JIMMY MARTIN**] When the folk music got real popular, and when they started calling it "bluegrass," is when Lester Flatt and Earl Scruggs got on *The Beverly Hillbillies*. Then me and the Osborne Brothers started getting it in the top-ten in country music. People like Lester Flatt and Earl Scruggs gave it the biggest shot that it ever was given.

Flatt and Scruggs's popularity with college audiences and their impact as national popularizers of bluegrass made the field blossom with talent. During the 1950s and 1960s, bluegrass songs regularly made the country charts. In addition to Monroe's contributions and the Flatt and Scruggs hits, notable radio records were created by Mac Wiseman (1959's "Jimmy Brown the Newsboy"), Jim and Jesse (1967's "Diesel on My Tail"), Wilma Lee and Stoney Cooper (1959's "Big Midnight Special"), Jimmy Martin (1964's "Widow Maker"), Reno & Smiley (1961's "Don't Let Your Sweet Love Die"), the Stanley Brothers (1960's "How Far to Little Rock"), the Louvin Brothers (1956's "I Don't Believe You've Met My Baby") and the Osborne Brothers (1968's "Rocky Top").

[**NAOMI JUDD**] Bluegrass music sets fire to the imagination. It's the ancestor of all music. Ralph Stanley of the Stanley Brothers—one of the architects of bluegrass music—is sort of my Elvis.

[**MAC WISEMAN**] That 1947 period when we started in Bristol on WCYB was also quite a turning point in my career. Unbeknown to me, Bill Monroe and the Blue Grass Boys—Lester Flatt, Earl Scruggs, and Chubby Wise—listened to my early morning program. I had an hour in the morning, just me and the guitar. One day, I went back to the studio, and this young man was sitting in the corner of the studio, and he wanted to talk to me a few minutes. He was Earl Scruggs. He said he and Chubby Wise were anticipating leaving the Blue Grass Boys and would like to hire in with me. In the spring of 1948, Lester decided to leave also. So Lester, Earl, and Cedric Rainwater called me, and we became the Foggy Mountain Boys.

[**DONNA STONEMAN**] I'd heard of Bill Monroe's playin', so I got some of his records and tried to copy. But I developed my own style on mandolin. I play too jazzy for traditional bluegrass pickin', but Bill Monroe was very inspiring to me. Jesse McReynolds, I love. I wish I could do his "cross pickin'."

[**JESSE McREYNOLDS, OF JIM AND JESSE**] I started out playin' like Bill

▲

Future country star Marty Stuart began his music career as a teenager in Lester Flatt's band.

FLATT AND SCRUGGS

~

MEMBERS
Lester Flatt (1914–79) and
Earl Scruggs (1924–)

HOME AREA
Tennessee (Flatt),
North Carolina (Scruggs)

SIGNIFICANCE
The bluegrass act that brought the style to
national prominence.

POPULAR SONGS WRITTEN
"Foggy Mountain Breakdown" (1949),
"Earl's Breakdown" (1950), "Roll in My
Sweet Baby's Arms" (1950), "Old Salty
Dog Blues" (1950), "Don't Get Above
Your Raisin'" (1951), "'Tis Sweet to Be
Remembered" (1952), "Flint Hill Special"
(1952), "I'll Go Stepping Too" (1953),
"Cabin in the Hills" (1959), "Crying My
Heart Out Over You" (1960), "Polka on
a Banjo" (1960), "Ballad of Jed Clampett"
(1962), "The Martha White Theme"
(1962), "Petticoat Junction" (1964),
"Foggy Mountain Breakdown" (1968)

INFLUENCED
Marty Stuart, Ricky Skaggs, Randy
Scruggs, John Hartford, Josh Graves

HONORS
Country Music Hall of Fame, 1985;
Grammy Award, 1968; IBMA Hall of
Honor: 1991 (Scruggs), 1992 (Flatt)

Monroe and Red Rector and Jethro Burns and Paul Buskirk. And then I heard Earl Scruggs come up with the banjo style; I thought, well, maybe I could do that on the mandolin. Someone in New York heard it and started callin it "cross pickin'" and tagged my name to it.

In 1967, the Stonemans won the CMA's first Vocal Group of the Year award. In 1971, the Osborne Brothers became the second bluegrass act to win the honor. Flatt and Scruggs won a Grammy in 1968, a feat repeated by the New South in 1983. A bluegrass category was added to the Grammy Awards in 1988. Two years later, the style's boosters created the International Bluegrass Music Awards. Monroe, Scruggs, Flatt, Martin, Wiseman, Reno and Smiley, the Stanleys, Jim and Jesse, and the Osbornes have since been inducted into IBMA's Hall of Honor.

[**MARTY ROE, OF DIAMOND RIO**] Dana Williams, our bass player, is the nephew to the Osborne Brothers. So to say he was influenced by bluegrass music would be an understatement. He says that he didn't know anything but Elvis and the Osborne Brothers 'til he was about fifteen years old. They had one of the biggest songs in the past twenty years in country music, and that was "Rocky Top" in 1968. Actually became an anthem for Tennessee and one of their state songs.

[**LYNN ANDERSON**] Most people expect me to say that "Rose Garden" is my favorite Lynn Anderson song, but when I travel around the world and do concerts in different countries, everybody knows "Rocky Top" just as well as they know "Rose Garden." That's the one that gets everybody stomping and singing and clapping and stuff.

[**PATSY STONEMAN**] We all learned to play because to begin with, we didn't have no toys. Nothing. We couldn't go to movies, and we didn't have no bicycles or balls or ballbats or nothin'. We had Daddy's instruments that he put together. What he didn't have, he made. If we wanted to go anywhere, we had to be sure we played music. 'Cause that's the way we got to go. Daddy would take us to play with him wherever he could get a job for us—nightclubs, anywhere they'd let children in. In the Washington, D.C., area, they had the child labor law. But Maryland didn't. We would play up at a little old place called Armstrong's, outside of Washington, D.C.; paid fifteen dollars a weekend and all the tips.

[**JIMMY STONEMAN, OF THE STONEMANS**] We went up there and was on the *Arthur Godfrey Talent Scouts* show in 1956,

when it was America's most watched TV program. And we won it. After we won, he kept us over for two weeks. Then he had us back on a Wednesday night special. After Arthur Godfrey passed away in 1983, he used us, the Stonemans, for his eulogy. And that is fantastic.

[**PATSY STONEMAN**] Homer & Jethro was on *The Tonight Show* with Johnny Carson one night. He asked Jethro who they thought was the best mandolin player they had heard. And he said, "Donna Stoneman." That made me proud. And Jimmy on that bass, there ain't no better. I'm braggin'. Can I brag some more? My brother Scott could play a fiddle with a coat hanger, a toothpick, a comb. Anything he could get his hands on. Daddy said, "I reckon that Scott's about the only child I got with a fiddle wrist. He'll be the fiddle player." Six months later Scott was at Constitution Hall. We were playin' up in Maryland when he won the national fiddle contest. They brought him back on their shoulders through the door of the club. Scott hollered, "Hey, I won, I won, I won, I won!" Nine times he was national champion.

▲

Dubbed "The Baron of Bluegrass," guitarist Lester Flatt is revered as one of the finest lead singers in the history of the style. Flatt and Scruggs were at their Grand Ole Opry peak on stage at the Ryman Auditorium in the late 1950s.

GOLDEN NUGGET

▲

*Singer/guitarist
Jimmy Martin left
Bill Monroe's band
to become one of
bluegrass music's
most colorful enter-
tainers. He entered
his field's Hall of
Honor in 1995.*

[**EDDIE STONEMAN, OF THE STONEMANS**] I believe he was the greatest fiddle player that ever lived. We's up on the stage playin' and somebody stole his fiddle bow. Nobody knew where it was at. He took a toothpick and played the "Orange Blossom Special" with a toothpick!

Scotty Stoneman died of alcohol poisoning in 1973. Van, Roni, Jimmy, and Donna were the mainstays of the Stonemans during the act's bluegrass heyday. After Pop Stoneman's death in 1968, Patsy assumed leadership of the band, and banjo-playing Roni went on to comedic fame on TV's Hee Haw.

With the exceptions of Wilma Lee Cooper, Delia Bell, the Lewis Family, and a handful of others, the bluegrass world was almost completely male dominated for roughly thirty-five years (1940–75). In 1957, Patsy Stoneman left the family group to become the first woman to lead her own bluegrass band, the Bluegrass Champs.

[**PATSY STONEMAN**] I didn't consider myself a boss. I just figured it was workin' together. If I liked what they was doin', I kept 'em on. If I didn't like it, I told 'em they was fired. That's about it.

[**LAURIE LEWIS**] It's true that women are a minority in bluegrass music, but when I first started playing the music out in the San Francisco Bay area in the '70s, there were many women musicians already kind of in the scene.

Ironically, this most male-dominated of country styles now finds its future largely in the hands of its female performers. Laurie Lewis, Rhonda Vincent, Lynn Morris, Tammy Sullivan, Suzanne Cox, Claire Lynch, and Alison Krauss are all indisputably bluegrass stars.

[**DOLLY PARTON**] I think there are cults of people that love true traditional mountain music, true traditional bluegrass. Alison Krauss is one of those people that everybody's talkin' about, that underground, cult following. And she could care less whether she records or not. She is just a true artist. She just wants to be what she is.

[**ALISON KRAUSS, 1994**] It isn't about money and fame. At the end of the day, the only thing that is left is the music. There is nothing else. And when you go home at night to face yourself, you want your integrity. We just want to play what we play—and try to do it better all the time. I'm not striving for a hit. We just want to play good bluegrass.

In 1993, Krauss became the youngest member of the Grand Ole Opry cast. Two years later, she made more history as the first bluegrass act to sweep the mainstream Country Music Association awards. An entire generation of country performers of the '90s was weaned on the bluegrass sound: Diamond Rio, Kathy Mattea, John and Audrey Wiggins, Joe Diffie, Kenny Chesney, Jon Randall, Mark O'Connor, Ricky Skaggs, Chris Hillman, and Clinton Gregory among them.

[**MARTY STUART**] If you'll look around, you'll see Travis Tritt, Vince Gill, Alison Krauss, Marty Raybon of Shenandoah. Bluegrass has a whole lotta new representatives and ambassadors inside of mainstream country music today. That can shed a lot of light and attention back on a beautiful art form, the purest music that we have in America.

Jim and Jesse (above) and the Osborne Brothers (below) are bluegrass mainstays on stage at the Grand Ole Opry to this day.

▲

*The Stanley Brothers
and their Clinch
Mountain Boys are
among the most
influential bluegrass
stylists of all time.*

*Bluegrass musicians weren't the only beneficiaries of folkies' interest. Louisiana's Cajun culture
also got a lift because of the new attention to the roots of country music.*

[JO-EL SONNIER] The Cajun people came from France to Nova Scotia. They
were deported from Nova Scotia in 1755 and went to different areas, Mississippi,
New Orleans, and part of Louisiana, and that's where the story starts.

*Isolated from mainstream culture by the Louisiana bayous, the Cajun people clung to their
ancestral music for generations.*

[JIMMY C. NEWMAN] A lot of people ask me about what makes the Cajun
sound. The first thing you need to really have the flavor of the traditional Cajun is
to be able to speak the language, because then you know what you're singing about.
But what is very important, too, is the instrumentation, the little Cajun accordion,
which Rufus Thibodeaux calls the "Mamou Air Compressor." You can get by without a Cajun-bred fiddle player, but it's very important, too. Those are the two

instruments that I say are the main ones. Now, to really get something exciting, add the scrub board. It's got a unique sound.

[**BEN SANDMEL, OF THE HACK-BERRY RAMBLERS**] Roy Acuff's "The Precious Jewel" was stolen pretty much and turned into a waltz. And then, on the other hand, Hank Williams took an old Cajun song and turned it into "Jambalaya." There's always been a big exchange between Cajun music and country.

Over the years, this has been demonstrated repeatedly. Mainstream country-Cajun hits have included "Jole Blon" (Harry Choates, 1947), "Jole Blon's Sister" (Moon Mullican, 1947), "Jambalaya" (Hank Williams, 1952), "Alligator Man" (Jimmy C. Newman, 1961), "Louisiana Man" (Rusty & Doug, 1961), "Bayou Talk" (Jimmy C. Newman, 1962), "Diggy Diggy Lo" (Doug Kershaw, 1969), "Cajun Baby" (Hank Williams Jr., 1969), "Boo Dan" (Jimmy C. Newman, 1969), "Big Mamou" (Fiddlin' Frenchie Burke, 1974), "Marie Laveau" (Bobby Bare, 1974), "Louisiana Saturday Night" (Mel McDaniel, 1981), "Tear Stained Letter" (Jo-El Sonnier, 1988), "Bayou Boys" (Eddy Raven, 1989), "Down at the Twist and Shout" (Mary Chapin Carpenter, 1991), "Adalida" (George Strait, 1995), and "Gonna Get a Life" (Mark Chesnutt, 1995). And Cajun acts were recorded commercially almost as early as hillbillies. One of the first to thrive was Louisiana's durable Hackberry Ramblers. The act has been going so long that

Ludarin Darbone says that every brick in his house represents a tune the band has played.

[**EDWIN DUHON, OF THE HACKBERRY RAMBLERS**] The Hackberry Ramblers were organized in 1933 by Edwin Duhon and Ludarin Darbone in Hackberry, Louisiana. We happen to be the oldest band participating in the United States at this

The soul-piercing harmonies of the Louvin Brothers (above) still have a profound effect on listeners today. The act was in its glory in the 1950s at the Grand Ole Opry. The Cajun act the Hackberry Ramblers (left) are country music's longest-lived string band.

time—been at it for sixty-one years. The Hackberry Ramblers was the first group of players that was playin' French and country/western. The reason why we survived so long is because we stayed with the trends, changed through the years, and we always did have rhythm.

[**LUDARIN DARBONE, OF THE HACKBERRY RAMBLERS**] We were neighbors. Edwin played accordion and guitar. He knew a lot of French numbers. And what I played mostly was hillbilly. And at that time, the main music in the southwest Louisiana was the accordion, guitar or fiddle, and the triangle, little irons. We are the oldest band with the original members.

In 1967 the Stonemans (above) were the first bluegrass band to win a Country Music Association award. Cajun Jimmy C. Newman (right) sings "Alligator Man" and wears it, too.

The resurgence of Cajun music began when college enthusiasts moved beyond bluegrass and the blues to explore other roots of America's music in the wake of the folk-revival movement. Tex-Mex sounds, zydeco, Cajun, polka, and Native American styles were given new dignity—and profitability—by the eager young audiences.

[**JO-EL SONNIER**] In my early years I started totally speaking French. In the third grade they told us we couldn't speak any other but English. If we spoke French, we would be punished. They wanted us to learn to speak English and not carry on as much what we were raised as Cajuns. We got hurt by that. A lot of the children were punished. They would take rulers and literally hit our hands. But the music stayed in French because of our listening to our peers, the music around the house, going to some of the clubs and parties we call "fais do-do."

Lauren Post was the college professor in San Diego, California. I'll never forget that. We were invited to come there to introduce French music to those students. I left my hometown because they wanted to hear Cajun music. I wanted to go 'cause I felt something inside me saying "go and reach. Show the people where you come from. Show where the music comes from." So I tell Mama, "I got to do this!" Lauren Post introduced the songs, explained the songs, and then I sung the songs in French, to explain to the students. It was really nice! And that's how it started, with the college students.

oretta lynn ∽ tammy wynette

dolly parton ∽ dottie west ∽

lynn anderson ∽ connie smith

∽ jeannie seely ∽ jan howard

donna fargo ∽ barbara mandrell

Loretta, Tammy & Dolly

∽ jeannie c. riley ∽ norma jean

melba montgomery ∽ jeanne

pruett ∽ barbara fairchild ∽

margo smith ∽ billie jo spears

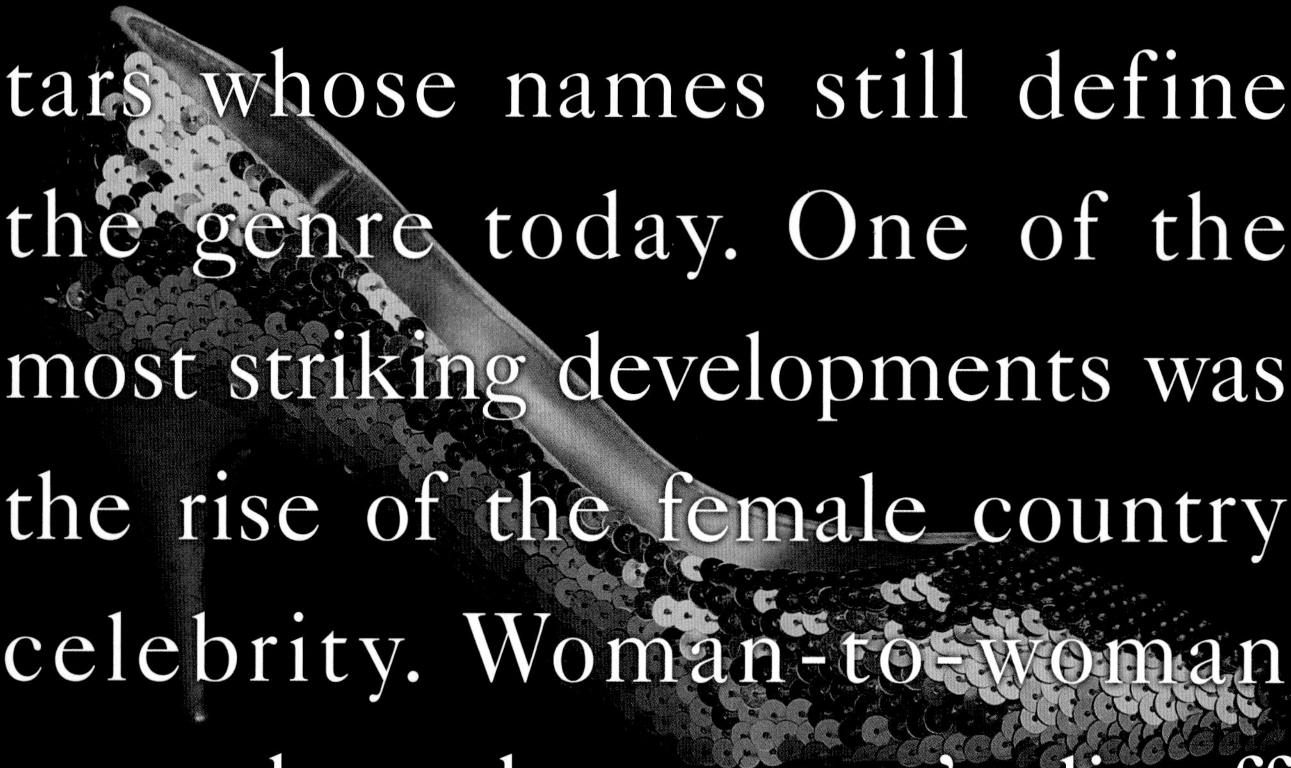

[As country music took the spotlight in the 1960s, it created a group of multimedia superstars whose names still define the genre today. One of the most striking developments was the rise of the female country celebrity. Woman-to-woman songs brought country's distaff entertainers into the hearts of a growing legion of fans.]

The trend was the mirror of society, for during this same era more women entered the work force than ever before.

The Carter Family, Lulu Belle, Minnie Pearl, Patsy Montana, Kitty Wells, Patsy Cline, and others in earlier eras had suggested that country had a "hidden" distaff side. But these women remained exceptions, distinct anomalies in a musical style that was 90 percent male until the '60s.

Without question, the three successors to Patsy who defined modern female country music were Loretta Lynn, Tammy Wynette, and Dolly Parton. All three launched their careers in the 1960s and survived into the '90s as million-selling stars.

⎯⎯⎯⎯◆⎯⎯⎯⎯

[**TRISHA YEARWOOD**] I don't wake up every day being "Miss Independent," "Miss I've-Got-the-World-By-the-Tail," you know, but I might wanna hear a song that makes me feel that way. When people say, "Now all of a sudden women are singing strong songs and more independent lyrics," I always reply, "Well, you must not have listened to Dolly Parton and Tammy Wynette and Loretta Lynn."

[**GAIL DAVIES**] I think those three ladies, along with Emmylou Harris, typify what is great about country music, and women.

Loretta, Tammy, and Dolly came to Music City in the wake of the breakthroughs of Kitty Wells and Patsy Cline. But instead of working in their shadows, these new stars of the '60s crafted highly individual songwriting and performing styles. These three all communicated distinctly assertive, feminine points of view, broke ground as female country headliners, and redefined what it means to be a woman in country music. Loretta Lynn came first, arriving in Nashville on the heels of her homemade 1960 hit "I'm a Honky-Tonk Girl."

[**LORETTA LYNN**] I think, really, to make it in this business you have to be great, different, or first. I think I was different when I come in writing about things that nobody would even talk about in public. And I didn't realize that they didn't. I was having babies and staying at home. I thought, "Well, gee, this is what's going on. I'll write about it." I was writing about life. I had a lot of songs banned.

Raised in Appalachian Kentucky poverty, Loretta married at age thirteen and began raising a family in Custer, Washington. Buck Owens had a local TV show in nearby Takoma and discovered her.

[**BUCK OWENS**] She was singin' around in the clubs of Takoma, and at the club, the Brittania, we had a talent show. This one night, in walks Loretta, and she's got on this blue suit with the white fringes, the white boots, the hat, and biggest smile you ever saw in your life. She won our talent contest that night. The club down the street had one also. She went down there and won their talent contest. She got a

"I think I'm part of bringing the ladies out of their shells and getting the girls all started, letting them know that they can have families and work, too."

LORETTA LYNN

▲

Loretta Lynn
belongs to the
first televised gen-
eration of country
performers. Millions
were exposed to her
when she became
a regular on the
Wilburn Brothers'
weekly TV show.

watch from both contests, real pretty, real goldy lookin', and they had a real nice case. She told me later on, "Neither one of 'em run."

[**LORETTA LYNN**] The first time that I got heels was when Teddy Wilburn locked my boots up in the trunk of the car. We were on tour. He locked my boots up in the trunk of the car and went out and bought me a pair of heels about that high—big, tall heels. So that was all I had to wear on the stage in Salt Lake City. I'll never forget it if I live to be 150 years old, which I will. There was a little gate that you had to walk through to get up on the stage, and I couldn't even get through that gate with them high heels on and my guitar. The disc jockey had to help me get up on stage. I know the people thought I was drunk. For the first two or three songs I was standing there and it was killing me. I thought, "I've got to let 'em know I'm not

drunk, 'cause I don't drink." So I pulled off my shoes, and I said, "Friends, I don't wear high heels. This is the first pair I've ever had. Teddy Wilburn has my boots out in the trunk of his car and won't give 'em to me. I can't wear these shoes. If you don't mind, I'll just finish my show barefooted." And that's the way I finished my show.

Her refreshing candor and unfailing good humor were infectious. In 1962 she became an Opry member, and by mid-decade she was an undisputed star. Loretta's strikingly original material took up for the neglected, abused housewives. "I sang it like the women lived it," she explained. By the late '60s even the mainstream mass media were taking note of her straight-talking, country-feminist style.

[**LORETTA LYNN**] Women are the ones mostly that buy the records. Or they did back ten years ago. The women were buying 'em, but the men were too. I sang to both. I would get hundreds and hundreds of letters, and they would want to talk to me, too, after the shows about how to work out their problems. They had problems just like me. And they would ask me about what they should do about their man. These are the letters I still get today.

[**PAM TILLIS**] Workin' with Loretta was unbelievable. I absorbed Loretta by "osmosis." Every now and then you can hear it in the way I'll say certain words and some of my phrasing.

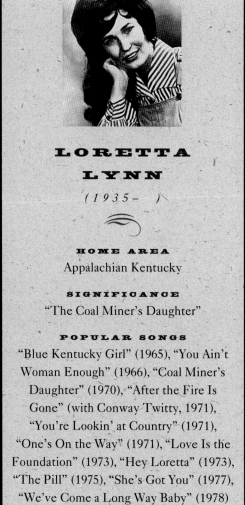

LORETTA LYNN
(1 9 3 5 –)

HOME AREA
Appalachian Kentucky

SIGNIFICANCE
"The Coal Miner's Daughter"

POPULAR SONGS
"Blue Kentucky Girl" (1965), "You Ain't Woman Enough" (1966), "Coal Miner's Daughter" (1970), "After the Fire Is Gone" (with Conway Twitty, 1971), "You're Lookin' at Country" (1971), "One's On the Way" (1971), "Love Is the Foundation" (1973), "Hey Loretta" (1973), "The Pill" (1975), "She's Got You" (1977), "We've Come a Long Way Baby" (1978)

INFLUENCED
Dolly Parton, Emmylou Harris, Crystal Gayle, Peggy Sue, Leona Williams, Pam Tillis, Naomi Judd, Connie Smith, Patty Loveless

HONORS
Country Music Hall of Fame, 1988; Nashville Songwriters Hall of Fame, 1983; eight Country Music Association awards; seven Academy of Country Music awards; ACM Artist of the Decade, 1979; two American Music awards; twenty-five *Music City News* awards; *Music City News* Living Legend award, 1986; Grammy Award, 1971 ("After the Fire Is Gone," with Conway Twitty); seven Gold Record awards; star on Hollywood Walk of Fame

Loretta beams proudly on the occasion of her 1960 breakthrough with "I'm a Honky-Tonk Girl."

I know a lot of the younger audience really isn't aware of Loretta except maybe as a personality. But the woman is so gifted and such an unbelievable vocalist. It may be so "country" for some people that they can't hear past the twang, but if you can just listen to the power and feeling in her voice, she's got an unbelievable instrument.

[**LORETTA LYNN**] Owen Bradley recorded me all my life. He's been a father figure to me; he's been a friend; he's been my producer; Owen Bradley is everything to me.

[**JEANNIE SEELY**] I didn't want to record "One's on the Way." Speaking of Owen Bradley, it was certainly one of the times when Owen was very frustrated with me. He said, "It's a great piece of material; people are going to identify. You need the number-one record." And I'm saying, "It would be a number-one record for Loretta Lynn. I cannot see me singing it." Loretta could identify with it, bless her heart. She has a wonderful family—and probably one day I'm gonna regret that I don't—but in the meantime, I couldn't handle "the screen door's slamming and one's on the way." I chose not to have children, and I could not lie. There again, the honesty. The fans would have known. I think the fans can tell the difference when you're telling the truth.

One of the earliest boosters of country's Fan Fair celebration was Loretta Lynn. And she's still there almost every summer to sign autographs. Attendees carry Fan Fair fans for relief from the southern heat.

▼

Ah, yes, the fans. No other style of music has such a special bond with its audience as country. And few entertainers have forged as intense a relationship with the fans as Loretta Lynn. Loretta's 1964–69 duet partner, Ernest Tubb, was a mentor to her and all the other stars of her generation when it came to fan etiquette.

[**JUSTIN TUBB**] My dad's relationship with his fans was unique. I think it started with the picnic where the fan club would all get together and he would go out and mingle with 'em and talk to 'em and eat dinner with 'em and sing a few songs. He told me, "I owe everything to those people that come to those shows and buy those records."

Loretta Lynn's 1960–95 fan club, headed by the Johnson sisters, Loudilla, Loretta, and Kay, served as the prototype for all other country-music fan organizations. It spawned IFCO, the International Fan Club Organization. Loretta Lynn and the Johnson sisters were early boosters of Nashville's Fan Fair. Begun in 1972 as a joint venture between

the Opry and the CMA, it is the annual "gathering of the tribes" of the country fan clubs.

In addition to concerts, autograph sessions, and fan-club activities, Fan Fair is also the week when the fan-voted Music City News awards are presented. These began in 1967. Loretta Lynn was named the fans' favorite female vocalist that year, and for the next eleven years in a row. She also won in 1980 and collected ten Duo of the Year trophies with Conway Twitty. No other female country artist has been so showered with honors by her audience.

Female stars seem to create legions of devotees. Reba McEntire's fan club is one of the most massive and best organized in the business. Dolly Parton has trunks and trunks full of

▲

Tammy Wynette contributed a stylish, ladylike image to country music.

TAMMY WYNETTE

Wynette Pugh
(1 9 4 2 –)

HOME AREA
Northern Alabama and Mississippi

SIGNIFICANCE
"The First Lady of Country Music"

POPULAR SONGS
"Apartment #9" (1966), "Your Good Girl's Gonna Go Bad" (1967), "D-I-V-O-R-C-E" (1968), "Stand By Your Man" (1968), "Til I Get It Right" (1973), "We're Gonna Hold On" (with George Jones, 1973), "Golden Ring" (with George Jones, 1976), "You and Me" (1976), "Near You" (with George Jones, 1977), "Womanhood" (1978), "Crying in the Rain" (1981), "Silver Threads and Golden Needles" (with Dolly Parton and Loretta Lynn, 1993)

INFLUENCED
Lorrie Morgan, Emmylou Harris, Wynonna Judd, Shelby Lynne

HONORS
Music City News Living Legend, 1991; Country Music Association Female Vocalist of the Year, 1968–70; Academy of Country Music Female Vocalist of the Year, 1969; Grammy Awards in 1967 ("I Don't Wanna Play House") and 1969 ("Stand By Your Man"); Gold Record award, Platinum Record award

fan mail and gifts. Jeanne Pruett invites fan club members to her house each Fan Fair, many of whom have been with her for twenty years. Kitty Wells and Patsy Montana have fan clubs that have remained with them even longer. Patsy Cline, dead more than thirty years, still has a fan club. Throughout Lorrie Morgan's motherhood, widowhood, divorce, hysterectomy, and career roller coaster, her faithful followers have provided solace and support.

The fans know everything about their favorites, even the most intimate details. They suffer and triumph along with their chosen stars. And few have provided as much raw material as Tammy Wynette. Tammy's five divorces, repeated hospitalizations, kidnapping, pill addiction, and rags-to-riches rise have fascinated millions. Her charismatic personality and electrifying voice have endeared her to fans around the world.

[**TAMMY WYNETTE, 1992**] I think they know when you're being really sincere, when you're really honest with them. Onstage and on record, I think it comes through. All my mistakes have been made in public.

I never want to go out there and be a threat to any woman. I had rather they know me, the truthful woman, than for me to be put on a pedestal, where I don't belong. I'd rather they know that I'm just a plain human being. I try to let them know that, "Hey, I'm average."

Raised on a Mississippi cotton farm, Tammy worked as a beautician, receptionist, and barmaid before arriving in Nashville as a divorced mother of three in 1965. She lived with her kids in a trailer, subsisting on bisquits and gravy while pounding on doors on Music Row.

[**TAMMY WYNETTE, 1983**] I left home at seventeen; had two kids when I was twenty. I had three girls by the time I was divorced. I wish my girls could go back to the farm one day and spend a whole day in the field, like we used to have to do. I think it would change every one of 'em's outlook on life.

Fragile? Good Lord, fragile I am not. I've been through an awful lot, but I wouldn't change anything at all. 'Cause I learned a valuable lesson from every mistake I made. You have to learn the hard way.

"Being a woman in this business today is such a privilege because we've come so far, and Tammy is the reason. She's such a superstar in my mind. She's like royalty. I have this big vision of Tammy as this Goddess of country music."

WYNONNA JUDD

Tammy Wynette has often joked that she's not country's best female singer, merely its loudest.

▲

*Dolly Parton was
a starlet from
East Tennessee
when Porter
Wagoner made her
a regular on his
popular TV series
in 1967.*

*The 1967–68 hits "Apartment #9," "I Don't Wanna Play House," and "D-I-V-O-R-C-E"
launched her career. Then, in 1968, Tammy sang "Stand By Your Man," reportedly the
biggest-selling single by a female country star. It became her signature song and the title of her
1979 autobiography and 1982 TV-movie life story.*

*Following her 1975 divorce from superstar George Jones, Tammy developed into a top-
notch showman, rousing audiences with gospel hand-clappers and sharing her diary-in-song in
intimate solo stage spots.*

[**GAIL DAVIES**] I am in awe of Tammy Wynette's voice. When I was a young girl
in Los Angeles and she was on the tube one night singing "Stand By Your Man," I
was singing along. And she just kept modulating until she went out of my range and
into the stratosphere. I was so impressed with the four-octave range.

[**GORDON STOKER**] "Stand By Your Man" was the first big shock we got with her
voice. The first time she went up and caught that bridge in rehearsal, she went up
past that. We thought, "Well, where does it stop?"

Tammy Wynette and Loretta Lynn teamed up with Dolly Parton, the third female country touchstone of the era, to sing trios on the 1993 album Honky Tonk Angels. *Tammy sang lead on the collection's single, "Silver Threads and Golden Needles," but she says that Loretta was the crucial figure on the project.*

[**TAMMY WYNETTE, 1994**] I had to put all the low parts on, 'cause Dolly and Loretta can't sing below me. Loretta put all the tenor parts on. She's got a higher voice than Dolly does. It surprised Steve Buckingham, the producer. She's got some kind of power.

[**LORETTA LYNN**] When me and Dolly and Tammy got together to do our trios, we were together long enough to get our songs picked out, and we had a good time while we were doing that. But then when it got right down to the nitty gritty, I had to go in and record 'cause I was a heading for Branson. Dolly, she was in Hollywood doing something. Tammy was in the hospital. So that separated us. So I went in and sung twenty-two songs five times— didn't hear 'em back—and did the harmony on all the choruses. When I left, I said, "Tell Dolly to take me off wherever she wants me off, and put her harmony on." I just did the best I could do, and I left.

[**DOLLY PARTON, 1987**] I just seem to have good luck working with other women.

In 9 to 5 *with Jane Fonda and Lily Tomlin; on* Trio *with Linda Ronstadt and Emmylou Harris; in* Steel Magnolias *with Julia Roberts, Shirley MacLaine, Sally Field, Olympia Dukakis, and Daryl Hannah, as well as on* Honky Tonk Angels *with Tammy and Loretta, Dolly has proved that statement time and again. Like her two celebrated contemporaries, Dolly is an up-by-her-bootstraps success story of grit and deter- mination. She moved to Nashville in 1964, but her start in show business happened years earlier when she became a ten-year-old child performer in her native Smoky Mountains.*

[**CHET ATKINS**] I first heard of her when she was eleven years old. Grant Turner, who's a great booster of country music, brought me a tape of hers. She had won a Pet Milk sin- gin' contest or somethin', and he played me this record of this little girl with a high voice. I said, "How old is she?" He said, "She's eleven;" and I said, "Well, let her go get an education first."

[**DOLLY PARTON**] My first time on the Grand Ole Opry was a lot different than a lot of people's first time. I had been makin' trips back and forth to Nashville with

One of the celebrated Parton wigs gets a dressing-room comb-out backstage.

▼

my uncle Bill Owens, anytime we could get enough money together for a tank of gas to come from East Tennessee. We'd just bug everybody to death every weekend to try to let me on the Opry. They had told me that I couldn't get on the Opry first of all 'cause I was too young and, second of all, I had to be in the union and, third of all, you had to be a member or you had to have been set up. And I said, "Well, I have to sing. My Daddy's back home listenin' to the radio, and I told him I was gonna sing on the Grand Ole Opry tonight, and I just have to." Finally I went up to Jimmy C. Newman. I said, "You've just got to let me sing. Please, please, please let me sing." So he did. He gave me his second spot on the Opry. And you know who introduced me? Johnny Cash. Now, how great can that be? I went out and I sang, and I knew then that I was gonna be a big star. I just got one encore after another with the only song I had to sing, and that was a George Jones song, "You Gotta Be My Baby." I only had the one, so I just kept singin' it over and over.

That night, after I got all the applause, I really thought that I had made it. I felt so proud that I was really on the Grand Ole Opry. All I could think about was the folks back home hearin' me on the Grand Ole Opry. You couldn't hit me in the butt with a red apple I had it so in the air when we were walkin' down through the parkin' lot. I just turned to my uncle Bill and said, "I'm a star, ain't I?" You gotta remember, I was a little kid. He said, "Well, if you ain't, you're gonna be."

Two years after arriving in Nashville, Dolly landed a recording contract and began making waves as a songwriter. Kitty Wells, Bill Phillips, Skeeter Davis, and Hank Williams Jr. were among the first to record her tunes.

[**HANK WILLIAMS JR.**] That song was "I'm in No Condition" [1967]. They said, "Why would you wanna cut a Dolly Parton song?" And I said, " 'Cause I love

Dolly whoops it up as she takes the reins of her solo career in 1975. "Jolene" (right) was her first number-one hit.

her, that's why." Dolly and I are almost exactly the same age, and, oh, I loved Dolly. Oh God! I had all these dreams about her. I lusted for her.

Me and her were there in the middle '60s when the big thing was the TV shows from Nashville that came on Saturday afternoon: *The Wilburn Brothers Show*, *The Ernest Tubb Show*, *The Flatt and Scruggs Show*, and *The Porter Wagoner Show*, which introduced Dolly to the world.

After joining the Grand Ole Opry in 1969 and apprenticing as Porter Wagoner's "girl singer," Dolly Parton struck out on her own in 1975.
[DOLLY PARTON] From the very time I left the Smoky Mountains, I did have big dreams. I did believe that I could be more than just a singer and a writer. I did want to travel around the world. I didn't wanna just be popular in Tennessee or just popular in Nashville. But even after I was a number-one singer and had number-one records on the radio and was on television, even after I was on Porter's show, I was still makin' very little money. One day, it just dawned on me, "This is the music business, so I have got to think of the business end of it." I took on that attitude in the early '70s of really thinkin' I'm gonna have to be very responsible. I can't depend on anybody else to make my life the way I want it to be. So I headed out to find better management, to find better producers, to find better labels, people that could see what I saw in me. And then to make the decision to cross over to the pop charts, even though people were complainin' about it and sayin' I was makin' a big mistake. I thought, "Hey, this is my life. I'm not leaving country music. I'm takin' it with me wherever I go."
[HOLLY DUNN] She's so far above so many of us. She's so deep, so free. She's a great broad. She's a role model for me and probably for a lot of people.

Dolly was a multimedia phenomenon by 1980. Already widely admired for her beauty and talent, she became almost as celebrated for her business sense. Her empire includes song publishing, real estate, restaurants, a theme park, a cosmetics line, and a movie production company.

During this era, a number of other women rose to power on Music Row. Song publishers Donna Hilley and Celia Froelig, record executive Martha Sharp, trade association heads Jo Walker-Meador

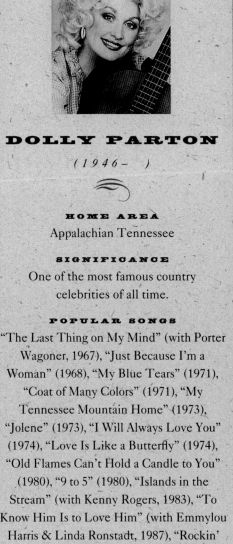

DOLLY PARTON
(1 9 4 6 –)

HOME AREA
Appalachian Tennessee

SIGNIFICANCE
One of the most famous country celebrities of all time.

POPULAR SONGS
"The Last Thing on My Mind" (with Porter Wagoner, 1967), "Just Because I'm a Woman" (1968), "My Blue Tears" (1971), "Coat of Many Colors" (1971), "My Tennessee Mountain Home" (1973), "Jolene" (1973), "I Will Always Love You" (1974), "Love Is Like a Butterfly" (1974), "Old Flames Can't Hold a Candle to You" (1980), "9 to 5" (1980), "Islands in the Stream" (with Kenny Rogers, 1983), "To Know Him Is to Love Him" (with Emmylou Harris & Linda Ronstadt, 1987), "Rockin' Years" (with Ricky Van Shelton, 1991)

INFLUENCED
Pam Tillis, Stella Parton, Holly Dunn, Reba McEntire, Emmylou Harris, Linda Ronstadt, Maria Muldaur, Alison Krauss

HONORS
Nashville Songwriters Hall of Fame, 1986; four Grammy awards; six Country Music Association awards; eight *Music City News* awards; five Academy of Country Music awards; three American Music awards; twelve Gold Record awards; five Platinum; *Ms.* magazine Woman of the Year, 1986; two stars on the Hollywood Walk of Fame

and Maggie Cavender, nightclub owners Tootsie Bess and Amy Kurland, and performance rights executives Frances Preston and Connie Bradley became some of the most influential people, male or female, in the country-music world.

Dolly, Tammy, and Loretta revolutionized country music. But they were not alone. They were part of an emerging army of female country talent of the '60s.

[**LORETTA LYNN**] There were a bunch of us girls that did it, not just one.

[**DOTTIE WEST, 1983**] I guess I've always loved a challenge. I wasn't afraid at all; had no doubts that I couldn't be the top singer. I mean, we were just going for it, that's all. I think I was most influenced by Patsy Cline. But, then, also I traveled a lot with the Carter Family [Maybelle, June, Helen, and Anita], and I really watched Mama Maybelle and those girls. I can remember a cold winter tour that we did together, and I rode right in the car with 'em. She would do all of the driving. She wouldn't allow any of us to drive. She was driving a Cadillac, and there was four of us girls with her. Mama Maybelle was just a really strong person, and she was very dedicated to her career, but she was also a very good mama. I mean, she really took care of those girls. I watched how she handled the business part, the stage, the performance part. I also watched how she handled the travel as far as being a woman. I learned how to be a mother in show business from her.

[**NORMA JEAN**] One of my favorite ladies in the country music business is

Entertainment dynamo Barbara Mandrell had the last successful variety show on network television.

▼

Jeannie Seely. I like what she's doing, getting the women to move ahead and not just stand still and be "pretty little ladies in a pretty little dress." She was instrumental in getting them to let the women emcee the Grand Ole Opry show.

[**JEANNIE SEELY**] Somebody asked me the other day, "Jeannie, are you getting old and set in your ways?" And I said, "No, I'm just getting old. I have always been set in my ways."

[**BILL ANDERSON**] I was at a little place called Frontier Ranch, a country music park, in August of 1963. They asked me, "Would you mind between the matinee performance and the night performance, helping us judge a talent contest?" So between shows I took my seat out in the audience along with a panel of judges to watch this talent. This little girl came on stage, just a tiny, tiny young lady with a guitar that was probably as big or bigger than she was, wearing a little homemade cowgirl outfit.

▲

Country queens
Lynn Anderson,
Dolly Parton,
Loretta Lynn,
Dottie West, and
Tammy Wynette
gather on the Opry
stage for a 1970s
TV special.

It was obviously homemade with fringe and a treble clef on the top of it, a little white outfit. When she opened her mouth, I said, "There is no way that that big voice could be coming out of that little, tiny lady." She was singing an old Jean Shepard song, "I Thought of You," and I had never heard that song sung any better in my life, with all due respect to Jean Shepard. I was just totally blown away.

Instantly, there was nobody that could win that talent contest but Connie Smith. When the contest was over, I went backstage and congratulated her and asked her if she had any desire to come to Nashville. Obviously, I thought this was what she'd want to do. She said, "No, I've got this little baby boy here. I go over to West Virginia sometimes on the weekends and sing on television. I'm a housewife, and I'm pretty happy. I don't think I want to be in the music business." I thought to myself, "What a waste of talent."

In January of '64 she came to see me in Canton, Ohio, at a concert and told me she was thinking it over pretty seriously and she had about decided maybe she did want to come to Nashville and give it a try. I first took her to Owen Bradley, because I was recording for Decca. Owen listened to her tape and said, "Boy, she

The emotional, full-throated gospel singing of Connie Smith is a highlight of any Grand Ole Opry show.

sings great, and I know she's probably going to be a big star, but we really don't have room for Connie Smith at Decca right now. We've got a new girl named Loretta Lynn that we're going to put a lot of our promotion behind." So then we took her to Chet Atkins at RCA, and he fell instantly in love with her and asked me, "We've got all these girl singers. We've got Norma Jean, Skeeter Davis, we've got this one and that one. Where are her songs going to come from?" I said, "I'll write them."

[**MARTINA McBRIDE**] Connie Smith is simply one of the greatest country voices of all time.

[**GAIL DAVIES**] Men may not understand what a woman wants to hear. "Round the Clock Lovin'" [1982], when it came out, the executives at the record label said, "You can't put out a song where a woman's demanding attention and sex from her husband." And I said, "Oh yes you can. That's exactly what women want to hear." They put the song out, and it was the biggest selling record I ever had.

[**NORMA JEAN**] We're still fighting for equality in any kind of business, and especially in the music business. The charts are still male dominated. On the Grand Ole Opry, it's just been within the last few months that they've let a woman emcee a show.

[**WYNONNA JUDD**] If you tell me, "No," that just hacks me off more and makes me wanna try harder. When somebody says, "You can't do that," it's like, "My mom said I could."

[**WAYLON JENNINGS**] When the "new thing" came along in the '90s, and men had to learn how to dance and look like hunks or whatever you call 'em, it took the pressure off the women. The women used to have to be sex symbols in order to get any play at all. Women, nowadays, the song is what they go for first. The men go for: "Will it make a good video?" Then second: "Is it danceable?" Then third: "Is it any good?" I think they got that wrong somewhere. But the women go for the song first.

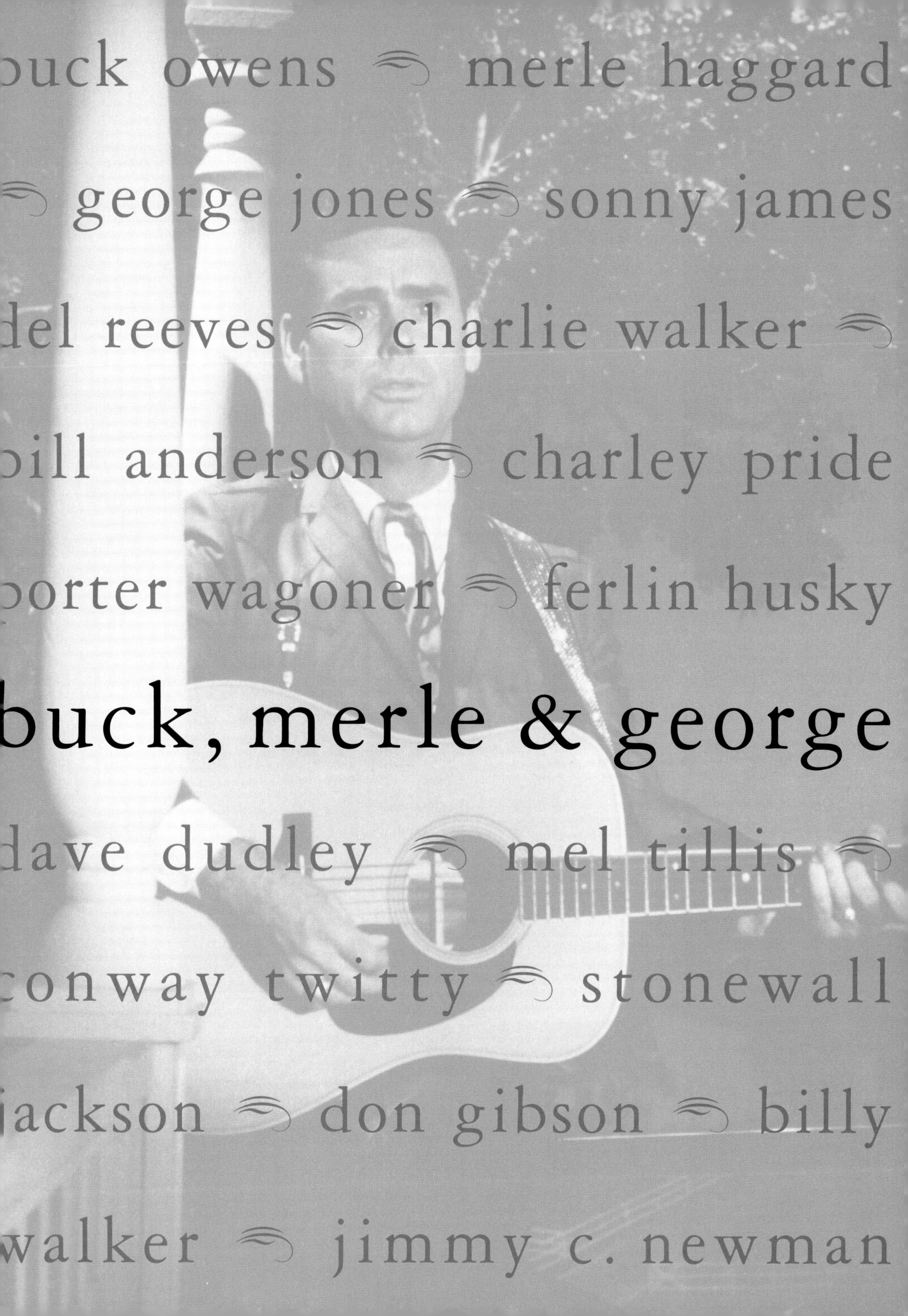

buck owens ☙ merle haggard

☙ george jones ☙ sonny james

del reeves ☙ charlie walker ☙

bill anderson ☙ charley pride

porter wagoner ☙ ferlin husky

buck, merle & george

dave dudley ☙ mel tillis ☙

conway twitty ☙ stonewall

jackson ☙ don gibson ☙ billy

walker ☙ jimmy c. newman

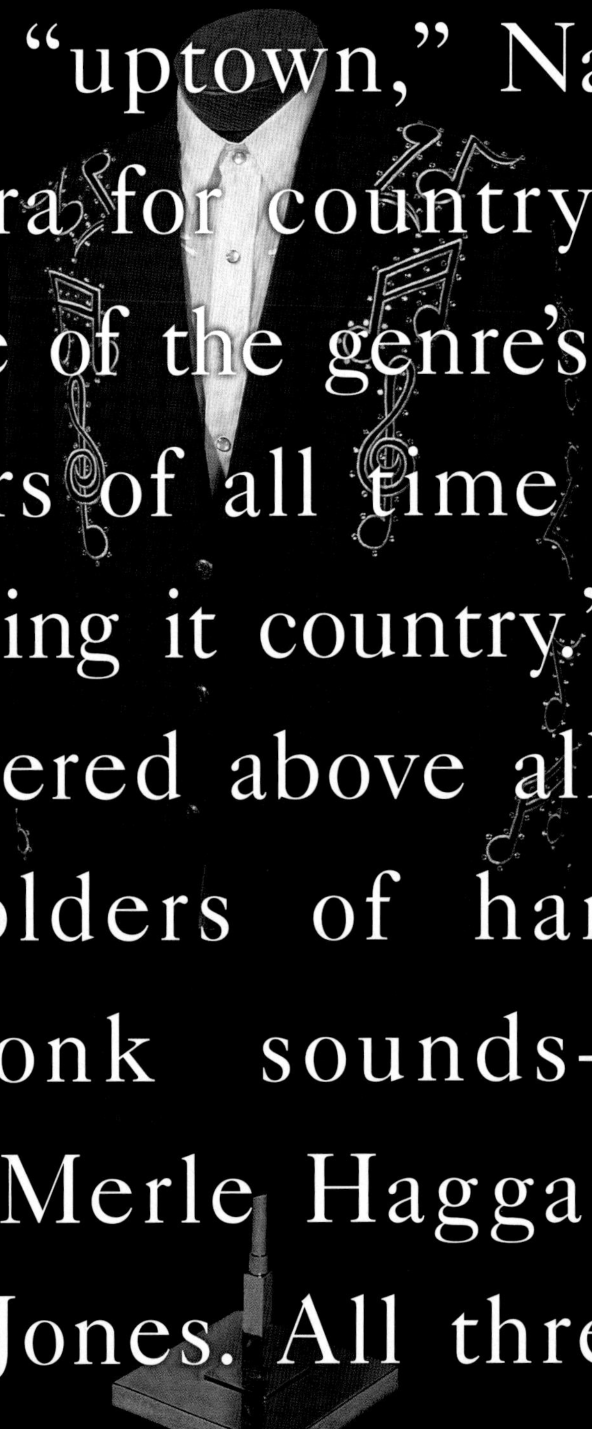

[The '60s are often thought of as an "uptown," Nashville Sound era for country music. But some of the genre's biggest superstars of all time thrived by "keeping it country." Three men towered above all others as upholders of hard-core honky-tonk sounds—Buck Owens, Merle Haggard, and George Jones. All three continue to exert a powerful stylistic influence today. ᔕ]

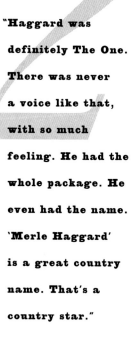

For Buck, hard-hitting honky-tonk came naturally. The son of a Texas sharecropper, he was picking guitar in country bars by age sixteen. He moved to California's San Joaquin Valley in 1951, continuing to work as a sideman for others. But by the late '50s, he was working steadily as a frontman.

———◆———

[**BUCK OWENS**] In Tacoma, Washington—I lived up there for two years—I went to work in a club and to work at a radio station. I remember this fellow; he walked into Channel 11 up there, KTNT, and told 'em he wanted to do a country-western show on Saturday afternoon. The guy says, "I don't have any money, we don't have any budget, but let me see what you got." So we gathered up and went in there. They had a little cable system. This was 1958 or '59.

Thousands of Dust Bowl migrants had settled around Bakersfield, California. This became Buck's headquarters. He made his chart debut with "Second Fiddle" in 1959, then teamed with emerging songwriter Harlan Howard to score such major early '60s hits as "Excuse Me (I Think I've Got a Heartache)," "Above and Beyond," "Under the Influence of Love," "Foolin' Around," and "I've Got a Tiger by the Tail."

Between 1959 and 1975, Buck took nearly fifty songs into the top-ten on the country hit parade. Several have endured as standards, as other singers have discovered their worth.

[**BUCK OWENS**] To have Ray Charles in those days do one of your songs was a financial pleasure. Long before Ray recorded "Crying Time," I was a fan. So to have him make such a huge, monstrous hit out of "Crying Time" in 1966 was sincere pleasure.

Ray Charles also brought Buck's "Together Again" onto the pop charts [1966]. Kenny Rogers and Dottie West did it as a duet in 1984. Emmylou Harris also repopularized "Together Again" [1976], and Buck sang with her on the 1979 tribute tune "Play 'Together Again' Again." Kay Starr revived "Foolin' Around" [1961]. Rodney Crowell brought "Above and Beyond" into the modern era in 1989. Dwight Yoakam teamed with Buck Owens to transform "Streets of Bakersfield" into a 1988 number-one duet. But the most famous reworking of a Buck Owens hit was when the Beatles did "Act Naturally" in 1965.

Buck became a visionary businessman, investing heavily in real estate and radio stations. Always very television-conscious, he starred for eighteen years on Hee Haw, *the most successful syndicated series of all time. He was also apparently the first country star to make music videos.*

Unlike most country stars of the time, Owens was a self-contained performing/recording unit. Then, as now, most country records were backed by an elite core of top-notch session musicians. In stark contrast to the Nashville Sound, Buck took his road musicians into the studio.

"Haggard was definitely The One. There was never a voice like that, with so much feeling. He had the whole package. He even had the name. 'Merle Haggard' is a great country name. That's a country star."

——————

TOBY KEITH

[**BOBBY BARE**] The Bakersfield Sound, in my opinion, was just a bunch of really good studio musicians. There was just a lot of country talent in Bakersfield, because whenever they migrated out there from Oklahoma and Texas and places like that, they landed in Bakersfield and brought all that great music with them. There were just great pickers. People don't realize what a good player Buck Owens is. These guys are really talented.

[**BUCK OWENS**] I never call it "Bakersfield Sound." People would call it "Buck Owens Sound" and "The Bakersfield Sound," then they'd call it "The California Country Sound." I called it the "freight-train" sound a lot of times, because that's what I wanted my music to sound like. That it had that much drive and that much "go" in it.

[**CHRIS HILLMAN**] The country music in California, I firmly believe what makes it a little different is the Hispanic influence. You can hear it in Buck Owens and the Buckaroos when they sing. I think there's always been more "edge" in the country music out of California than Nashville.

Buck Owens (above) poses with his distinctive red, white, and blue guitar in front of TV's famed Hee Haw *cornfield. His Buckaroos band (below) featured such standouts as Don Rich and Tom Brumley.*

You cannot mention Bakersfield or California country without adding the other outstanding name, Merle Haggard. Born in a railroad boxcar to a pair of Dust Bowl migrants, Haggard grew up fast. His father died when he was nine. He ran away from home at fourteen, began performing in bars at age fifteen, married at seventeen, and was sent to prison for burglary at age twenty. California governor Ronald Reagan pardoned Haggard in 1960.

[**JOHNNY PAYCHECK**] Back in my drinkin' days, whenever I wanted to get a beer and sit down and listen to some music, I always listened to Merle. I think Hag's one of the pillars of this industry.

[**BILLY WALKER**] Merle Haggard and I worked some shows out in California together. He came to me after working one night and said, "Billy, I think I might accidentally have a hit." He had out a song called "(My Friends Are Gonna Be) Strangers" [1965], which was his first hit. He was kind of shy and laid back, very withdrawn, until he got out on stage.

[**MERLE HAGGARD**] The workin' people in this country have supported Merle Haggard. I was probably ten number-one songs

into my career before I realized just how much they were really supporters. That's
what "Workin' Man Blues" [1969] was all about.

[**ALAN JACKSON**] The thing I like about Merle is he's, well, he's an American
poet. He's a common person. I think that's his connection with everybody.
Everybody wants to write a song like Merle Haggard.

[**BILLY DEAN**] I was a Merle Haggard fanatic when I was growing up. Haggard
was like Elvis. Had the charisma. He's the one that just really had it all for me. In
fact, one of the few books as a teenager that I ever read all the way through was
Sing Me Back Home, Haggard's autobiography.

In Merle's book, it says he used to hobo, jump on trains to go see Lefty
Frizzell. So I got this big idea that I was gonna go out to California and meet
Merle Haggard. I put together some money, left all my clothes and everything to
my junior college roommate, and went down to where the freight trains were coming through. I snuck on the train, and the train took off. I had this big lump in my
throat: "I'm off to California; I'm going." The freight train went three miles to the

*The Buckaroos
had a driving,
punchy stage sound.
Leader Buck Owens
invested in country
radio stations
like KBUC.*

BUCK OWENS
(1 9 2 9 -)

HOME AREA
born in Texas, raised in Arizona,
settled in California

SIGNIFICANCE
Leader of the Bakersfield Sound. The top
country hit maker of the 1960s.

POPULAR SONGS
"Under Your Spell Again" (1959), "Above
and Beyond" (1959), "Foolin' Around"
(1961), "Loose Talk" (with Rose Maddox,
1961), "Kickin' Our Hearts Around" (1962),
"Act Naturally" (1963), "Love's Gonna
Live Here" (1963), "My Heart Skips a
Beat" (1964), "Together Again" (1964), "I
Don't Care (Just as Long as You Love Me)"
(1964), "I've Got a Tiger By the Tail"
(1965), "Crying Time" (1965), "Waitin' in
Your Welfare Line" (1966), "Tall Dark
Stranger" (1969), "Big in Vegas" (1969), "I
Wouldn't Live in New York City" (1970),
"Rollin' in My Sweet Baby's Arms" (1971),
"On the Cover of the Music City News"
(1974), "Play 'Together Again' Again" (with
Emmylou Harris, 1979), "Streets of
Bakersfield" (with Dwight Yoakam, 1988),
"Act Naturally" (with Ringo Starr, 1989)

INFLUENCED
Dwight Yoakam, Joe Diffie, Emmylou
Harris, Buddy Alan, Rodney Crowell

HONORS
Academy of Country Music Pioneer Award,
1988; star on Hollywood Walk of Fame;
Gold Record (*The Best of Buck Owens*)

other side of the town and unloaded its lumber, and then three miles back to the other side of town. Freight trains don't go across country anymore. I didn't know that. I told Haggard that story when I got a chance to work with him this year, and I'd never seen him laugh so hard.

[**HAL KETCHUM**] He's had fifty-one number-one records. When a lot of us roosters get to thinking we're something after eight or nine top-ten records, we should all look over our shoulders and bow to Mr. Haggard.

[**MERLE HAGGARD**] The bus, the bus, the damned ole bus. The bus is everybody's home that lives on the road. Somebody said the other day, "What are you gonna do with that bus when it's all over?" I said, "Well, I don't know if I'm gonna wait 'til it's all over or not, but I been thinkin' about hirin' one of them big ole helicopters and takin' it up about five thousand feet and droppin' it." But it's been a great thirty-five-year bus ride, so far.

People have no idea, you know. It looks like it would be different than what it is. Sometimes it's one of the most exciting ways to live, and then other times it's the most confining. It's like bein' in jail. It's much like havin' a cell.

By the 1990s, Haggard was a bona fide icon, the idol of an entire generation of country entertainers.

[**JOHN ANDERSON**] He is one of the biggest reasons that I moved to Nashville and am a country singer today.

[**SUZY BOGGUSS**] Buying his records was one of the best things I ever did as far as makin' an investment in a songwriting career.

[**CLINT BLACK**] Merle Haggard started out bein' the person that I was emulating the most with my songs. My earliest recollection of listenin' to country music was listenin' to Merle Haggard, "Okie from Muskogee" [1969].

Clint Black topped the country charts in 1994 with "Untanglin' My Mind," a song he cowrote with the legendary Haggard.

[**MERLE HAGGARD**] A legend is just another name for an old country act.

Uncompromising honesty wasn't exclusively in Bakersfield. Music City kept pace throughout this era by growing its own crop of peerless country stylists. In Nashville, the ultimate honk-tonker remains

◀

Merle Haggard
gave Nashville
a taste of his
West Coast style
during the Capitol
Records Show at
the Country Music
Week festivities
of 1967.

George Jones. "The Rolls Royce of Country Singers" began his career in the late '50s, achieved stardom in the early '60s, hit his stride as a chart topper in the early '70s, and created his biggest hits during a career revival of the early '80s. Nicknamed "The Possum," Jones has seen it all, from the dingiest barroom of 1955 to the glitziest showroom of 1995.

[**JOHNNY PAYCHECK**] Actually, I formed George's band. He didn't have a band when I went with him. We started out in a '59 Chevy or something. It was just me and him, and we worked a long time that way. Then I quit and went on my own, just ramblin' around the country. When I came back the second time, then I formed the Jones Boys for him. Him, Hank Williams, and Lefty Frizzell, I guess, were the three main influences in my life.

*Country icon Merle
Haggard endured
into the 1980s
on the charts with
hits like "Big City,"
"Natural High," and
"That's the Way
Love Goes," and into
the '90s as a 1994
inductee into the
Country Music Hall
of Fame.*

[**JOHNNY RODRIGUEZ**] When I came up here I only had about four pairs of
pants and three shirts and a guitar. I was livin' out of the trunk of my car, literally,
back in those days. Tammy Wynette used to cook real well back then when her and
George were married, so I used to go over there to eat supper. We were finishin' up
eatin' one time and George said, "I got a Spanish lookin' suit back here that I want
you to try on." Tammy'd been cookin' a lot; he'd gained quite a bit of weight. So we
walked back to the closet; he pulls it out; I tried it on; it fit just right. He said,
"Well, that looks real good on you. Why don't you just go ahead and take this whole
damn closet right here?" He had a ton of these Nudie suits, a bunch of 'em. I've

still got 'em, and there ain't no tellin' what they're worth. I wouldn't part with 'em for nothin'.

[**JO·EL SONNIER**] I got to see George Jones when I was seven years old, right there in Crowley, Louisiana, at the Cajun Club. He sang a song with so much heart and so much feeling. I didn't know where he was taking me, but that's where it all started for me. I was nicknamed after George Jones. I was "The Cajun George Jones."

For twenty-five years, Jones rampaged through the country-music world. His binges on alcohol and drugs became nearly as celebrated as his music. His erratic, unpredictable behavior on the road earned him the unflattering title of "No-Show Jones." Like his idol Hank Williams, George Jones didn't just sing honky-tonk music, he lived it.

Everyone in country music idolizes Jones, and everyone, it seems, cherishes the dream of one day getting to harmonize with him.

[**BRENDA LEE**] In 1984, I did a duet with him called "Hallelujah I Just Love Him So." Of course everybody wants to sing with George, or sing like George, and I got to sing with him.

[**SAMMY KERSHAW**] George is the biggest hero I have in

A young Merle Haggard signs autographs after a concert in the '60s. In later years, he saluted forerunners Bob Wills, Jimmie Rodgers, and Elvis Presley with tribute albums.

MERLE HAGGARD
(1937 –   )

HOME AREA
Northern California

SIGNIFICANCE
"The Hag." One of the most influential singer-songwriters in the history of country music.

POPULAR SONGS
"Sing a Sad Song" (1963), "Strangers" (1965), "Swinging Doors" (1966), "I'm a Lonesome Fugitive" (1966), "Sing Me Back Home" (1967), "Mama Tried" (1968), "Hungry Eyes" (1969), "Workin' Man Blues" (1969), "Okie From Muskogee" (1969), "The Fightin' Side of Me" (1970), "If We Make It Through December" (1973), "Old Man from the Mountain" (1974), "Kentucky Gambler" (1974), "Ramblin' Fever" (1977), "I'm Always on a Mountain When I Fall" (1978), "Rainbow Stew" (1981), "Big City" (1982), "Are the Good Times Really Over" (1982), "Going Where the Lonely Go" (1982), "Pancho & Lefty" (with Willie Nelson, 1983), "Twinkle Twinkle Lucky Star" (1987)

HONORS
Country Music Hall of Fame, 1994; Nashville Songwriters Hall of Fame, 1977; Grammy Award, 1984; twenty-five Academy of Country Music Awards; six Country Music Association Awards; eight Gold Record awards; BMI Songwriter of the Year, 1976

GEORGE JONES

(1931–)

HOME AREA
East Texas

SIGNIFICANCE
Often cited as the greatest
country singer on earth.

POPULAR SONGS
"Why Baby Why" (1955), "Color of the
Blues" (1958), "White Lightning" (1959), "A
Girl I Used to Know" (1962), "The Race Is
On" (1964), "Love Bug" (1965), "Walk
Through This World with Me" (1967), "If My
Heart Had Windows" (1967), "A Good Year
for the Roses" (1970), "The Ceremony" (with
Tammy Wynette, 1972), "A Picture of Me
Without You" (1972), "We're Gonna Hold
On" (with Tammy Wynette, 1973), "Once
You've Had the Best" (1973), "(We're Not)
The Jet Set" (with Tammy Wynette, 1974),
"The Grand Tour" (1974), "We Loved
It Away" (with Tammy Wynette, 1974),
"The Door" (1974), "Golden Ring" (with
Tammy Wynette, 1976), "Bartender's Blues"
(with James Taylor, 1978), "Two Story
House" (with Tammy Wynette), "If Drinkin'
Don't Kill Me" (1981), "Who's Gonna
Fill Their Shoes" (1985), "I'm a One
Woman Man" (1988), "I Don't Need
Your Rockin' Chair" (1992)

HONORS
Country Music Hall of Fame, 1992;
Academy of Country Music Pioneer Award,
1992; *Music City News* Living Legend Award,
1987; Grammy Award, 1980

music. Buddy Cannon and Norro Wilson are my producers, and, of course, they had been knowing ever since I met 'em that I wanted to sing with George Jones, do a duet. It's one of them lifelong dreams. It only took us really about forty-five minutes to cut the song, and if you could have bottled the energy that was in the studio that day, we could have ran the lights in Nashville for a year. I have never felt like that in my life. I mean, my hands are getting wet right now just talking about doing a duet with George Jones [1994's "Never Bit a Bullet Like This"].

[**PATTY LOVELESS**] He could definitely just bring me to my knees every time I'd hear him sing something like "He Stopped Loving Her Today" [1980]. There's no other person that can phrase that way.

[**GEORGE JONES, 1993**] I guess you could call me a die-hard. I love the business and I love the music, and I'm not ready to give it up. You know, a lot of artists my age just hang it up and quit. But I just love it. I would go crazy if I was sitting around.

Buck Owens, Merle Haggard, and George Jones thrived during an era when some of the biggest country stars in history were active.

[**CHET ATKINS**] I guess when a history is written on country music years from now, I'll be remembered 'cause I signed Charley Pride, which was a great civic thing to do in those days. No black country singers around.

[**CHARLEY PRIDE**] A lot of people ask you, "Why do you feel it is so few black country singers?" To me, that would be like asking, "Why do you think there's so few black presidents of the United States of America?" I think it's so obvious to why there happen to be people like myself that ends up the first black in this and the first black in that. That's like asking, "Why is it, Charley, that we had slavery?" asking me to answer for all of our ills.

"Mississippi Cotton Pickin' Delta Town" [1974] was written about my hometown, Sledge, Mississippi, by a guy that grew up there, Harold Dorman. He's passed away now, but he worked for the grocery store where we got our groceries every weekend. If you grew up at the time that I grew up in

"George Jones is the world's greatest country singer. George Jones reaches in and takes your heart out while it's pounding and shows it to you. And is kind enough to give it back."

HAL KETCHUM

George Jones tunes up in solitude backstage in the '60s. He posed with future wife Tammy Wynette on the cover of a 1969 album (far left).

▲

*Charley Pride sings
one of his '60s hits.
Despite his break-
through, country's
sizable African-
American fan base
remains largely
unexploited by
Music Row.*

Mississippi, nine times out of ten, you picked cotton. That's about the ball game there. But I just never believed in sittin' around feelin' sorry for myself. I always worked hard and felt that, yes, there was something else out there.

Pride's first attempt to escape his childhood poverty was as a professional baseball player. During off-season, he worked construction in Montana and sang part-time.

[**CHARLEY PRIDE**] As far as bein' discovered, what you're getting at is meeting the two people that encouraged me to go to Nashville, the late Red Foley and Red Sovine. The night that I met them, I went backstage at a concert in Montana and picked up a guitar and did "Heartaches by the Number," that Ray Price had out as a big hit, and "Lovesick Blues" by the great Hank Williams. They looked at one another and said, "You oughta go to Nashville. You're country." So that's what I did.

Producers Jack Clement, Chet Atkins, Felton Jarvis, and Bob Ferguson brought Pride some of the greatest country songs of the era—1966's "Just Between You and Me," 1967's "Does My Ring Hurt Your Finger," 1968's "The Easy Part's Over," 1970's "Is Anybody Goin' to San Antone," 1971's "Kiss an Angel Good Morning," and the like. By 1984, Pride had thirty-one top-ten blockbusters and was a titan of the industry.

[**CHARLEY PRIDE**] When I first came aboard in country music, if you sold fifty thousand or sixty thousand albums, you were a success. But then I was very fortunate. At one point, they was pressin' three hundred thousand copies of every Charley Pride release.

Thanks to hits like "Homecoming" (1969), "Ballad of Forty Dollars" (1969), "The Year That Clayton Delaney Died" (1971), "Harper Valley PTA" (1967), "Watermelon Wine" (1973), and "A Week in a Country Jail" (1969), Tom T. Hall became known as "The Storyteller," a poet of the common man.

[**TOM T**. **HALL, 1995**] All I know is just don't judge anybody. God made everybody different. Be honest. That's the main thing. Just tell the tale. I am not a judge. I am a witness.

After establishing himself as a Nashville songwriter, Mel Tillis began scoring big hits as a singer with 1966's "Stateside," 1967's "Life Turned Her That Way," and 1968's "Who's Julie." TV appearances that transformed his stuttering into a comedic device, and a string of '70s hits like "Heart Over Mind" (1970), "Memory Maker" (1974), and "Good Woman Blues" (1976), led to country's biggest awards.

[**MEL TILLIS**] Tennessee Ernie said, "And the winner of the CMA's 1976 Entertainer of the Year Award is—and I love him—Mel Tillis!" I was in the audience, and I had a pipe, and I was smokin' it. I didn't expect to win 'cause I was up against Milsap, Dolly, Willie, and Waylon. I said, "There ain't no way for me to win this thing." But I won, and I took the pipe and stuck it in my tux. I got up on stage and, man, it started burnin' up in there. I hurried my acceptance speech.

The era also produced the star who had more number-one hits than anyone in history, Conway Twitty. After his stint as a rockabilly and pop idol, in 1965 Twitty returned to his original love, country music.

[**CONWAY TWITTY, 1982**] They said I was crazy. My management said, "You're going to go from selling hundreds of thousands of records to selling thirty or forty thousand records, going from making thousands of dollars a day to making one hundred to two hundred a day. You're out of your mind."

I was right in the middle of a show that night, in this huge club in Summer's Point, New Jersey, where all the college kids came. And all of a sudden, I just couldn't sing another song. I finished with a song, took my guitar,

Flashy rhinestone suits and aw-shucks sincerity remain the hallmarks of Porter Wagoner's stardom.

▼

set it down, and told the band to finish up the set. I had never done anything like that in my life. I told the band, "We're headin' south, and we ain't comin' back." And, sure enough, in a week or two I was pickin' in them little clubs, makin' one hundred to two hundred dollars, just like they said I would.

Twitty hit the country charts with classic honky-tonk performances such as 1970's "Hello Darlin'" and "Fifteen Years Ago," 1968's "The Image of Me," 1969's "To See My Angel Cry," and 1974's "There's a Honky-Tonk Angel." In the '70s he challenged country's lyric

boundaries by bringing frank sexuality to the fore on such smash successes as "I See the Want-To in Your Eyes," "Linda on My Mind," and "I'd Love to Lay You Down." Conway also waxed passionate in a series of 1971–81 duets with Loretta Lynn. They became the most awarded duo in the history of country music.

[**LORETTA LYNN**] We were over in London, and we were playing at the Palladium. He'd be in one dressing room singing, and I'd be in the other one singing just as loud as I could, trying to drown him out, just for meanness. So him and I got together with some harmony over there. We recorded for the same label. So he said, "Loretta, why don't we record?"

Women loved him. He could hit the stage and give one little twist, throw that hand up in the air, and the women would scream. I loved Conway like a brother, with all my heart. We had a duet thing going where we would get in the studio and try to outsing each other. We sang together better than we did apart.

To many fans, country music will always mean people like Loretta, Dolly, and Tammy, icons like Conway, Charley, George, Merle, and Buck. They defined an era and captured the imagination of the mass media like no other stars since.

[**CHARLEY PRIDE**] Back when I was fortunate enough to win awards, there was some heavy competition. I was in some heavy company. When I came along, the people that I was openin' shows for were all new faces comin' along.

[**MARTINA McBRIDE**] I grew up listening to real traditional country music. I didn't know there was any other kind of music until I got to be a little older. Merle Haggard, Buck Owens, Conway Twitty, and George Jones. That's who I grew up listening to. That's who I associate country music with.

▲

A severe stuttering problem made Mel Tillis initially shy as a stage entertainer. Minnie Pearl urged him to turn it into a comedic device, which turned him into a superstar.

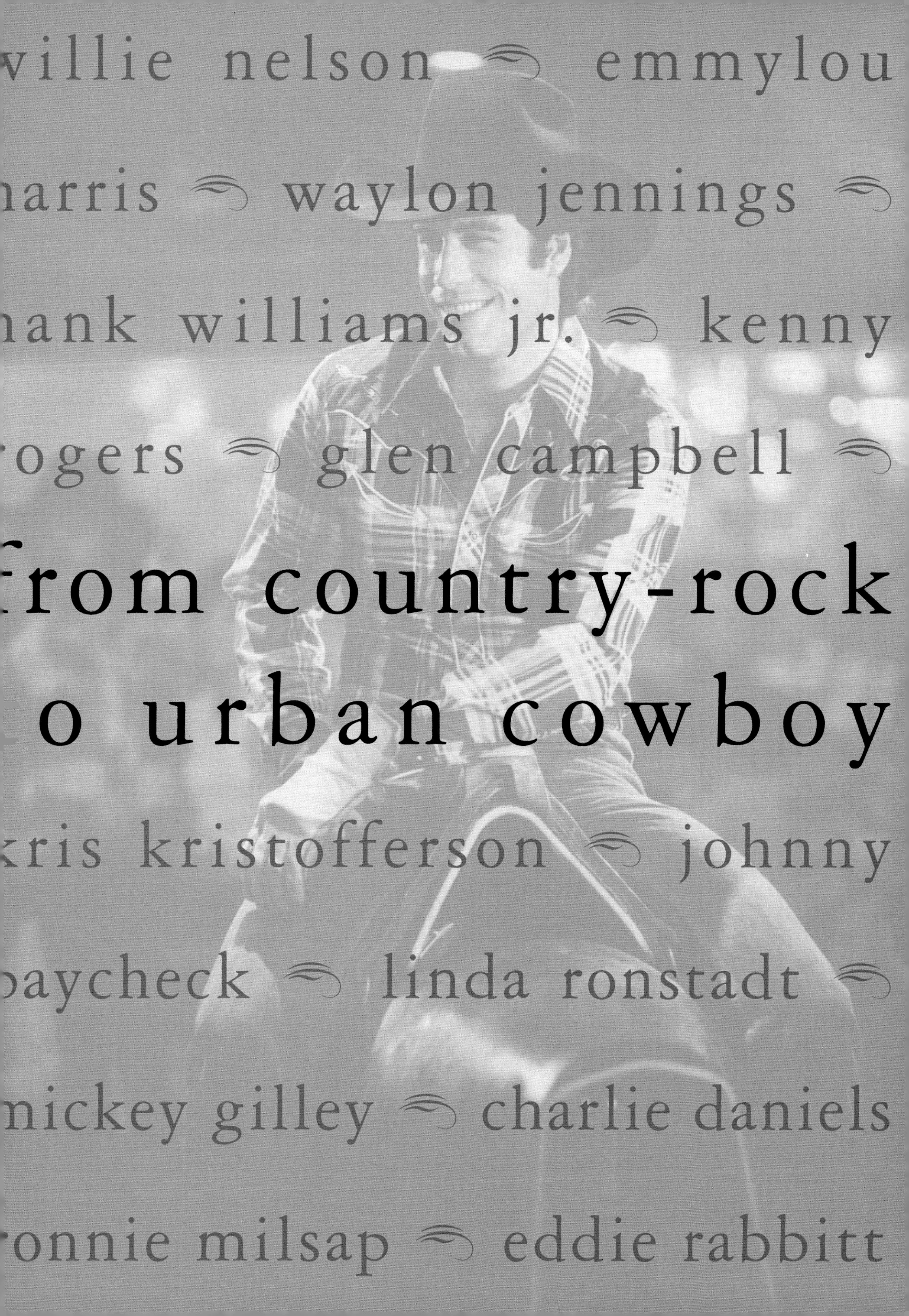

willie nelson ☙ emmylou

harris ☙ waylon jennings ☙

hank williams jr. ☙ kenny

rogers ☙ glen campbell ☙

from country-rock

to urban cowboy

kris kristofferson ☙ johnny

paycheck ☙ linda ronstadt ☙

mickey gilley ☙ charlie daniels

ronnie milsap ☙ eddie rabbitt

During the late '60s and early '70s, pop/rock stars, principally on the West Coast, began embracing country songs and instrumentation. They were among the first to understand that country could be successful with young audiences. They created a fusion style using creamy harmonies, steel guitars, and rock 'n' roll energy. Pundits dubbed it "country-rock."

In the 1970s a series of musical movements swept through the country-music world that brought the genre dramatically increased sales, wider renown, and ever more prominent media exposure. Country-rock stylists from California, pop-crossover sounds on Music Row, a youth movement from Texas, "outlaw" music in Nashville, and feature films from Hollywood all played a part in country's increasing popularity.

◆━◆━◆

[**JOHN McEUEN**] It felt like we could actually effect a change. That's I think the impression that came on me, hearing the Byrds [in 1968–69]. Jackson Browne is tryin' to get a record deal. Linda Ronstadt's hanging out in the clubs, trying to convince people she could sing. Hoyt Axton's smashing his guitars on stage at various times when people weren't listening. Something was happening, and you were in the middle of it.

[**PETER ROWAN**] It's hard to speak for Jerry Garcia, but I will say in connection with this idea of how country became popular among rock musicians, one of the things that brought us together was that we were all really on a quest for the roots of music.

[**CHRIS HILLMAN**] Gram Parsons came from a very wealthy family in Florida and had gone to Harvard briefly, but he got enamored with country music and had really become familiar with the real pure country music of the '50s and early '60s. When I met him, I had found an ally in the stuff I liked. I was in the Byrds, and I had sort of stopped listening to it, but I had this great love for Buck Owens and Merle Haggard. I found this young guy who shared similar musical tastes.

Clarence White, Peter Rowan, John McEuen, Jerry Garcia, and Chris Hillman had all worked in California bluegrass, folk and/or country bands by the mid-'60s. Groups like Shiloh, Nashville West, Hearts and Flowers, the International Submarine Band, Dillard and Clark, and Longbranch Pennywhistle were also part of the emerging country-rock scene. But the figure who was the catalyst was Gram Parsons, and the album that defined the style was Sweetheart of the Rodeo, *made when he, Hillman, and White were all members of the Byrds in 1968.*

[**CHRIS HILLMAN**] *Sweetheart of the Rodeo* was not my favorite album in the Byrds, but it's been listed as one of the great albums of all time, which is beyond me. I guess it was a good door opener.

[**JOHN HARTFORD**] When "Gentle On My Mind" got hot, I used to get called for a lot of sessions just to pick that rolling banjo style. I wound up playing on the Byrds' *Sweetheart of the Rodeo.*

[**EMMYLOU HARRIS**] As far as what was happening with the "country-rock movement," Gram Parsons initially called it "American cosmic music." He didn't

"The *Urban Cowboy* soundtrack introduced people to what country's really all about. All these young acts that are on now, *Urban Cowboy* had somethin' to do with. It opened the doors for a lot of people."

───────

MICKEY GILLEY

EMMYLOU HARRIS

(1947–)

HOME AREA
Virginia, Maryland, and Washington D.C.

SIGNIFICANCE
Leader of the country-rock movement. The single most important performer in making country music "hip" with pop/rock audience. More Grammy Awards than any other country female.

POPULAR SONGS
"If I Could Only Win Your Love" (1975), "The Sweetest Gift" (with Linda Ronstadt, 1976), "One of These Days" (1976), "To Daddy" (1977), "Two More Bottles of Wine" (1978), "Beneath Still Waters" (1980), "That Lovin' You Feelin' Again" (with Roy Orbison, 1980), "If I Needed You" (with Don Williams, 1981), "Born to Run" (1982), "In My Dreams" (1984), "To Know Him Is to Love Him" (with Dolly Parton and Linda Ronstadt, 1987), "Those Memories of You" (with Dolly Parton and Linda Ronstadt, 1987), "We Believe in Happy Endings" (with Earl Thomas Conley, 1988), "Heartbreak Hill" (1989)

HONORS
Six Grammy Awards; ten Gold Records

like the term "country-rock." To him, it implied something that was lesser than the sum of the parts.

[**CHRIS HILLMAN**] It's unfortunate he didn't have the discipline to sustain a career. I think he got seduced by all the trappings, instead of really put his heart in it and work at it. He was good. He was a very important link. Whenever I hear Dwight Yoakam, I see what Gram could have been if he'd-a stuck around.

[**EMMYLOU HARRIS**] The Byrds were doing *Sweetheart of the Rodeo* and then Gram Parsons went on with *The Flying Burrito Brothers* albums; Linda Ronstadt was recording and doing wonderful things. And I didn't know any of these people. I was an outsider. I was a single mother—waiting tables and just trying to make a living—and had pretty much given up on music when Gram Parsons came through town. We met up, and my real education began musically. Gram was a person who forged all those pieces together and gave me the sense of direction that I was lacking.

[**CHRIS HILLMAN**] When I was in the Flying Burrito Brothers, I was working in Washington, D.C. There's a great club that used to be there called the Cellar Door, and we were working there. This is after Gram had left the group. There was a young fellow in the band named Rick Roberts who said, "There's a great girl singer down the street. You gotta go listen to her." So I go down, and there's Emmylou singing, this girl with a guitar doing folk stuff, maybe a Joni Mitchell song. And when she'd start in on an old country song, it was really magical. She came back and sat in with the Burritos that night. I ran into Gram Parsons a few months later. He had come back from living in England. And I was going out of the Burrito Brothers into Manassas with Stephen Stills. Gram wanted to get something going. I said, "There's a girl singer in Washington, D.C., you need to go hear." We were in Virginia; and [he] went up and saw her the next day, as far as I can remember. But it worked. It launched both of them. It got him back on his feet. He made two great albums and her career took off after that.

[**RODNEY CROWELL**] I'd have to rank Emmylou Harris very

Emmylou Harris (left) embraced traditional country yet attracted a sizable audience of "hip" rock 'n' rollers. Her vision came from Gram Parsons, pictured second from right on the Flying Burrito Brothers LP jacket (opposite below).

high in contemporary country music. She's a watershed artist. It had a lot to do with her idealism as an artist. She really loved country music. She loved it with her soul and a fierceness like a mama lion.

[**KATHY MATTEA**] Emmylou was a major historical figure, I think. She had the whole Gram Parsons rock 'n' roll connection. But at the same time, she had this real deep appreciation for the really pure stuff, the roots.

[**JEFF HANNA, OF THE NITTY GRITTY DIRT BAND**] In the late '60s and early '70s in Southern California, there was a kind of "graduating class," a lot of people [who] became real instrumental figures in the beginning of country-rock, people like Jackson Browne, Linda Rondstadt, and the guys that became the Eagles,

▲

The Eagles made the country charts with "Lyin' Eyes" in 1975 but weren't really recognized for their country-rock contribution until a collection of their songs won Album of the Year from the Country Music Association in 1994.

the Flying Burrito Brothers, Poco. The Byrds had just gone through a transformation and done an album called *Sweetheart of the Rodeo*, which was something that we all bought and went, "This is it! This is a great direction for music."

We were a jug band back in '68, right before we started playing country-rock music. We happened upon the song "Mr. Bojangles" when I was returning home from a rehearsal in 1969 in the summer. It was late one night on an FM station, I heard this great song. I pulled the car over to the side of the road and cut it off so I could hear it better, and it just blew me away. The next day I came into rehearsal and started talking about this tune, but I really couldn't remember the title of it. Jimmy Ibbotson said, "I know that song." He ran to the trunk of his Dodge Dart that he had driven from the East Coast the summer before, and pulled up this spare tire. Underneath was this old 45 of "Mr. Bojangles" that somebody had given him. It was so scratchy that when we put it on to get the words off it, we missed some of them. Messed up the lyrics a little bit, but Jerry Jeff Walker, who wrote it, didn't penalize us.

[**JIM MESSINA, OF POCO**] We were rebelling against "acid rock," and we all grew up with country music. So we tried the combination of putting country music, which was our roots, and rock 'n' roll together to try to form something new in Poco. I kind of think of country-rock like a 1965 convertible Mustang. It's out of production, but it's very much in demand. Poco never had a hit record and yet every place we played in America was a full house.

Poco, Rick Nelson's Stone Canyon Band, Firefall, Pure Prairie League, and others took the country-rock sound onto the pop charts of the 1970s. The Eagles and Linda Ronstadt translated their success with the style into superstardom.

[**TRISHA YEARWOOD**] If not for the country-rock movement, I don't know what I would be doing. Because when I heard Linda Ronstadt for the first time, that's when I said, "This is what I wanna do." And it was country to me.

[**SUZY BOGGUSS**] I didn't listen to Linda Ronstadt until after I was aware of Emmylou's stuff. The very first time I heard her voice I was knocked out. I listened to the Eagles a lot. Their music to me was not "country-rock." All I knew is I loved all that beautiful harmony.

[**PATTY LOVELESS**] Linda Ronstadt was a real big influence on the music that I do today. I feel like I'm a mixture of Loretta Lynn, Dolly Parton, Linda Ronstadt, and Ralph Stanley, one of the fathers of bluegrass.

[**JIM MESSINA**] The Eagles is still one of my favorite groups, even though I was a little jealous with their success when we were in Poco. The Eagles is a real success story of what country-rock music finally became. They were able to take the country elements in their music and make it more palatable to mainstream rock music.

[**CLINT BLACK**] The Eagles, to me, are the American Beatles. They had a profound effect on me. They wrote songs that made me think, songs that made me explore my own feelings and what I was goin' through, songs like "Desperado." The Eagles made great music.

[**TRISHA YEARWOOD**] Don Henley's voice is so unique. I grew up listening to the Eagles, so I listened to that voice through some very influential years in my life. I was amazed and shocked when he called me. He knew who I was and had such an interest in my music. When he came in to sing on "Walk Away Joe" and "Hearts in Armor," I had to continue saying, "I can't believe this voice that I grew up listening to is in here singing with

Chet Atkins (left) produced the 1970–71 discs that took protégé Jerry Reed onto the pop charts, "Amos Moses" and "When You're Hot, You're Hot."
▼

my voice." I never got used to it. I was in such awe of his voice. I'm so proud that I have that on tape, that we have a video. I'm so proud to say I did this, very proud of the fact that I got to sing with him.

Although it had little commercial impact on country music of the time, the country-rock movement left a lasting mark on the genre. Emmylou Harris, Chris Hillman, and the Nitty Gritty Dirt Band graduated from it to become major country hit makers of the '70s and '80s. Today, a huge part of the contemporary country sound is derived from country-rock. Carbon copies by other country artists of the Eagles' pop hits won the CMA Album of the Year award in 1994, and an entire generation of stars was introduced to country music thanks to the West Coast experiment.

While the hippie Californians were exploring country-rock, Nashville was in pursuit of "pop-crossover" hits, records that could be equally at home on country or pop charts. The success of the Nashville Sound in the '60s made Music Row hungrier for the big dollars that could be made when a country record made the "crossover" into the pop world.

[LYNN ANDERSON] When we did "Rose Garden" in 1970, I had no idea that it would be anything but a country record. It turned out, of course, it did cross over and became number one on the pop stations.

I've always been a songwriter person. I always listen to songwriters' albums. I got an album from a fellow named Joe South who was a writer. "Don't It Make You Wanna Go Home," "Walk a Mile in My Shoes," and "Games People Play" [of 1969–70] were just tremendous songs in this album. My husband was my producer, and I said I love this "Rose Garden" song. He didn't want me to do "Rose Garden." He said "Rose Garden" was a man's song. He said "No woman would say, 'I could promise you things like big diamond rings.' " Later, we were in the studio all day and ran out of songs. So I brought "Rose Garden," and as soon as we started that song, we couldn't get rid of the band. They called their wives; they went and got six packs and came back and listened. We stayed in the studio till way, way after midnight listening to that.

[**JIM FOGLESONG**] The town was starting to change a little bit. Kris Kristofferson songs were becoming very popular. Ray Price had used a big string section on his "For the Good Times" [1970]. Musically, there were some new people in town. They were bringing in some fresh—not always popular—ideas to country music.

[**GLEN CAMPBELL**] That was me, "Rhinestone Cowboy" [1975]. The part that really hooked me on the song was, "There's been a load of compromisin', on the road to my horizon." I was goin' through marriage problems at that time. And in the next verse it said, "But I'm still gonna be where the light is shining on me." What a signature song to have, you know?

[**ANNE MURRAY**] Glen's kind of an aw-shucks, guy-next-door kinda guy. The thing that attracted me to him in the first place was his wonderful voice. He can sing anything, I believe. And I love a good singer. He heard "Snowbird" [1970] and wanted me on his television show. I became a semi-regular on the show; and it was a great experience for me. It was frightening, but it was great.

[**FREDDY FENDER**] "Before the Next Teardrop Falls" [1975], I don't think I could ever finish talking about what it has done for me. It was written by Vivian Keith and Ben Peters here in Nashville. The tape ended up in Houston with Huey Meaux, who was my manager for many years. He said, "Freddy, I want you to record this song." At that time I was doing a rhythm & blues album there. I said, "No, man, I don't like hillbilly music." He said, "Come on, Freddy, do this song, brother." I said, "Look, I'll do it for you if you let me go back to my rhythm & blues." He said, "Okay, man. Put some Spanish words into the song." So I put in about four lines of Spanish. It took me twenty minutes to record it, and I forgot about it. To this day, the rhythm & blues project that I was doing is still somewhere on the shelf. I won the Best Single of the Year in 1975 with a CMA award.

Glamorous Crystal Gayle had a sound that was worlds apart from sister Loretta Lynn's. She topped the pop charts with the dreamy ballad "Don't It Make My Brown Eyes Blue" in 1977.

▼

[**RICK BLACKBURN**] I came to Nashville in 1974 to be involved with Monument Records. We had some success back then. Monument was to some degree a country label as well as a pop label. We were trying to be all things to all people. When you talk about "crossover," as you think back on it, we almost ruined country music by doing that. And I'm as guilty as anybody. We thought that if we could sign country music artists and make pop-sounding records, we could fool a lot of people into thinking they're really pop. We brought in Crystal Gayle, for example, who was a fine country music singer, but our whole mission was to make pop-sounding records.

[**CRYSTAL GAYLE**] It was so neat to be a part of that time in Nashville, where things were changing. Having a crossover record was wonderful. I was so lucky to have a song that went all the way up the country charts, as well as the pop charts, "Don't It Make My Brown Eyes Blue" [1977]. A song like that, for a country artist, opens so many doors. I had so many letters, and I still do, where they would tell me that my music made them open up to country music.

[**RONNIE MILSAP**] I grew up in western North Carolina in the Smoky Mountains, in bluegrass and country and gospel music. When I was six years old, I was sent to the Governor Morehead School for the Blind in Raleigh, and one of the things that happened there was somewhat of a culture clash. I was thrown from Flatt and Scruggs and Bill Monroe and the Stanley Brothers to Mozart, Bach, and Beethoven. I think the exposure made all the integration of the different types of music into my brand of country music. I went on to play in jazz bands and rock 'n' roll bands, blues groups; and that all makes up my kind of country.

Nineteen seventy-seven was an incredible year for me. I had a record that was what they called a "crossover" record, "It Was Almost Like a Song." That year the CMA awarded me the Male Vocalist of the Year, Album of the Year, and Entertainer of the Year. So it was a "triple crown," and a very high point in my life.

Between 1970 and 1985, dozens of Nashville acts made the leap into the pop top ten. Sammi Smith's "Help Me Make It Through the Night" (1971), Donna Fargo's "Funny Face" (1972), Charlie Rich's "The Most Beautiful Girl" (1974), Jessi Colter's "I'm Not Lisa" (1975), Anne Murray's "You Needed Me" (1978), and the Oak Ridge Boys' "Elvira" (1981) typify the country-to-pop crossover era. Between 1977 and 1983, Kenny Rogers ruled as the crossover king with hits like "Lucille" (1977), "She Believes in Me" (1979), and "Lady" (1980).

The idea was to shed country music's low-class image, to adopt the trappings of mainstream, variety-TV entertainment. This was also the aesthetic behind the presentations at

▲

Memphis resident Charlie Rich was "the Silver Fox" on smoky-voiced ballads of 1973–74 like "Behind Closed Doors," "The Most Beautiful Girl," and "A Very Special Love Song."

"Willie Nelson

may be the most

influential man

of this century

in country music.

That's the way I

think about him.

He's written

some of the most

significant songs.

The borders he's

crossed, the way

he's brought things

together, and his

ability to always

be there when

somebody needs

somethin'. I can't

say enough about

Willie Nelson.

I'm a fan."

MERLE HAGGARD

WILLIE NELSON

(1933–)

~~~

HOME AREA
Abbott, Texas

SIGNIFICANCE
Music Row composing great who reinvented
himself as a country "outlaw."

POPULAR SONGS
"Family Bible" (1960), "Hello Walls"
(1961), "Crazy" (1962), "Night Life" (1963),
"Blue Eyes Crying in the Rain" (1975),
"Good Hearted Woman" (with Waylon
Jennings, 1975), "Mamas Don't Let Your
Babies Grow Up to Be Cowboys" (with
Waylon Jennings, 1978), "Georgia on My
Mind" (1978), "Blue Skies" (1978), "My
Heroes Have Always Been Cowboys"
(1980), "On the Road Again" (1980),
"Always on My Mind" (1982), "To All the
Girls I've Loved Before" (with Julio
Iglesias, 1984), "Seven Spanish Angels"
(with Ray Charles, 1985), "Highwayman"
(with Waylon Jennings, Johnny Cash,
Kris Kristofferson, 1985), "Living in
the Promiseland" (1986)

HONORS
Country Music Hall of Fame, 1993;
Nashville Songwriters Hall of Fame, 1973;
Grammy Living Legend Award, 1989;
Academy of Country Music Pioneer
Award, 1991; five Grammy Awards;
seventeen Gold Records; eleven
Platinum/Multi-Platinum Records

Nashville's musical theme park, Opryland. It, too, developed during this "crossover" era.

[**IRVING WAUGH**] In looking at the Ryman Auditorium, I felt it was run down and getting worse. I felt it would be too costly to try to make the Ryman a fireproof theater. Also, I wanted a theater with better sight lines and larger seating capacity. So I began to think, "How could I talk a conservative insurance company into building a major theater for a radio show that was on twice a week?" A thought occurred to me that a new Opry House could be the centerpiece for a project in Nashville, like the castle was Disney's centerpiece in Anaheim [at Disneyland].

So I did come up with a project that we called Opryland, in which the centerpiece would be a new Grand Ole Opry house; and we would have a theme park and possibly a hotel. The park opened in '72. The Opry House didn't open until '74, and the hotel in 1977.

In the mid-'80s, Music Row decided to bring back the man who had originally done so much to put country tunes on the pop charts, Ray Charles. His duets with George Jones (1984's "We Didn't See a Thing"), Willie Nelson (1985's "Seven Spanish Angels"), and Hank Williams Jr. (1985's "Two Old Cats Like Us") became the biggest country hits of his career. But not everyone in Nashville benefited from the genre-bending country-pop experiments. Many refused to record in the new style or objected to the dilution of traditional country sounds.

[**JEAN SHEPARD**] In the '70s, when country music started drifting away from what I thought it should be, I got an awful lot of flak when I stood up and I said, "Hey, we're losing it. This is not country music." They told me that I was old-fashioned and it was "sour grapes" and everything. I had nothing to be sour about. Country music had been to good to me. But the slicked-up records that they put out, that wasn't Nashville, and that wasn't country music. They were wrong.

By the late 1970s, the hippie country rockers and Nashville's old-guard honky-tonkers were equally vocal in their dislike of "country-politan" sounds. A group of artists became especially rebellious about the status quo. They demanded artistic integrity, courted a younger audience, and reinvented country with stripped-down instrumentation, poetic lyrics, and a punchy backbeat. Music Row dubbed them "outlaws."

[**LACY J. DALTON**] When country music began to change for me in the '70's, it was when I began listening to Willie and Waylon. They called themselves "outlaws" at that time because they weren't doing the slick stuff. They were doing really earthy songs about cowboys, which for a long time hadn't been the thing to do in country. Country was getting more pop sounding. I'd kinda grown away into folk and rock. What brought me back was listening to Willie and Waylon and Kristofferson.

[**JOHNNY PAYCHECK**] I think the outlaw movement came with people who got tired of bein' told how to do things. Back then, there was a certain way you were supposed to dress. There was a certain kind of song you were supposed to sing. The movement came when we said, "We don't care what you say; that's the way we're gonna do it." Because we did that, we became what was known as "outlaws."

[**WILLIE NELSON**] The Berlin Wall fell for the same reason. A lot of people wanted to see that happen. They wanted to see the artist have a little more

▲

Willie Nelson's well-worn guitar bears the names of dozens of pickers and pals. His "Blue Eyes Crying in the Rain" (1975), "Stardust" (1978), and "Always On My Mind" (1982) were major breakthroughs.

control. And the fight still goes on, every time you go to the studio. Sometimes the artist knows what he wants, knows what he's doin', and doesn't get a chance to do it. And I think that's sort of sad.

The change began when Willie Nelson left Nashville in 1971, moved to Texas, let his hair grow, and found a new audience.

[**WILLIE NELSON**] Big G's in Round Rock, Texas, was a highly redneck place back in those days, but there were a few little long-haired cowboys that were comin' in there. Of course, they got the shit kicked out of 'em a couple of times. But they kept comin' back, kept showin' up. I heard about a place called the Armadillo World Headquarters in Austin. They were also hangin' out over there, where they didn't get the shit kicked out of them. They were welcome over there. So I realized that there were young people who wanted to hear not only my music, but a lot of good country music, that weren't being exactly welcomed with open arms in all these beer joints around. So I said, "Well, why don't I go down to the Armadillo and see how they like what I do?" The manager said, "You'll do fine," and was real optimistic about it. And sure enough, there was a whole lot of young people that showed up. There were a few of the cowboys from Big G's who had ventured in there, just because they'd never been around a bunch of the "dope smokin', hippie, goddamn cowboys." Anyway, they came in there, and they mixed around. They looked around and drank a beer together, and they wound up not disliking each other at all. It's not hard to like Hank Williams and Ernest Tubb, and they found out that there was a lot of common ground.

Nelson's Shotgun Willie *and* Phases and Stages *albums of 1973–74 were the earliest indications of the emerging "outlaw" country subculture. Meanwhile in Nashville, Waylon Jennings was developing an ever more rebellious image. Destined to become the new movement's figureheads, the two had met years before.*

[**WILLIE NELSON**] I was in Phoenix doin' a tour in the '60s, and doin' one-nighters. Waylon was at another club over there called J.D.'s—a great job, makin' a lot of money. We'd never met, but he called me, and he said, "Since we're both from Texas, I thought we might have a little in common. Do you wanna get a cup of coffee?" So we went down to the Holiday Inn twenty-four–hour restaurant and started talkin'. He wanted to know what I thought about him leavin' Phoenix and goin' to Nashville. I said, "You've got to be crazy. You've got a good job. Stay with it." Because I was out there travelin' around with a six-piece band all over the world tryin' to make it, and I wasn't makin' as much money as he was right there at J.D.'s. 'Course, we all know that's not the important thing. He wasn't out there where he needed to be. So he naturally didn't pay any attention to me, went right on to town, and did pretty good.

[**WAYLON JENNINGS**] The first time that I noticed there was a difference in the audience, that there was a lot of young people there, was when Willie Nelson called me. He said, "Waylon, you gotta come down here to Texas. I think I've found something. He booked me in the Armadillo Club. I got down there, and I was backstage. Willie and his family were out front. I looked out from the curtain and there's all these long-haired kids. I thought, "Man, what's he got me into this time?" I said, "That's a bunch of kids, Willie! Are you crazy?"

Mac Davis parlayed success on both pop and country charts into TV and movie stardom.

▼

That's the first time I had been before almost an all-teenage audience. And spread from right there, I swear, from that club across the country. We were right at the right place at the right time.

[**RICK BLACKBURN**] Willie would have a series of "picnics." They all took place in Texas, little towns like Dripping Springs that nobody ever heard of except Willie. And about a million people would show up. The industry was amazed.

[**WAYLON JENNINGS**] The name "Outlaw" was kind of attached to me before we ever did the album *Wanted: The Outlaws* [1976] in the so-called "outlaw movement." I did an album called *Ladies Love Outlaws* [in 1972], so when they came up with that idea, I said, "Why don't you call it outlaw music?" Don't say, "outlaws," 'cause I thought it was corny. Besides, there was a rock 'n' roll group called the Outlaws, and I didn't think it was fair to them.

Assembled by RCA's Jerry Bradley, Wanted: The Outlaws *became the first Platinum Record in country music history. It included tunes by Jennings, Nelson, Jessi Colter, and Tompall Glaser.*

Nelson and Jennings were soon followed by others. David Allan Coe, Johnny Paycheck, Kris Kristofferson, and a host of Texas mavericks pushed the outlaw movement to the forefront.

[**LACY J. DALTON**] Kris Kristofferson's songs have changed my life drastically.

[**FARON YOUNG**] Johnny Paycheck came to Nashville with a kid named Darrell McCall. They called theirself Darrell and Donny, the Young Brothers. I hired Johnny for about two years to work for me, but I never could make Johnny behave hisself. He was too wild. He was wilder than me. That's getting on with it, if you can outdo me. So I had to let Johnny go.

[**JOHNNY PAYCHECK**] Billy Sherrill brought me the song "Take This Job and Shove It" [1977] and said, "I think we got us a hit."

[**RAY BENSON**] There was the movement that Michael Murphey, Jerry Jeff Walker, and Willie Nelson called "progressive" country music in Austin in 1973; we used to say we were "regressive" country music. I felt that there was so much that was being lost to the modernization of country music. The Sons of the Pioneers, Jimmy Wakely, Hank Thompson, Merle Travis, these kind of people had been passed over for country-politan. I first moved to Texas upon the urging of Willie Nelson. I said, "Oh? Do you think we could work there?" He said, "Shoot, you could work four nights a week. Come on down." The first six months I lived in Texas, I never left the border except to go to Louisiana once and Oklahoma once.

Kenny Rogers's love songs made him the king of "country-politan" in the '80s.
▼

[**CHARLIE DANIELS**] I didn't identify with the outlaw movement that much. At the time it was going on, the only place you'd find our records was in the rock bins. I used to say I'm not an outlaw, I'm an outcast. Country has liberalized quite a bit since then. Although we would come up with a song once in a while like "The South's Gonna Do It" [1975], or "The Devil Went Down to Georgia" [1979], or "Long Haired Country Boy" [1975], or something that country radio would play, our guitar sounds were a little hairy for 'em. So most of the time our records were in rock.

With one foot in country and one in southern rock, Daniels became a key figure during this era. For many years he united rockers and country fans at an annual Nashville concert marathon called the Volunteer Jam.

The rebellious spirit of the outlaws and the volume of the southern rockers came together in the work of Hank Williams Jr. After imitating his legendary father as a teenager, Hank broke free of the Nashville mold in the late '70s. By 1990 he'd sold more than 20 million

▲

The songs of Kris Kristofferson revolutionized Music Row. They were profoundly literate, explored intimate subject matter with extraordinary insight, and eventually took on a highly political dimension.

"I totally identified with Waylon Jennings. He had irreverence, which is what the youth of America has to express. They call it arrogance. They call it bein' cocky. They call it bein' American. But whatever it is, he brought that back into country music; and thank God he did."

MARK COLLIE

Waylon jennings sold more than 20 million records with his "outlaw" sound.

records, become the voice of TV's Monday Night Football, and developed into one of the most powerful stage performers in the history of country music.

[**MERLE KILGORE**] Hank Williams Jr. wants everyone to stand up and have a party. Whatever has been bothering them all week long, he wants them to get rid of it at his show. He loves it when the audience gets up.

I started with Hank when he was fourteen years old in 1964 as his opening act and emcee of his road show. He would do his father's songs, and he would do a patter that they told him to do. It was really convincing, but he got tired of the same old thing over and over and over. He made the decision that he was going to do what he really wanted to do, and that was rock like Charlie Daniels, Toy Caldwell, the Marshall Tucker Band. Waylon was his big hero, and he wanted to do things like that.

In 1975, he fell off the mountain [in a hiking accident in Montana]; and that slowed him down. I got a job with George Jones at the Possum Hollow Club in Nashville. When he was ready to come back on the road almost two years later, he said, "Okay, brother, we are ready to go." I said, "I can't leave. I'm king of Possum Hollow. They give me free drinks." He said, "Oh no, you're not staying at Possum Hollow. You're going with me."

He took me on the road, and he had a band that I had never heard before. I don't where he got these people. They didn't know one country song 'cause I was opening and all those old country songs I had written they had never heard of. I said, "I don't think it's going to work out with these guys." He said, "Well, you gotta understand what kind of audience I'm reaching."

There was a time when he played "Sweet Home Alabama" when I swear to you he could empty a five thousand-seat auditorium. There'd be three hundred left. He kept right on going. I said, "Doesn't that bother you?" He said, "No, because the word is going to get out; and those that want to hear that kind of music are going to come to see me." It took over a year on the road before we started creating enough crowd to pay the promoter. And then he had "Family Tradition" [1979], and that brought them in. That song told exactly what Hank had in mind. He created his style of music and sold millions and millions of records.

WAYLON JENNINGS

(1937–)

HOME AREA
West Texas

SIGNIFICANCE
Brooding presence and pioneer in producing own records made him leader of Nashville's "outlaw" movement. First country star to earn Platinum Record award and Quadruple Platinum Record award.

POPULAR SONGS
"(That's What You Get) For Lovin' Me" (1966), "Only Daddy That'll Walk the Line" (1968), "Good Hearted Woman" (1972), "I'm a Ramblin' Man" (1974), "Dreaming My Dreams with You" (1975), "Are You Sure Hank Done It This Way" (1975), "Luckenbach, Texas" (1977), "There Ain't No Good Chain Gang" (with Johnny Cash, 1979), "Mamas Don't Let Your Babies Grow Up to Be Cowboys" (with Willie Nelson, 1978), "I've Always Been Crazy" (1978), "Amanda" (1979), "Theme from the Dukes of Hazzard" (1980), "Storms Never Last" (with Jessi Colter, 1981), "Never Could Toe the Mark" (1984), "Highwayman" (with Kris Kristofferson, Johnny Cash, Willie Nelson, 1985), "Will the Wolf Survive" (1986), "Wrong" (1990)

HONORS
Fourteen Gold Records, seven Platinum/Multi-Platinum Records

If you look back, he started the revolution of "young country." He influenced so many of the stars today, like Travis Tritt, Alan Jackson, Clint Black. So many of them have said, "Hank Williams Jr. inspired me to do this song, do this way." Most of them have been in his audience many times as a paying member. When he started with the outlaw music, he broke the mold.

[**HANK WILLIAMS JR**.] If you're enjoyin' the music business, then that's fine. But don't let it own you. Then the bad things happen. No matter which bad thing that is, that's when they start, whether it's early death or not payin' attention to your albums or whatever. When the fun part is gone, then it ain't good. Keep that little edge there. Keep that freshness there. I think that's the important thing.

Country music's boundaries were expanding dramatically. Journalists, scriptwriters, TV producers, and lifestyle observers became fascinated with its culture.

[**SNUFF GARRETT**] Why do I think country music got popular in the '80s? They did some films. The earliest I was proud to be a part of were with Clint Eastwood, *Every Which Way But Loose* [1978] and *Any Which Way You Can* [1980]. I think that Clint Eastwood played a pretty good hand in popularizing country music.

Eddie Rabbitt put a rockabilly tinge on "Drivin' My Life Away" and "I Love a Rainy Night" in 1980.

▼

[**RAY CHARLES**] "Beers to You" was the name of the song that I did with Clint Eastwood for the 1980 movie *Any Which Way You Can*. I'm a great fan of Clint's anyway, so it was a wonderful treat, just havin' fun with a guy that was enjoyin' himself as much as I was enjoyin' myself.

[**RONNIE ROBBINS**] In June of 1982, Marty Robbins got a phone call either from Snuff Garrett or Don Blocker wanting to know what he would charge to sing a title song for a movie. Daddy said, "Who's in the movie?" They said, "Clint Eastwood," and he said, "I'm not gonna charge anything, but I want a part in the movie." 'Cause he was a big fan of Clint Eastwood. I don't know how the powers-that-be made that happen, but he got to play a part of session musician in the scene where Clint gets kinda overcome with tuberculosis. It was called *Honky-Tonk Man*, and it was about a singer in the early '40s who was in the process of dying as his record was becoming a hit on the radio. It was a big thrill for Daddy, because he had always wanted to be a singing cowboy.

On the morning that they were to have the premiere here in Nashville for *Honky-Tonk Man*, I got a call from my mother. She said that Daddy was havin' another heart attack. I got to the hospital about ten-thirty or eleven, and they were just bringin' him in, in the ambulance. He was conscious, and I could tell he was in

a great deal of pain. They decided to have a quadruple bypass, and we didn't know, at that point, what the outcome was gonna be. The premiere was scheduled to be that night. Several people were tellin' me that at the point in the movie where Daddy took Clint Eastwood's place at the session, where Clint was being struck with his illness, they said it seemed like the whole movie got quiet. They said it was just a real eerie feeling.

We felt like, "He's gonna come through this. He's always come through." Unfortunately, it wasn't meant to be that way this time. What was happening to Clint in the movie actually happened to Daddy, more or less.

[**JERRY REED**] I was doing the Glen Campbell TV show in L.A., and I asked our agent, "If you ever hear of a movie somewhere happening, I'd like to read for it 'cause I'd like to do some pictures." He called me and said, "Burt Reynolds is doing *W. W. and the Dixie Dancekings* [1975] in Nashville. Why don't you go over and read?" So I went over and got the part of "Wayne" in the movie. Don Williams was in it, too. We had a wonderful time together. Burt is a sensational dude.

▲

Waylon Jennings rouses a crowd at Farm Aid, the annual music festival staged by his pal Willie Nelson to benefit America's beleaguered agricultural families.

Country titan Hank Williams Jr. has won three Emmy Awards for his rowdy theme for TV's Monday Night Football. *In the late 1980s, he developed country's most thunderous stage show.*

The surprise came next when he asked me to be the heavy in *Gator* [1976]. That was an incredible experience for me, a shock to my central nervous system. And talking about a shock, nobody had any idea *Smokey and the Bandit* [1977] was going to wind up to be the phenomenon that it was. Are you kidding me? We were just down there having fun, wrecking equipment, tearing trucks and cars up, and watching Jackie Gleason.

[**MEL TILLIS**] Burt Reynolds put me in *W. W. and the Dixie Dancekings*. I played a gas station attendant. Then he put me in the *Smokey and the Bandit* movies, in *Cannonball Run* [1981], in all those. And then I did *The Villain* [1979] with Kirk Douglas, Arnold Schwarzenegger, and Ann-Margret. I did one not too long ago with my buddy Roy Clark, which he and I produced ourselves. It was called *Uphill All the Way* [1985]. He played played "Bean," and I played "Booger." I enjoyed that.

[**JO·EL SONNIER**] The biker character that I did in *Mask* [1985] was very interesting for me. It was exciting to be on location with real, true bikers. I couldn't do the "Brando" deal. Just too tough on me. I couldn't ever get the motorcycle to start. I said, "You sure you want me to be a biker?"

Almost all of the country movies made before 1970 were cheaply made "B" movies, secondary features for rural theaters and drive-ins. Now the cinema community began treating country culture with more respect. Glen Campbell starred in True Grit, *and the Nitty Gritty Dirt Band were featured in* Paint Your Wagon, *both in 1969. Tammy Wynette's music was woven into 1970's* Five Easy Pieces; *1971's* Cisco Pike *introduced Kris Kristofferson as a movie star.*

The soundtracks of Deliverance *and* Pat Garrett and Billy the Kid *used country music in 1973.* Payday *(1973),* Nashville *(1975),* Honeysuckle Rose *(1981),* Honky-Tonk Man *(1982),* Songwriter *(1984), and* W.W. and the Dixie Dancekings *(1975) were all about country music, itself.* Ode to Billy Joe *(1976),* Harper Valley P.T.A. *(1978),* Take This Job and Shove It *(1980), and* Middle Age Crazy *(1980) were inspired by country hits.*

Eastwood returned in the rodeo-themed Bronco Billy *(1980).* Hard Country *(1981) introduced Tanya Tucker and Kim Basinger to the screen. The lives of Hank Williams Jr. (1982's* Living Proof*) and Tammy Wynette (1981's* Stand By Your Man*) became successful TV movies, as did Kenny Rogers' 1980–91 series of movies inspired by* The Gambler.

Robert Duvall won an Oscar for his portrayal of a faded country star in 1983's Tender Mercies. *Jessica Lange was Oscar nominated for her 1984 portrait of Patsy Cline in* Sweet Dreams. *Sissy Spacek's role as Loretta Lynn in* Coal Miner's Daughter *(1980)*

Country went to the movies in 1980 when Dolly Parton starred with Jane Fonda, Lily Tomlin, and Dabney Coleman in 9 to 5, *and when Sissy Spacek won an Oscar for portraying Loretta Lynn in* Coal Miner's Daughter.

HANK WILLIAMS JR.

(1949–)

HOME AREA
Nashville

SIGNIFICANCE
"Bocephus," the king of rowdy, rocking, Southern-boogie country.

POPULAR SONGS
"Standing in the Shadows" (1966), "Cajun Baby" (1969), "Pride's Not Hard to Swallow" (1972), "I'll Think of Something" (1974), "Family Tradition" (1979), "Whiskey Bent and Hell Bound" (1979), "Dixie on My Mind" (1981), "A Country Boy Can Survive" (1982), "This Ain't Dallas" (1985), "Country State of Mind" (1986), "Born to Boogie" (1987), "Young Country" (1988), "There's a Tear in My Beer" (with Hank Williams, 1989), "Good Friends, Good Whiskey, Good Lovin'" (1990)

INFLUENCED
Travis Tritt, Confederate Railroad, Clint Black, John Michael Montgomery, Mark Chesnutt, Alan Jackson

HONORS
Country Music Association Entertainer of the Year, 1987–88; Academy of Country Music Entertainer of the Year, 1987–88; Grammy Award, 1989; fifteen BMI Songwriter Awards; three Emmy Awards (sports), 1990–92; seventeen Gold Records; four Platinum/Multi-Platinum Records

---

won filmdom's highest accolade, and Owen Bradley's soundtrack was the first Nashville recording to be Oscar nominated.

The country star who became most active on the big screen was Dolly Parton. Her title tune for 9 to 5 *was Oscar nominated in 1980; and she went on to star in 1982's* The Best Little Whorehouse in Texas *(with Burt Reynolds), 1984's* Rhinestone, *1989's* Steel Magnolias, *and 1992's* Straight Talk.

[**DOLLY PARTON**] Who woulda ever thought that country music would have had this kind of success? I've always wanted it to be accepted, that it would at least be respected and appreciated. Whereas before, people'd say, "Oh, I don't like that old shitkickin' music, that old corn-poney twang, twang, twang. Now people don't look at it like that. Even people that didn't even know what country music was now have their favorites. At least now I know it's been acknowledged, and I'll always be happy to be the goodwill ambassador.

The film that unofficially named the whole era was 1980's Urban Cowboy, *a portrait of Texas dancehall life that centered on Gilley's, the Houston nightclub operated by Mickey Gilley.*

[**BRUCE HINTON**] *Urban Cowboy* did take country music in a mass appeal sense that we had not had before. Also brought a lot of radio stations into the country music format.

[**MICKEY GILLEY**] Actually, the only reason why Gilley's came about was because I threw the towel in as far as my recording career was concerned. I opened Gilley's in 1971 with a gentleman in Pasadena, Texas. If I'd-a ever dreamed that I'd have a hit record, I would have never went in the bar business.

[**ANNE MURRAY**] I think that was a great era for country music. It brought a lot of attention to country music and was the precursor of what's goin' on right now. "Could I Have This Dance" [the love theme from *Urban Cowboy*] is probably the most recognizable song I have—I mean, certainly as recognizable as "You Needed Me" and "Snowbird."

[**EDDIE RABBITT**] I guess we were lucky enough with the mechanical bull, the *Urban Cowboy* movie with John Travolta. Country at that point became very in vogue.

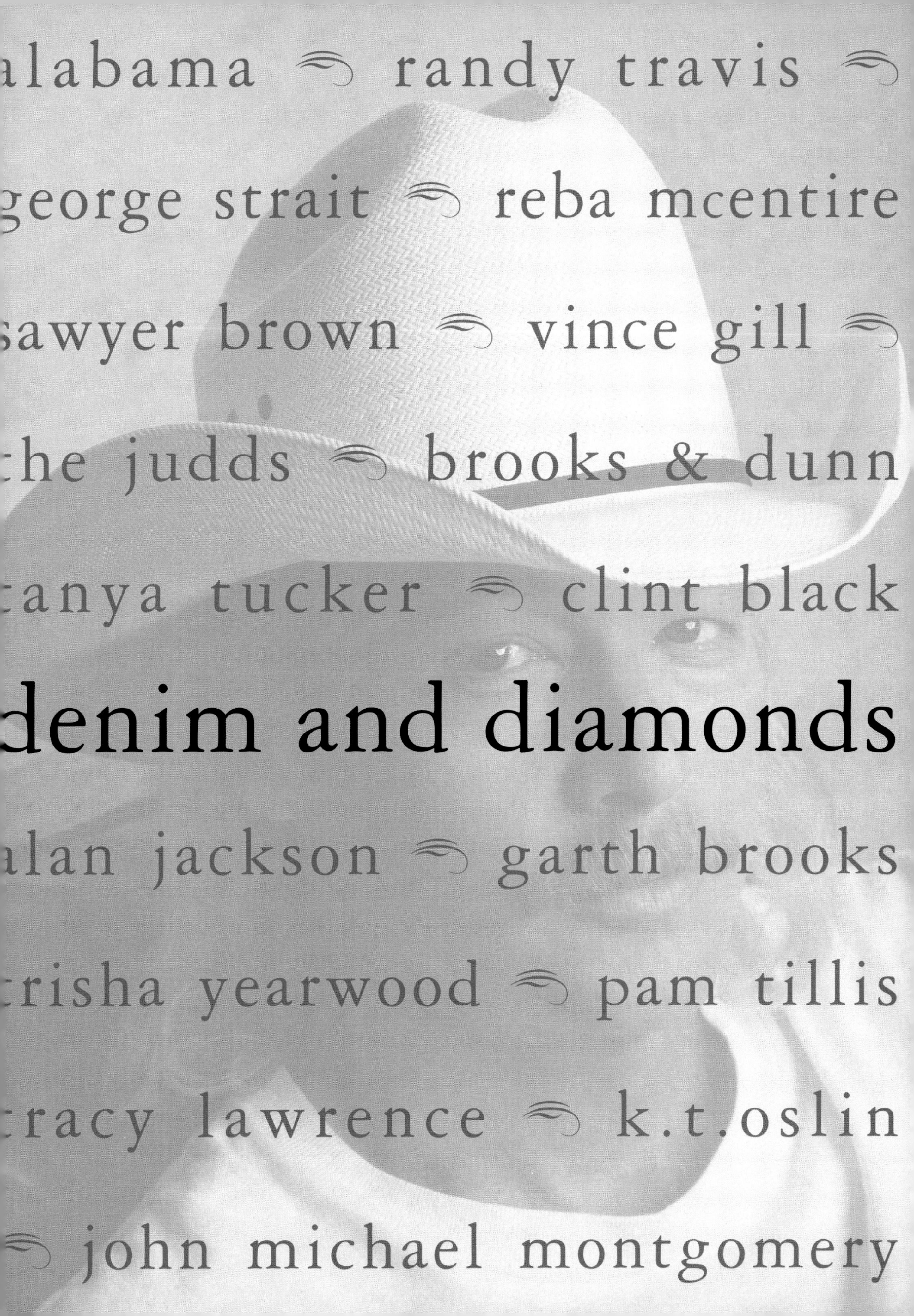

alabama ∾ randy travis

george strait ∾ reba mcentire

sawyer brown ∾ vince gill

the judds ∾ brooks & dunn

tanya tucker ∾ clint black

denim and diamonds

alan jackson ∾ garth brooks

trisha yearwood ∾ pam tillis

tracy lawrence ∾ k.t.oslin

∾ john michael montgomery

In the late 1980s and early 1990s, country music developed a huge new stable of young, attractive superstars. These artists took the style's established traditions and updated them with elements of rock music, showmanship, video images, and youth appeal. For the first time, country outgrew its hayseed image to become music for all America.

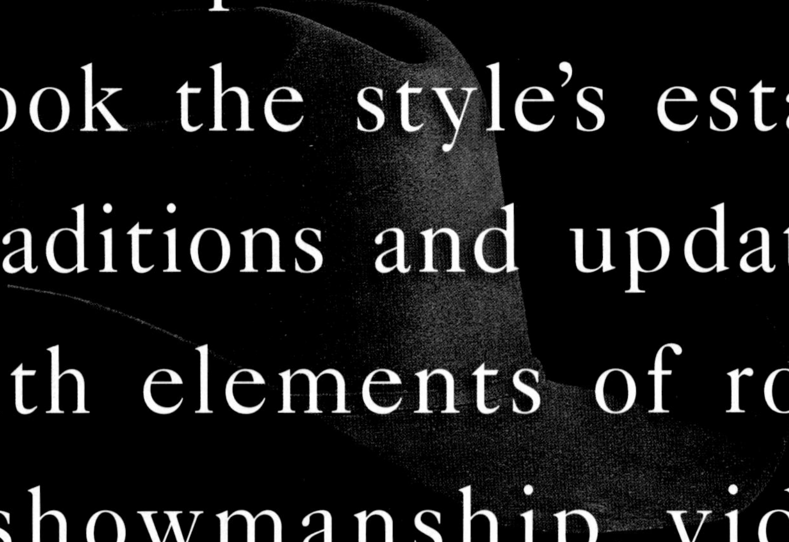

After the "Urban Cowboy" boom ended, country sales dipped. But not for long. This new generation of stars created what was dubbed "new country." More an attitude than a consistent sound, it detonated an explosion of popularity among young people.

The earliest of the "new country" acts to emerge was the biggest-selling band in country-music history, Alabama.

⟷◆⟷

[**RANDY OWEN, OF ALABAMA**] We started working at Myrtle Beach, S.C., at a little bar there on the beach, right on the ocean. One night you'd have three hundred college kids, the next night you'd have some NASCAR race fans there; you'd have mill workers from up in the upper part of South Carolina, or you'd have the coal miners from West Virginia. All these people had different songs that they wanted to hear, so we adapted to changin' from night to night. We had to, we worked on tips.

Alabama's style was laced with country-rock elements. Others were taking the back-to-basics lessons taught by Emmylou Harris and her generation, and applying them in Nashville. At the height of the pop-crossover era, a group of youth-appeal artists emerged who respected country traditions.

[**JOHN ANDERSON**] "Swingin'" [1983] was different from the very first moments when Lionel Delmore and I wrote the song. We didn't really know what was different about it; and we surely didn't know that it would become as successful a record as it ended up being.

[**KIX BROOKS, OF BROOKS & DUNN**] Randy Travis wasn't far behind. He was a guy who just stood there and sang great. But he really brought in a young crowd.

[**ALAN JACKSON**] When I moved to town, Randy Travis had just hit [in 1985], and I thought, "Man, this is it." Randy Travis opened the door for the "new traditionalists," as they call us.

[**RANDY TRAVIS, 1987**] When I first got to town, I was turned down by just about every record label in town.

Travis revolutionized Music Row in the mid-'80s by waving the banner of hard-hitting honky-tonk sounds. He stunned everyone when his sales far surpassed the sea of supper-club stylists then active. He sold more than 17 million albums in six years and collected more than fifty awards. In his wake, record labels scrambled to sign dozens of handsome young "new traditionalist" stylists. In the late '80s and early '90s, Randy Travis and his followers made country the music of young America.

[**RANDY TRAVIS, 1994**] I had my point of view. I didn't want to do anything else than hard-core country music, and I haven't.

[**RICK BLACKBURN**] Around that time when sales were down I signed this kid

"The one thing that me and my contemporaries all have in common is that we were listenin' to all the country greats. That defines us. And there are so many of us. There's young blood out there workin' the road."

CLINT BLACK

ALALABAMA

MEMBERS
Randy Owen (1949–), Teddy Gentry
(1952–), Jeff Cook (1949–),
Mark Herndon (1955–)

HOME AREA
Ft. Payne, Alabama

SIGNIFICANCE
The biggest country band in history;
with 50 million in sales, one of the
ten biggest selling bands in the annals of
popular music. Touched off country
youth explosion in the '80s.

RANDY TRAVIS

Randy Trawick

(1 9 5 9 –)

HOME AREA
Marshville, North Carolina

SIGNIFICANCE
Emerged in mid-1980s to lead the
movement back toward hard-core country.

out of Emmylou Harris's band named Ricky Skaggs, who was so traditional. It was not a popular thing to do at that time, and nobody was amazed more than we were that within ten months, in 1981, the album sold over a million units. We started to getting the message, "Maybe country music is alive and well, and maybe we ought to start cutting country records instead of pop-crossover sounds."

Shortly after that, RCA came out with the Judds, which was also a traditional country sounding record with enormous success.

[**NAOMI JUDD**] When Wynonna and I moved to Nashville in '79, we were really disturbed about country music. It was slick. It was as if they had taken our genuine, authentic, real music and started mass producing it. I honestly think that one of the reasons why the Judds attained whatever success we may have is that we strike a universal chord with people. Wynonna and I began singing together, frankly, because there were times when we couldn't talk to each other. We represented the modern embattled family, with all its defects and its glories. I was a single working mother, and Wynonna was a very rebellious teenager.

The advent of the "new traditionalists" coincided with the birth of the cable TV industry. The MTV music video channel went on the air in August 1981, creating a new breed of rock star. Nineteen months later, Nashville launched two full-time cable networks which dramatically altered the country-music landscape. Television favored younger faces, better images, more showmanship. The record companies responded to the video revolution by marketing a stampede of attractive cowboy-hatted young men, dubbed country's "hot hunks" by the media.

[**RAY BENSON, OF ASLEEP AT THE WHEEL**] George Strait is a matinee idol, a good lookin' guy with a great voice. George is the real thing. He's a singing cowboy.

[**RICK TREVINO**] If there was ever an alien or somebody that came to earth and wanted to know what's country music all about, I would say, "Go see George Strait and the Ace in the Hole Band."

[**BUCK OWENS**] I began to hear about Dwight Yoakam. I heard quite a few of his records, and people would send me things that he'd said in the paper about Buck Owens. He was sayin' things like, "You guys have forgotten about Buck

Owens. Buck Owens *was* country music." One day I'm sittin' in my office, and my secretary comes in and says, "There's a guy here says he's Dwight Yoakam." I said, "Well, is he?" She said, "Well I think so." I said, "Well bring that dude in here!"

Dwight reminds me of an uncurried stallion. He's always plungin' off in all these rebellious, outspoken directions. When I say, "Now, Dwight, don't do that. You don't need to say that," he'd say, "Well I oughta be able to say it. You did things like that."

[**CLINT BLACK**] My father is a huge country-music fan. We sort of butted heads. He said, "Be lookin' for songs," and I said, "I wanna write the songs." He said, "You haven't done enough livin'. You haven't spent enough time in barrooms to write real country songs." I think I was about twenty-four at the time. I went home and

Randy Travis poses atop his palamino, Trigger. Roy Rogers sold him this descendant of his original movie horse. The two appeared together in Randy's 1991 video "Heroes and Friends."

wrote "Nothing's News" [1990]. It's a song on my first album, which was my way of saying that you don't have to stick your hand in the fire to know it'll burn you.

[**JACK GREENE**] I'm always excited to hear a new act. Travis Tritt and the people that's from down around Atlanta and Georgia—these young kids come in with a new enthusiasm and new excitement. Great songs, great voices. And they fear nothing.

Travis Tritt was part of a country invasion from Georgia that occurred in the early '90s. Doug Stone, Confederate Railroad, Stephanie Bentley, Trisha Yearwood, Rhett Akins, John Berry, and Jeff Foxworthy all emerged from the Peachtree State to become hit makers. Biggest of all was Alan Jackson.

[**ALAN JACKSON**] I grew up in Georgia. We weren't starvin' poor or anything, but we weren't that well off. We grew up more backwards than we did poor. We were like the Waltons. When I moved to Nashville in 1985 I didn't know anybody. I didn't even know what producers did or what publishers were. Didn't have a clue. My wife had just started flyin' with airlines, and she saw Glen Campbell and his band waitin' for a flight in Atlanta. We'd never been around any stars or anything. So she just went up and introduced herself and told him that we were thinkin' about movin' to Nashville and if he had any advice. I didn't even have a tape. He was real nice and gave her a business card, Marty Gamblin's. He runs his publishin' in town. So I came to Nashville, and that's the first place I went. Knocked on his door. Marty said, "Well, I don't know what to tell you to do. You're here." He said I oughta get a job and start writin', singin' demos, and that kind of stuff. And that's what I did.

In Nashville, the most widely beloved of the "hot hunks" is Vince Gill. A dazzling instrumentalist, gifted songwriter, and brilliant tenor singer, Gill is also renowned for his tireless charity work.

[**VINCE GILL**, **1990**] I'm just a human being. I write. I sing songs. I don't put on

Mark Miller (right) led Sawyer Brown to enduring popularity as a country band. The Judds (below) became the most honored female act of the '80s, thanks to Naomi's vision. Daughter Wynonna (at right) became a '90s solo superstar.

any pretensions. As you see me now, that's the way I'll be ten years from now, and the way I was ten years ago.

At my second Fan Fair, in 1985, this girl came up to me and said, "I just think you're the greatest singer in the world. Someday I'm gonna record. I'm coming to town, and that's what I want to do." And it was Patty Loveless. So there's a real special kinship between the two of us.

[**PATTY LOVELESS**] To sing with Vince Gill was a dream come true for me. The first time I met him, he came in to sing on my first single, and I just almost fell to the floor.

Vince is an Oklahoman, one of dozens who have revitalized modern country music. Others include Joe Diffie, Wade Hayes, Brian White, Reba McEntire, Toby Keith, the Tractors, and Ronnie Dunn. So is the man who transcended country to become the biggest music artist of his era, Garth Brooks.

[**MICKEY GILLEY**] Garth Brooks has taken country and rock 'n' roll, like Elvis did, and intertwined it all together and made something really, really big out of it.

[**GARTH BROOKS**, 1995] People say, "What do you think is going on right now?"

▲

Kix Brooks (left) and Ronnie Dunn turn a concert into a country party with their rollicking Saturday-night sound. The duo helped kick off the country dance craze with "Boot Scootin' Boogie" in 1992.

"Garth taught me just by watching him. I watch him with people. He is the biggest star in country music, yet he never makes you feel that way. He is always kind with people. He takes time for the people that got him where he was."

TRISHA YEARWOOD

In 1996, Garth Brooks became the biggest-selling male star in the history of popular music.

The answer is, "There is no way to say." It's not fair. Only twenty years from now can you look back and say, "Was Garth Brooks good for country music or not?" Was John Travolta and the "Urban Cowboy" era good for country music?

Garth, Vince, and Alan detonated a '90s explosion of talent. They made headlines for selling records in the multiple millions in the early '90s. By mid-decade, this was commonplace for

acts like Tim McGraw, Brooks & Dunn, Billy Ray Cyrus, Clay Walker, and John Michael Montgomery. Between 1989 and 1991, the country-music business doubled, from $500 million annually to a billion. In the two years following, it nearly doubled again. By the dawn of 1996, two-thirds of the albums on the country charts had been declared Gold, Platinum, or multi-Platinum for their sales accomplishments. What's more, over a quarter of the top-two hundred albums on the pop charts were country products. Many observers believe that the genre's mass acceptance is due to its changing sound, a hybrid of past rock elements.*

[**GAIL DAVIES**] In the '70s, you started having this generation who grew up with the Beatles and Bob Dylan, like myself, but whose parents listened to country music. And this merge happened. And in the generation behind us, they don't see a barrier between buying a Garth Brooks album and buying a ZZ Top or a Nirvana.

Pop and rock became less and less dance oriented. In the mid-'90s, country capitalized on this neglect by creating new dance steps, making danceable ditties, and promoting dance clubs nationwide. A craze erupted.

[**JUSTIN TUBB**] As they used to say on the Dick Clark show, "It's got a good beat, and you can dance to it." They've invented dances to go along with the music now, and people are having fun doing it. It's party music.

[**DON VON TRESS**] Billy Ray Cyrus had the one little move that he did to "Achy Breaky Heart," the one little thing that kind of ended up in the line dance. The label was talking about marketing and thought, "Well, shoot, let's do a dance," and the whole thing just kind of took off. They marketed an instructional video of the dance and the video of "Achy Breaky Heart" to hundreds of dance clubs around the United States in 1992. It was a brilliant move on their part. The rest is history, I guess.

[**RONNIE DUNN, OF BROOKS & DUNN**] They didn't wanna release "Boot Scootin' Boogie" [1992] because, "People in the North aren't gonna know what boot scootin' means." And we go shootin' up there on some tour and, bingo, they're havin' boot scootin' contests in all the clubs.

▲

Tracy Lawrence (top) and Travis Tritt are among stylists labeled "new country" because of their

GARTH BROOKS

(1 9 6 3 –   )

HOME AREA
Yukon, Oklahoma

SIGNIFICANCE
The biggest-selling country act of the modern era. Brought new dynamism to country concerts.

GEORGE STRAIT

(1 9 5 2 –   )

HOME AREA
San Marcos, Texas

SIGNIFICANCE
Father figure to an entire generation of Texas/Oklahoma cowboy-hatted stylists. Generated "hot hunk" appeal of country male stars, making looks as important as sound.

Unlike their rock and pop counterparts, country stars tour constantly. In the '90s, dynamic, rock-inspired showmanship was added to country concerts. Videos, the dance phenomenon, increased showmanship, enormous profitability, and youth appeal have made country something it never was before. Long sneered at as the music of rednecks, the genre now has a dramatically different image.

[**NORMA JEAN**] I don't believe there's a soul in the world that doesn't know about country music today. I'm happy that now it's all-American music. When I started out, there were very few people that liked country music. Then, it was hard to be in it. People would ask me what I sang, and I told 'em, "country music," and I was a little bit ashamed to say it. I wasn't ashamed of my music, but I was ashamed to say it. And now it's worldwide, and I'm so proud, proud of everybody in country music.

[**BUCK OWENS**] It reminds me so much of the rock of the '50s and the early '60s. It seems like the first thing they say

If country has ever produced the female equivalent of Elvis Presley, it's smoky-voiced Tonya Tucker, a free spirited good ol' girl with a yen to rock.

is, "Well, how tall is he?" "He's five-foot-eleven." "That's pretty good. How much does he weigh?" "Well, he weighs 145." "That's good; he's slim, then. How's he look in jeans?" "Well, he looks okay in jeans." "Does he wear a hat?" "Yeah, he'll wear a hat if we want him to." And the last thing they ask, "Oh, by the way, can he sing?" I think that's happening.

[**FARON YOUNG**] I think today's singers are so much alike. They're too homogenized. It's hard to tell one from the other one.

Although many older artists complain about being shoved aside, their opportunities are also greater than ever. Branson, Missouri, has become a country-music tourism mecca by showcasing the mature artists in its many theaters. But whether in Branson, Nashville, or Dallas, the focus of country remains on its fans. The culture has historically valued close fan interaction, making its stars more accessible to the public on the road.

[**MIKE McGUIRE, OF SHENANDOAH**] In rock 'n' roll music, they never get close to their fans. Country-music fans and country-music artists have a kinship,

▲

Tender of heart, full of fun, and blessed with talent, Vince Gill is Nashville's picker/ singer/songwriter supreme. His moving composition "Go Rest High on That Mountain" has become a eulogy at funerals nationwide.

somehow. Country-music fans always hang out by the bus, and they're always bringing food. They'll bring cookies, they'll bring cakes, they treat you like you're their next-door neighbor or a first cousin or somethin'. They feel like they know us.

At the beginning of the "hot hunk" era, female stars lost a lot of ground. But by the mid-'90s, many became country's most challenging and artistic performers. At a time when men were increasingly homogenized, Mary Chapin Carpenter, Alison Krauss, Shania Twain, Lorrie Morgan, Faith Hill, Pam Tillis, and others forged powerful new songs and images.

The most successful of all the women was unquestionably Reba McEntire. With top-grossing tours and skyrocketing record sales, she went head-to-head with almost any male in her field.

[**REBA McENTIRE, 1989**] I'm very competitive, very ambitious. The thing that helped me so much in the music business is that I'd competed with men as a rodeo cowgirl. It got me ready.

[**SHELBY LYNNE**] Reba McEntire sums up everything that country music is about, as far as females go. She has it all. She's got the show. She's got the songs. She's got the hair. She's got everything.

[**REBA McENTIRE, 1989**] I know what it's like when you dream about a star and you idolize them and all this. You dream that they're perfect. But she's just a human, just an old, everyday person. Only she was blessed with a God-given talent. I try to let fans know all the time, "Hey, I'm not perfect."

[**BRUCE HINTON**] Reba McEntire's relationship with her audience is unlike anything I've ever seen in all of my years in music. She might not get home until four A.M. the next morning, but she will see every last person in the Municipal Auditorium that wants to see her.

The most enduring of all the female stars is Tanya Tucker. Her first top-ten hit was in 1972, and she is the only woman from the '70s who was still in the top-ten in the mid-'90s.

[**TANYA TUCKER, 1983**] I've had to do basically everything myself. I've had to sort of "fake it" and feel my way through the business. I'm a fun-loving girl, a Texas girl, a "good ole girl." But if I had done half the things that people say I do, I'd be dead.

[**PATSY MONTANA**] I worked with Tanya Tucker not long ago, and she invited me on her bus to see it. Whoo, was it like a big powder puff! All the lace, mirrors, and stuff. I just started laughin'. We used to ride with the four boys, myself, and a big bass fiddle in the car. But, you know, you can't miss nothin' you never had. A bus? We didn't make that kind of money.

Perhaps now more than ever, country music has captured the imaginations of musicians everywhere. As we roll toward the twenty-first century, they are still coming to Music City. Guitars in their hands, hope in their hearts and dreams in their heads.

[**MARK COLLIE**] We all come to try and make money outta nothin,' out of imagination—Garth Brooks, Aaron Tippin, Billy Dean, Alan Jackson,

ALAN JACKSON
(1958 –)

HOME AREA
Newnan, Georgia

SIGNIFICANCE
Champion of hard-core honky-tonk. Most prominent of the so-called "hat acts" of the '90s.

VINCE GILL
(1957 –)

HOME AREA
Norman, Oklahoma

SIGNIFICANCE
"Sweet Pea." The most beloved country star of his generation.

REBA McENTIRE

(1955-   )

HOME AREA
Chockie, Oklahoma

SIGNIFICANCE
Biggest country female act of 1990s.

TANYA TUCKER

(1958-   )

HOME AREA
Seminole, Texas/Phoenix, Arizona

SIGNIFICANCE
"The Texas Tornado." Brought sexuality
to female country.

and I, payin' our dues. There is a camaraderie, a support group. Everybody pulls for everybody to score, because if one guy scores, it keeps the dream alive. One day he's waitin' tables at Mac's and then, six months, he's got the number-one record on the charts.

[**TRACY LAWRENCE**] What's coming out is "young country." And it's hot, it's hip, and it's happening. It's fresh and it's exciting. It's cool now to ride around on a Saturday night with country music cranked up in your pickup truck.

[**DAN SEALS**] Country music is still one of the few places where you can find genuine lyrics, lyrics that tell a story, lyrics that move you. I look at some of the other musics, and I don't see that. It's the last place to go for great lyrics. That's probably one of the reasons that so many people love country today.

Pam Tillis toiled for years as a studio singer in Nashville before breaking through as as star in 1991. "I love this town!" she exclaimed when she was named Female Vocalist of the Year in 1994.

yesterday and tomorrow

———————◆———————

[**ALAN JACKSON**] What is country music? Country music is America's common-man poetry.

[**JUSTIN TUBB**] It's Americana. It's the music of the working man, the farmer, the trucker, the factory worker.

[**DOLLY PARTON**] I think that what makes country music so popular is the same thing that we loved about cowboy movies, western movies. It's like the natural heroes of the earth. There's just somethin' about the dirt, somethin' about horses, somethin' about the land, somethin' about honesty, somethin' about the music.

[**MARTY STUART**] Country music to me is a very spiritual thing, a callin' from heaven. It's a gift from God that He allows me to play country music.

[**EDDIE STONEMAN**] Without music, you wouldn't have nothin' to look forward to.

[**FRANCES PRESTON**] Country music writers wear their souls on their sleeves. It's the music of everyday life, hard times and good times. They tell it all.

[**MERLE HAGGARD**] I'm a little worried about country music. I don't hear enough emotion. I hear a lot of people in tune, and I hear a lot a perfect records, but I don't hear a lot of emotion. I wish we could get a little more emotion back in it.

But I'm a great nostalgist. That's kind of my department, tendin' to the roots of country music. And I'm doin' everything I can to preserve what I know.

[**BROTHER OSWALD**] I don't call this country music what they're doin' today. They call it that; but I don't.

[**GRACE STONEMAN**] There's very few of 'em that really play country music anymore.

[**ALAN JACKSON**] "Hello Darlin'" came on the radio, Conway Twitty. And me and this guy were goin', "Man, we love that song." This radio guy looked at me and said, "What song is that? I don't think I've ever heard that." And I almost fell out of my chair. There's a lot of the people that are runnin' record labels and programmin' radio stations and producin' records who didn't really listen to country music much.

[**STEVE WARINER**] One thing I hope a lot of young artists always remember is the roots and the heritage of country music, where it all began and the pioneers that paved the way for all of us.

[**EMMYLOU HARRIS**] We can't know where we're going until we know where we've been. And the music of the past is not just to study and put in a museum. The way to study it is to put it on the damn stereo and turn it up as loud as you can.

[**JEAN SHEPARD**] Friends, give me Lefty Frizzell and Bob Wills and Hank Thompson and Hank Snow and Ernest Tubb and Kitty Wells. Man, I can live on it. I just want to be remembered as a good ole country gal that sang a good ole country song.

[**JIMMY DICKENS**] Country music is bigger today than it's ever been in history. It's the metropolitan people who listen to country music now. I can remember back to where we were singing and entertaining basically the rural people. Today, we're entertainin' everybody all over the world.

[**JOHNNY CASH**] If the young people that are comin' into country music don't know a little about their tradition in the music they love, they really are missin' their inheritance. I love to hear the new stuff, but I love to hear some of the old stuff too, like Gene Autry and the Carter Family. I was talkin' to Gene Autry not long ago in California, and we were reminiscing about the old songs. So Willie and Kristofferson and Waylon and I and June were sittin' around, singin' old songs from Gene Autry's days. It was one of the greatest times in our lives, and it would be wonderful if country fans could do that today, sit around and swap those old songs.

[**MARTY STUART**] There will never be another time in country music like there is on this side of the twenty-first century, where you can still go and see Bill Monroe tonight and go see Garth Brooks and Dwight Yoakam or me or Travis Tritt tomorrow night. It's a precious time.

[**WANDA JACKSON**] I'm so very proud of our new generation of country music singers and performers and pickers. I tell the whole world, "Country music is in good hands. Don't you worry about it."

[**JACK GREENE**] They're still singing about life. They're still singing about love, tragedy, loss and gain, happiness and sadness. That's what country music is. It's stories of life put to music.

[**ROY ACUFF**] I think we're in business: We're selling a product, we're selling country music, we're selling our way of life. We're trying to let people know that we love 'em and want them to come to visit us. If the boys and girls stop doing that, we'll go down the creek.

[**CHARLIE DANIELS**] It's train whistles and church bells and babies crying, broken marriages and fulfilled dreams, love affairs that go right and go wrong; eighteen-wheelers, some guy riding on a tractor out in the middle of Kansas, some cowboy out in the middle of nowhere on his horse chasing some old cow. That's what country music is to me.

[**HAL KETCHUM**] Country music is simply three chords and the truth.

ARCHIVE PHOTOS: pp. 9, 12 (bottom), 13 (bottom), 16, 18 (left), 23, 27, 28, 30 (top, bottom), 31, 34, 36 (top), 37, 40, 44 (bottom right), 55, 66 (top), 71, 96 (top), 108, 110 (bottom), 111, 113 (bottom), 114, 118 (bottom), 123 (bottom), 124, 131, 146, 148, 149 (top, bottom), 150 (bottom), 190, 201, 206 (top), 208, 218, 222, 232 (top left).

AUTRY MUSEUM OF WESTERN HERITAGE, LOS ANGELES: p. 61 (top, bottom).

BROWN BROTHERS: pp. 35, 67.

CORBIS-BETTMANN: pp. 32, 52, 62 (top), 105, 106, 112 (top), 121, 129, 133, 135, 169, 206 (bottom).

COUNTRY MUSIC FOUNDATION, INC.: pp. 13 (top), 15, 17, 18–19, 20 (top, bottom), 21, 22, 25, 26, 33, 38 (right), 44 (top), 45 (top), 47 (bottom), 50 (top), 54, 63 (top), 68 (bottom), 69 (top), 75 (top), 76 (top), 77 (top), 78 (left, right), 79, 83, 85 (bottom), 86 (bottom), 87, 88 (top), 90 (top, bottom), 94 (top, bottom), 95, 98, 100, 101, 104 (top), 107, 110 (top), 113 (top), 115, 118 (top), 119, 122, 123 (top), 130 (bottom), 132, 134 (left), 140 (top, bottom), 143, 150 (top), 156, 163, 164, 166, 167 (top, bottom), 172 (top), 173 (bottom), 175, 184, 188 (bottom), 189, 193 (top), 197.

COUNTRY MUSIC **MAGAZINE COLLECTION**: p. 183.

BETH GWINN: pp. 152, 212, 231 (top), 232 (bottom right), 234, 236 (left center).

LES LEVERETT: pp. 24 (top), 38 (left), 43 (bottom), 44 (bottom left), 46, 48 (bottom), 49, 68 (top), 74 (top left), 76 (bottom), 77 (bottom), 82 (top), 84, 86 (top), 89 (top, bottom), 91, 92, 93, 109, 120, 125 (top), 126, 127, 128, 134 (right), 142 (top), 144 (bottom), 147 (top, bottom), 151, 153, 157 (top), 159, 160, 161, 165 (top, bottom), 182, 185, 191, 195, 196, 198, 213, 214.

LIBBY LEVERETT-CREW: p. 157 (bottom).

LGI PHOTO AGENCY: p. 177; Richard Corkery: p. 202 (top); George Dabrowski: p. 73; Mark Davitt: pp. 215, 219; Dean Dixon: pp. 29, 103, 117, 192, 194 (top), 226 (top), 235 (top right); Lynn Goldsmith: p. 226 (bottom); Stephen Harvey: p. 11; Mick Hicks: p. 228 (top); Chuck Jackson: pp. 220, 235 (bottom right); Tim Mosenfelder: pp. 203, 229; Marc Serota: p. 236 (bottom right); Marko Shark: p. 217; Bryan Smith: p. 204.

MUSIC CITY NEWS: pp. 178, 180 (bottom).

TOM NEFF: pp. 158, 168 (bottom).

SCOTT NEWTON/AUSTIN CITY LIMITS: pp. 231 (bottom), 236 (top).

MICHAEL OCHS ARCHIVE: pp. 58–59, 85 (top), 125 (bottom), 162.

ROBERT K. OERMANN COLLECTION: pp. 2, 12 (top), 14, 24 (bottom), 36 (bottom left, bottom right), 39, 42 (top, center, bottom), 43 (top), 45 (bottom), 47 (top), 48 (top), 50 (bottom), 51, 53 (top, bottom), 56, 63 (bottom), 64 (top, bottom), 66 (bottom left, bottom right), 75 (bottom), 82 (bottom), 88 (bottom), 96 (bottom), 99 (top, bottom), 112 (bottom), 113 (center), 130 (top), 138, 139, 142 (bottom), 144 (top), 168 (top), 172 (bottom), 173 (top), 174 (insert), 176 (top, bottom), 180 (top), 181, 194 (bottom), 202 (bottom).

ONYX: George Lange: p. 235 (bottom left); Steven Pumphrey: p. 209; Lara Rossignol: p. 228 (bottom).

OUTLINE: M. Borham: p. 179; E.J. Camp: pp. 97, 227, 233; Deborah Feingold: p. 225; Pat Harbron: p. 216; Chris Little: p. 171; Paul Natkin: pp. 41, 137; Stephanie Pfriender: p. 57; Ken Sax: p. 65; Mark Seliger: p. 145; Harry Siskind: p. 211; Brian Smith: pp. 6, 223; Mark Tucker: p. 230.

PHOTOFEST: pp. 58 (top), 59 (top), 60, 69 (bottom), 70 (left, right), 199, 221 (left, right).

HOPE POWELL: pp. 174 (top), 188 (top), 193 (bottom).

ERIC SCHAAL, *LIFE MAGAZINE*: p. 141.

SOUTHERN FOLKLIFE COLLECTION, UNIVERSITY OF NORTH CAROLINA, CHAPEL HILL, N.C.: p. 104 (bottom).

J. STOLL/TBS, INC.: pp. 10, 62 (bottom), 72, 74 (bottom right), 80, 102, 116, 136, 154, 170, 186 (jacket courtesy of Manuel, Nashville, TN), 200, 224.

SYGMA PHOTO NEWS: p. 232 (bottom left).

COURTESY OF TBS, INC.: pp. 205, 207, 210; Chris Cuffaro: pp. 81, 155, 187.

FRONT COVER (clockwise from top): Archive Photos, Archive Photos, Outline/Brian Smith, Les Leverett, Archive Photos, Robert K. Oermann Collection, Archive Photos, Robert K. Oermann Collection, Outline/Mark Abrahams, Les Leverett, Corbis-Bettmann, Corbis-Bettmann.

BACK COVER (clockwise from top): Onyx/Loren Haynes, Mark Hill/TBS, Inc., LGI Photo Agency/Lynn Goldsmith, LGI Photo Agency/Marc Serota, Frank Ockenfels 3, Onyx/Lara Rossignol, LGI Photo Agency/Dean Dixon, Beth Gwinn.

COVER ART: Gary Tanhauser.

EDITOR
Alan Axelrod

COPY CHIEF
Lauren Emerson

DESIGNER
Carol Farrar Norton

PHOTO RESEARCHER
Marty Moore

PRODUCTION MANAGER
Anne Murdoch

ASSISTANT PHOTO
RESEARCHER
Kerry Barnett

ASSISTANT
COPY EDITOR
Jim Davis